HEALING THE BLUES

Dorothea Nudelman
David Willingham, MSW

HEALTH INFORMATION PRESS
Los Angeles, California 90010

Library of Congress Cataloging-in-Publication Data

Nudelman, Dorothea, 1940-
  Healing the Blues: An account by patient Dorothea Nudelman and therapist
David Willingham.
  p. 236 + xiii
  Includes bibliographical references. 3 p.
  ISBN: 0-940168-3145
  1. Depression, mental-Treatment-Case studies. 2. Psychotherapy-Case studies.
3. Theory of depression. I. Willingham, David. 1938- II. Title.
  RC537.N83 1994   94-12688
  616.85'27065 l-tic 20   CIP

Printed in the United States of America

ISBN: 1-885987-10-2

Health Information Press
4727 Wilshire Blvd.
Los Angeles, CA 90010

DEDICATION

DOROTHEA

To my parents, Vincent and Dorothy Grottola, who always believed in me and to Michael and Kathryn, who have always loved me exactly as I am.

DAVID

To my mother, Isabell Willingham, and the memory of my father, John Willingham. They gave me everything I needed.

TABLE OF CONTENTS

Odd-numbered chapters by Dorothea Nudelman.
Even-numbered chapters by David Willingham.

PREFACE

    DOROTHEA vii

    DAVID ix

ACKNOWLEDGMENTS

    DOROTHEA xi

    DAVID xiii

CHAPTERS

    1. IN A DARK TIME 1

    2. DIAGNOSING DEPRESSION 15

    3. SEPTEMBER 3, 1949 25

    4. BLOCKED EMOTION 35

    5. IN THE CHILDREN'S WARD 43

    6. CHILDHOOD TRAUMA 51

    7. COMIC RELIEF. 57

    8. HUMOR AND PERSPECTIVE 67

    9. BODIES ARE TO LIVE IN 73

10. OVERCOMING ALIENATION 85

11. NIGHTMARES, DREAMS, AND TREASURES 91

12. THE UNCONSCIOUS MIND 101

13. THE BEAUTIFUL WOMAN 107

14. BREAKING OLD PATTERNS 119

15. THE VOICE OF ANGER 131

16. EXPRESSING THE NATURAL SELF 141

17. ACCEPTANCE 149

18. COMING TO TERMS 165

19. LEAVE TAKING 173

20. INTEGRATION, CREATIVITY, AND CLOSURE 183

AFTERWORD

    DOROTHEA 189

    DAVID 191

SUGGESTED READING 193

EPILOGUE 197

DOROTHEA NUDELMAN

PREFACE

".. go into yourself and see how deep the place is from which your life flows..."
—Rainer Maria Rilke in Letters to a Young Poet,
February 17, 1903

The summer of 1949, my parents rented a cottage on the beach in Manasquan, New Jersey. The ocean was a magical treat for me, a nine-year-old used to playing in a city park. The heat waves ebbed and flowed. My days rolled out like a lazy carpet with simple patterns of daily beach play interrupted only by meals and the required rest period after lunch to ward off the polio "scourge" of summer.

With about twenty other beach kids we made and broke alliances almost daily. When the thrill of endless summer days wore off, one mother organized a neighborhood carnival. We sold raffle tickets all over town. I liked that part and soon gained a reputation for fearlessness. I would stand on anyone's porch, ring anyone's bell and say, "We're raising money for the National Foundation for Infantile Paralysis. Would you like to buy a raffle ticket for our carnival? The tickets are one for a dime and three for a quarter." Because I liked snooping in other people's houses, my boldness sold more tickets than anyone.

The carnival was a huge success. When it was over, we had raised $305.82 for polio victims and we had our picture in the small town newspaper.

One morning three weeks later I awoke in terror, paralyzed from neck to toes with polio. In the hospital the next day, I saw the kind face of an old Irish nurse who said she thought she recognized me. She asked if I had sold her a raffle ticket at the beach the month before.

On September 3, 1949, the end of my childhood came in a moment. There followed years of intense work, inching forward to recovery. My efforts paid off and I achieved a fulfilling life—a fine education and a successful career in teaching, a happy marriage and motherhood—always in spite of the aftermath of polio.

Then, almost forty years later, I gradually noticed a marked loss of strength and mobility, insatiable fatigue, and low-grade chronic pain. I read about post-polio syndrome and grew anxious. Medical examinations confirmed that the loss of strength was real, the effect of increasing deterioration of my muscles, and that this condition, over time, might continue to reduce my level of physical capacity.

During the following months I became increasingly depressed and fearful. Finally, I sought the help of David Willingham, a psychotherapist, hoping he would suggest some new ways of coping. This book is the story of the remarkable private conversations that took place between us. The therapy resolved my depression and led me to a different understanding of my past as well as the meaning of polio in my life. Reaching the end of my therapy, I saw that fear crippled everyone in some way. I imagined connecting with and helping other people touched by depression through telling my story.

I invited David Willingham to write with me because of his special place in this story. As a highly competent and compassionate professional, he guided me through the intensity of psychotherapy. I was blessed to have a trusting, capable, caring person to share the journey. His commentary gives an objective dimension to my account and connects it to the universal human story.

DAVID WILLINGHAM

PREFACE

P sychotherapy is in part a series of private conversations that allows a person to set aside his or her concerns about the judgments of other people. The privacy provides a place where one can examine life without fear of censure and criticism.

Therapy is also private for the therapist who is bound by the rules of confidentiality. A therapist's personal experiences with clients are not often shared, making the daily life of the therapist a lonely one. The therapist spends each hour sitting with a patient, listening, probing, and guiding the examination of a life. Although not actually alone, there is an essential aloneness in the work, for the therapist is focused on the patient and certain tasks that the patient must accomplish for his or her successful treatment. Unlike many other professions, there is little opportunity for unfocused or unstructured activity. One life after another passes before the therapist who witnesses the psychological change that takes place through the therapeutic conversation.

On the other hand, the life of a therapist is incredibly rich and textured. We vicariously experience a multitude of lifetimes in a unique way. We glimpse the intimate memories, thoughts and feelings of all kinds of people, travel with them as they sort through their involvement with every imaginable life experience: childhood, family and marriage, culture and sub-culture, business and profession, achievement and failure. I have always wanted to be able to share the complexity and grandeur of this human landscape with others.

In this book, Dorothea Nudelman sets aside her privacy and shares the adventure of her life examination. She tells eloquently of the struggle she had with depression. In the process, she graphically recounts the terrifying experience of childhood poliomyelitis and her courageous journey to overcome its aftermath in order to live a full and dynamic life. Hers is a fascinating life story.

I joined Dorothea in telling my side of this story so readers can see both sides of the therapeutic process. The therapy which took place is a particularly good demonstration of how the examination of a life can result in "additive change," or transformation. She resolved a persistent depression, but more, she uncovered and reclaimed portions of a rich life which had been filed away as too painful to contemplate. In the process, she discovered powerful, unused facets of her personality and unleashed a creative explosion in herself which was totally unexpected.

I invite the reader to join me in the consulting room, to listen in on my memories, thoughts and feelings, and to watch this rich therapy unfold. Most of what I have written is the story of her psychotherapy. I have included some personal experiences from my own life and treatment vignettes from other patients, all of which illuminated my understanding as the work proceeded. Interspersed are theoretical reflections about clinical issues which I hope will provide information useful to the reader about depression and psychological approaches to treating it.

I believe that the emotional disturbances of depression, as discomforting as they are, are more than clusters of symptoms to be eliminated. Contained within them is information that may be vital to the further development and maturation of the individual. This book describes an experience of finding the meaning behind a depression through conversations which had a powerful impact on one person's life. I hope that through this story readers will understand why so many of us who do psychotherapeutic work never lose our excitement and fascination for the task—to guide a distressed person toward a more satisfying life.

DOROTHEA

ACKNOWLEDGMENTS

Many thanks to David Willingham, without whom I would not have been able to claim my story or write this book collaboratively. I also appreciate the friends and colleagues who have helped me throughout the writing of *Healing the Blues*. I owe special thanks to those who read the entire manuscript and encouraged me to seek publication. They include Marjorie Lightfoot, Ann Connor, Mary Jane Moffat, Georgia Logan, Barbara Kent, Liz Keefe, Rae Cole, Edith Collin, Kim Wolterbeek, April Flowers, Alison Wilson, Maureen Mitchell, Sue Shaffer, Valerie Beatts, and Michael Grottola. True friends, all.

Thanks also for creative inspiration from Jim Fetler, Joe Gallo, and Nick Keefe; for research help from Karen Gillette; and to Bill Walker—writer, colleague and friend par excellence—who simply said, "You must write this book."

Thanks to Doubleday Books for permission to quote from *The Collected Poems of Theodore Roethke* (Doubleday, New York, 1966).

Great thanks to Foothill-DeAnza Community College District for granting me generous accommodation which allowed me to maintain a rewarding 32-year career on a physically challenging campus, and for providing me with a sabbatical leave during which I was able to write this book. And thank you to all the participants in the 7th International Post-Polio and Independent Living Conference, 1997, for giving me the inspiration to network more fully within the powerful disabled community.

I thank my family for generous and sustaining support. Their love encouraged me when I needed it. My sister, Lois Dupre, read portions of the manuscript and enriched my memories; my brother, Michael Grottola, had zeal enough to ignite my imagination.

I owe deepest appreciation and gratitude to my husband and daughter. Thank you, Michael—best friend, incisive editor, first class professional, and playmate. Thank you for all the conversations that made the dream of this book a reality. Thank you for nourishing me through our wonderful and challenging journey for 26 years. Thank you for the laughter and love that sustains. Thank you, Kathryn, for your larger-than-life faith and pride in my work, for your depth and breath of beauty, and for the daily joy of you—here and now and always.

DAVID

ACKNOWLEDGMENTS

First of all, I want to thank Dorothea Nudelman for her courage in abandoning her privacy to share the conversations in this book. Also, many thanks to Joanie Wread, for reading the roughest drafts and liking them, to Margaret Simpson, reader of the first manuscript, for very helpful comments and support; to Abbe Stump-Hopkins and John McGovern, my friends and former office-mates, for steady companionship; to Marty Klein, for good conversations about writing; to Eileen Bobrow, colleague and intellectual explorer, for her energy and spirit; to Karen Harber, long-time colleague, for years of warmth and inspiration.

I have always been sustained by time spent with so many loving friends who pull me away from excessive work and lead me into laughter and renewal. Grateful thanks to Ray, Patricia, Nikki, David, Dan, Mary Anne, Nancy, Craig, Mike, Jennie, and more.

Gratitude to my three children: Andrea, Laura, and Alexander, who have filled my life with joy and taught me so much about love.

To Alex, for his lively intellectual enthusiasm and his amazing computer consultations, my admiration.

To Joan Willingham, wife, colleague, best friend, and most challenging teacher and consultant, very special appreciation for nearly 30 years of adventure and love.

And finally, to all of the clients who granted me permission to include vignettes from their therapy experiences (disguised for confidentiality), thank you for sharing your lives with me and with the readers.

1

DOROTHEA

IN A DARK TIME

"In a Dark Time, the Eye begins to See..."
—*T. Roethke*

I had carried David's phone number around all summer. On a late August afternoon, I was alone and exhausted from the fierce heat of the California sunshine. My daughter had gone swimming with her friends, and I sought relief in the shaded master bedroom of our new home. I set a cold glass of ice water on the night stand, leaned my crutches against the wall, and sat down on the edge of the bed.

Lying back on the cool comforter, I felt the heavy achiness in my legs. The right leg trembled with fatigue. The left one perspired in the aluminum and plastic brace that enclosed it. I took a deep breath and sighed, feeling fatigue move through my body. Something wasn't right, but what?

Following our family vacation in the Pacific Northwest, I had expected to feel refreshed and renewed. Instead, I was exhausted and near despair. The trip had been rough. Physical barriers had challenged me everywhere in spite of my well-developed skills with crutches and leg brace—remnants of my childhood bout with polio. Our summer cabin at Crescent Lake had stairs too narrow for me to climb without help. Walking to view wild flowers on Hurricane Ridge was hard work because of the steep slope of the land. Unexpectedly, I had needed assistance boarding a ferry boat to British Columbia.

I sat up and sipped the icy water. The facts were there. My general health was fine, but my stamina was flagging. Middle-aged slowdown was one thing, but this was ridiculous. I was an expert at coping and adjusting, yet nothing had seemed enough this past year. In another three weeks I had to return to my community

1

college teaching position. But I was worn out, afraid of injury, afraid I was falling apart. I have to get some help, I thought, staring at the stony face of the bedside telephone.

Though I had carried his phone number for months, I was reluctant to call David Willingham. I would have to say my name and what I needed. What could I say? "Help? I'm drowning?" Silence filled the room and suddenly I knew I had waited too long already. I snatched the phone and dialed the number. When his answering service told me he was on vacation, I mumbled my name and number, banged down the phone, and wept in despair.

About a week later, I was washing vegetables at the kitchen sink when the phone rang. When I heard David Willingham announce that he was returning my call, something collapsed inside me, like a tall tower of wood blocks crashing down.

"Oh, thank God you called!" I cried, and immediately felt foolish spilling over to this stranger. We set our first meeting for September 4th—one day beyond the 38th anniversary of the day I got polio. I wondered if I could say that to him about the polio. It wasn't the sort of thing one dropped into a casual conversation.

Sitting in David's waiting room, I felt awkward and nervous. I had no idea how to talk to a complete stranger, a "shrink," about my real self. Anxiety had gotten me there early enough to look around and search for clues which would reveal this man. The room was narrow but homey. Nothing really matched. A handsome oriental rug lay atop a dark blue carpet. A corner table held magazines and one book, *The Way Things Work*. Across from two of the three chairs was another table with coffee pot and cups, inviting visitors to relax and feel at home. Warm yellow light streamed from a table lamp and soft classical music filled the tiny room. I liked the place. It wasn't sterile.

Still, I trembled and sucked in some air at the turn of the doorknob. There stood a tall broad-shouldered man, about my age, framed for a second in the doorway. Smiling warmly, he came toward me, extending his hand. "Hello, Dorothea, I'm David Willingham. Nice to meet you." His voice was friendly and his use of my given name sounded familiar. He didn't comment on my cold hand. As I rose to follow him into the office, I trembled. How would I begin or sustain an hour long conversation with him?

It helped that his office resembled someone's living room—spacious, colorful and light. David moved around casually, offering me a comfortable chair facing his own. He asked a few simple questions in an easy conversational tone. I was grateful for his help and in a short time I lost the feeling that I was "facing off" with someone.

2

I talked at length summarizing details of my life. Born, reared, and educated in New York City, I was the second of three children and the first in my family to complete college. I mentioned my childhood polio experience at age nine. But my focus was more on the present loss of power in my legs.

For several years I had read scattered news articles about something called post-polio syndrome, a deteriorating condition occurring about twenty five years after the onset of the original illness. Since polio had become an antiquated disease after the Salk vaccine, it no longer caused alarm in the general population. But I was alarmed by my aches and pains, the increasing difficulty of each step, and the enormous daily fatigue. What would happen to me next? And, worst case, what would I do with my life if I could no longer cope physically? I shuddered and kept this anxiety to myself. I was afraid to risk saying aloud to a stranger what I most feared. And there was no reason to think David could possibly understand what this new threat meant after a lifetime of living with polio.

David nodded thoughtfully as I spoke and then returned to an earlier thread in the conversation. "When did you move West?" he asked.

"When I got a university to pay my way to graduate school. I saw my big chance to leave home!" We both laughed. "You see, to teach, I needed both a graduate degree and a job. To be independent, I needed a gentle climate where I could get around on crutches without worrying about snow or ice."

It was an ancient litany to me. But I went on. "I got my Master's degree and my first job. After two years of teaching, I moved into my present community college position. I've taught for over twenty years now. Even met my husband at work. Michael and I have been married for 16 years, and our daughter, Kathryn, is ten." I was proud and satisfied.

"Are there any other children?" he asked.

"No, only Kathryn. I always tell people, 'Do it once. Do it perfectly. And you never have to do it again!'" It sounded hollow to me and I dropped the bantering. "She is the joy of my life, really."

I described the heaviness of my mood and asked. "What do you think? Any ideas about what's wrong? Why I feel so rotten? I mean, this isn't like me!" I wanted to turn the tables and challenge him. I wondered what he'd say but never expected his questions about the distant past.

"Well," he began, "I've a few more questions. Tell me about your childhood polio. How long were you in the hospital when you first got sick?"

"Almost a year. From the third of September, when I was nine years old, until the end of June. It was like a long school year. Very long." I laughed feebly. He didn't. "The corrective surgeries came later, through my teen years. But they got done mainly during summer vacations."

David stared at me, engrossed, thoughtful. "And did you see much of your family during that time? Your parents? Your sister and brother? What happened with them?"

"That was one of the hard parts. We were allowed visitors twice a week. And only parents or grownups. My little brother was five and he drew pictures and sent them with my Mom. And once my sister, Lois, came. They smuggled her in to see me. She was tall for eleven. Mom let her dress in high heels and wear lipstick. She looked strange and uncomfortable and mostly stared at me. We didn't know what to say to each other.

"After a couple of months, around Thanksgiving, I was well enough to sit up in a wheelchair. They let me go home for occasional weekends after that. It got much better then. I lived for those weekends."

I let out a deep breath and remembered the trips in the back seat of the car, racing up the West Side Highway to get home to my mother's food and the smell of my own bed in the room I shared with my sister. The return trip on Sunday evening was unbearable, especially in the winter. Darkness fell early and I watched warm yellow lights come on in the tall apartment houses on Riverside Drive. I imagined all those families sitting down to supper and then my own family eating without me. The trip back to the hospital always seemed faster than the one home.

"And after that?" David prompted.

"I came home in July and had another whole year of rehabilitation until I could walk well enough to go back to school. I was so happy to rejoin my classmates in seventh grade."

"I'll bet you were!" he seconded. There were more questions about polio that I answered. Privately, I was always amazed at the quality and fullness of my recall of that time...sights, sounds, odors, but mostly the sensation of paralysis. David listened attentively, took some notes, and often nodded his head conveying both understanding and sympathy. This story was new to him and he was engaged. He appreciated my humor and had shown some of his own. I liked that he had managed to put me at ease almost immediately.

He had striking eyes. I had looked intensely at others, but no one had ever held my gaze quite like this. He was really looking at me, waiting for me. I feared that those eyes would look right down inside my own and find me. I needed to look away, but I didn't know why.

When I looked back, his expression was reflective. He furrowed his brow, pursed his lips, and tapped his pen on the lined tablet resting on his knees. "Well, I have an idea about what may be happening here. It's early, of course, but this is a possibility. You said you finished building your new house a year ago, didn't you?" I nodded affirmatively. "Your life seems to be stable now, even though you've gone through some very stressful experiences lately. Is that accurate?" He paused and looked straight at me. Again, I nodded.

"Dorothea, sometimes when life is very hard for a person, some parts of the experience don't get finished. This unfinished emotional business gets put on a back burner or on a shelf. It may sit there for years. The person gets to a point in life where he is no longer striving so hard, and life calms down enough where there's time and energy available for the unfinished business. Then the back burner issue moves forward. Sometimes, an event occurs to bring it forward."

Unfinished business? What was he talking about anyway? I took brief stock. My life was in order. I had taken care of things. What did he mean? I shook my head and waited.

"From what you've said, it sounds like you've never grieved for the loss that occurred with your childhood polio, grieved the loss of function in your legs." His words hung in the air. "I don't mean you never experienced polio, only that there wasn't a way, then, to express feelings about what was happening to your body. Is that right?"

"Of course," I agreed. "But I can tell you I had a lot of pain, and went through a long, tough rehabilitation. God, I struggled—ten years before I was back on my feet, totally independent. I think this post-polio weakness has brought the old memories back. And, frankly, I can't endure it again, alone." It was such a long hard battle, I thought. Maybe I need new coping skills or another way to survive what's coming now, whatever that is. "That's why I'm here," I added. "To do something nice for myself, finally."

As I spoke, David held my gaze. He nodded reassuringly and smiled. He said nothing but seemed to understand. I looked down, clasped my hands, and felt a little breathless. Panic rose in me again as it had so often in the weeks before.

"Do you really think that's what's wrong?" I said. I heard my voice, thin and faraway. I wanted him to reconsider. I just couldn't see any possible relationship.

"Yes, I do. But as I said, it's just a hunch. I don't know what else might ...."

"I was afraid you'd say something like that!" The words just shot out of me and I laughed nervously. Truly, I felt like groaning. What did he know, anyway? Sounded like a crock to me. I didn't want to sit around talking about what happened

5

to me almost forty years ago. I probably dwelled on that post-polio stuff too long. Misled him.

Yet, ending the hour, I didn't deliberate about returning the following week. I was falling apart and had to get back in control. So what if David had gone off on this polio tangent. People had done it all my life. They were curious. He was easy enough to talk to and he knew how to listen. There was nothing to lose.

I first learned about post-polio syndrome in 1980, in my optometrist's waiting room. Scanning a health magazine, the word *Polio* caught my eye. It had been ages since I'd read anything about the disease. To my surprise, the article focused on polio survivors in middle age who were experiencing some alarming new symptoms: muscle aches and pains, sharp decreases in mobility and strength, frequent and longer lasting fatigue. The cause of these symptoms was unknown. While some feared a reactivation of the original virus, another theory was that overworked compensatory muscle groups were wearing out.

Two facts particularly alarmed me. From the figures gathered, about 25 to 40 percent of the polio population were reporting such symptoms. And the losses of ability were severe. People who walked on crutches now needed wheelchairs. People who walked with a slight limp were now using braces. The changes were noticeable and dramatic.

I dropped the magazine when the optometrist called me into his office. I was happy to put the story aside, grateful that I wasn't among that chosen group. I set my teeth together and gave a little shiver. "Well, that's never going to happen to me, thank God!"

In May, 1982, I broke my leg. The recovery period was arduous. After four months I was walking again, but much more tenuously. My husband Michael noticed that my gait was different, slower. His comments annoyed me and I snarled defensively about not being fully recovered from the accident. But my palms bore red pressure points from leaning on my crutches and the phone rang a few extra times before I could get there to answer it.

In the summer of 1985 I read another article on post-polio syndrome, this one on data being gathered at the Warm Springs Institute in Georgia. People who had sustained weaknesses from polio were encouraged to write for further information. I received a packet of information, including an invitation to come to Warm Springs for a physical evaluation, and a request for personal information on noteworthy changes I had observed. My name was entered into the Warm Spring Registry and I was promised current information as it became available.

It was clear from the Warm Springs material that no new research was being done. My own generation had been "mainstreamed" back into school and the work force. Earlier generations of polio victims had been left to wither. In 1954, five years after I got polio, the Salk Vaccine arrived. I remember the headline of the New York World Telegram and Sun: *MAN CONQUERS POLIO*! But post-polio syndrome did not threaten society the way polio epidemics had in the past or AIDS does in the present. The material from Warm Springs signaled no headlines. I tossed it out.

In the summer of 1986, Michael and I were nearly finished building our new home. While Michael oversaw and participated in the new building, I maintained family life at the old house, and carton by carton packed for the move. One day, I packed 44 cartons of books. That night, I felt like an old crank-up record player winding down. My fatigue was insurmountable. I feared I was overworking and losing ground.

On September 1, 1986, we moved. That afternoon, I first walked across the blue carpet on our family room floor. I concentrated on each step and noticed how much bigger the house was than I had anticipated. I felt sure my exhaustion would subside with time and rest.

As the year progressed, the house was finished inch by inch. I felt like an inch worm moving through vast new territory. I moved slowly. I counted telephone rings and hang-ups that year. People weren't rude. It just took longer and longer for me to reach any of the three telephones spread through the larger house.

I consulted my internist, then my orthopedist, noting my observations carefully. They each checked me for other possible problems that might explain the fatigue and slowdown. They had heard of post-polio syndrome, but neither of them had first-hand experience with it. They gave me reassurances, speculated that middle age and difficult physical challenges made everyone more tired, and recommended moderate exercise. Other medical professionals had similar replies. I kept reading and began to feel like the expert. One day I put post-polio out of my mind. It was too depressing to think about.

In August, 1987, the family vacationed at Crescent Lake on the Olympic Peninsula, in Washington. There were boats to rent, wild flowers everywhere in abundance, a world of spacious beauty. Everything was stamped with perfect rustic peace. Here was the vacation that would restore me, I thought.

I was doing practically nothing, getting plenty of rest, but still stumbling over myself, and still tiring out fast. Our cabin had four narrow steep steps and no handrail. I was barely able to clear the steps with my good leg and the slight unevenness from the warped wood made balancing precarious. Climbing up, I teetered on each step. Descending, I was sure I'd tumble head over heels. In the end, Michael had to construct a makeshift handrail so I could steady myself.

One evening at twilight while our daughter explored the lake, I sat on a log at water's edge, nursing a glass of wine and wondering aloud to Michael about what was happening to me. "I'm scared," I whispered, turning the glass in my hands. "I don't know what to do, what's happening. And I don't know where to turn."

He looked concerned and uncomfortable. "Well, I sure as hell don't know what's going on either. But you're tense and exhausted. You're struggling to do things you used to do easily." Together we reminisced about our honeymoon trip through this same area, sixteen years before. The memories were sweet but they slipped away. Michael had married a capable person, someone beyond all this polio struggle. He wasn't prepared for this. And neither was I.

We held hands and I could feel my eyes cloud over. "Remember when I had my last surgery—I said I didn't think I could go through the painful medical stuff anymore without support?" He nodded. "Well, I don't know what's happening physically, but I feel heavy and sad. I can't go on alone. I need some help. I mean, if I still feel this way when we get home, I think I should find someone—go talk about this, whatever. I've got a number here. What do you think?"

"I think it's a good idea," he said. He sounded pleased and relieved. I knew he must have been feeling as troubled as I was. "But don't worry. We're good at working out the tough stuff. We'll work this out too." I heard his uncertainty.

The word wasn't in yet on post-polio syndrome, but it was time for me to move. I hadn't been enjoying life for a long time. As my physical efforts became greater, mental exhaustion threatened to overtake me. I felt tired and sad. I lacked vitality. And lately, I was becoming conscious that I was afraid of what was to come. If I didn't get my feelings and attitudes sorted, I'd be stuck sitting on a log, on the Olympic Peninsula, missing all the fun.

I had been seeing David for almost a month and nothing had gotten better. Though I doubted his ideas about "grieving the loss," I had to continue trying to relieve my growing distress.

While I largely ignored his "back burner" idea, I continued the meetings hoping to feel better and still curious about what I would discover. This strange new experience of sitting around talking about myself wasn't entirely unpleasant.

It was a little like getting acquainted with an old friend from the past, someone I hadn't thought about for years.

We discussed my Italian-Catholic background and my traditional Catholic education. David continued to ask questions about my illness and the long difficult recovery. Frequently, he remarked on my bravery in the face of such adversity. I flinched and blushed as I always did when people said things like that.

I had no corner on the courage market. I had forged ahead because it was expected and because the alternative was terrible. I remembered the nun who had called me "the sterling example of the seventh grade" after I'd returned to school again. Remarks like that separated me from other kids by my physical difference. Made my polio my specialness, and then assigned me special spiritual strengths that I didn't have. I began striving to live courageously from very early on. It was expected. I wondered if David would expect it too. I still wasn't sure how therapy worked or how I could help myself in these hours we spent together.

More and more I noticed the enormous energy it took to cope with the daily demands of living in the new house. I continued to be exhausted. I talked about feeling uncomfortable where I lived. The house had cost a fortune and we had designed it with my limitations in mind. Still, I was overwhelmed and felt ashamed that I could not walk its length easily. Asking family members for more help felt like giving in. I hated that. Besides, Michael and Kathryn loved the rustic beauty we had created, loved the way the redwood house nestled into old oaks on our country acre. I, too, admired its beauty. But I often drove by our old comfortable home on an ordinary suburban street, longing for what I had left behind.

One overcast morning in late September, I awoke feeling uneasy, as if from some bad dream I couldn't remember. At breakfast, I warmed my hands on a coffee mug and watched the young birch trees from the kitchen windows. A little time remained before my appointment with David, and Michael sensed my mood. "Wanna talk?" he said, slipping his arm around me.

"Oh, God, yes!" I sighed. "I feel so rotten this morning. So irritable. And I don't know why. I've got this appointment and I don't even know what to say to David. I have nothing left to say. Tell me something to say!" I begged.

Michael looked at me and we laughed about my uncharacteristic loss of words. But he had encouraged me to seek help. "Well," he mused. "You're miserable enough all right. Why not just say that? Tell him you're depressed about the polio coming back. About the house being too much to manage. All that stuff."

He sounded so sane as he listed items. As he piled them higher and higher, I became more miserable. By the time I arrived at David's office, I was in despair. His cheerful greeting left me cold.

"I don't know how to begin today," I said. "I'm irritated. And really tired of feeling so miserable." I recounted the earlier discussion with Michael and then just blurted out, "I don't think I can stand living with this heavy feeling much longer. I need help. Please, can you help me?" I heard my voice cry out in a whisper and I swallowed back tears.

"I can help you," he said gently. I looked straight at him while he explained that he wanted me to pay attention to what was going on inside. "Dorothea, your unconscious mind contains whatever you need to know. It won't hurt you. If you give yourself a chance, you can see what's in your mind." It sounded strange, like another kind of thinking. But I listened anyway.

"I'd like you to close your eyes, breathe normally, and just relax." He paused for a moment and I felt alone in the quiet. "Now visualize a movie projector casting images on a screen. Just let the pictures come. Go inside and look," he said softly. "And let them go. Let them pass through. Mostly they won't mean anything special. Eventually, you'll stop at one. Or a picture might return again and again. Look carefully. You'll know when it happens." He was quiet.

I watched and waited as the frames passed. I saw a little naked girl sitting on steep concrete steps watching old home movies. A white light glared and jumped on the screen, then pictures of the city street and park where I lived and played as a child. The screen went blank again except for the glaring light. My mind wandered and I began feeling self-conscious, knowing David was watching me while I did this dumb thing he called "going inside and looking."

Then the glare of light illuminated a child on an operating table below it. I was that child, dizzy and hot with fever, dangerously nauseated. I saw the kind eyes of Dr. Ping and her assistant preparing me for a spinal tap. I saw them through the harsh light in my eyes, through the headache that was splitting my head with pain. I was alone and afraid, lying naked beneath a starched sheet.

In a high pitched, delicate voice, Dr. Ping said, "We are going to turn you on your side now, for this special examination. You won't have to do anything." I believed her and assumed it wouldn't hurt. I smiled bravely and said nothing.

In one swift motion the assistant, a tall curly-haired man, put his huge hand under my neck, scooped up my legs from beneath my knees and turned me on my side in a U-shaped position, head touching knees. The shock and pain of having my totally stiff body moved overcame me. I gave a sharp scream and then tumbled down into blackness.

Watching the scene was stunning. I remembered being told that I passed out during the spinal tap—that I was lucky because spinal taps were so painful. Now, all grown up, I saw again the horror, the pain, and the fear. My mouth went dry and I had difficulty breathing. As I struggled to regain control, I heard David's calm voice telling me I was all right. I felt my face contort and my hands tremble, but I couldn't look up. This felt awful. I reached out my hands for something to hold onto, and David caught them in his own.

"It's all right now. You can hold on. You're okay. Open your eyes and look around." I did, and I told him what had just happened. After a while, I felt a little like my old self, but something was different. Despite his reassuring tones, he was outside of me and I was still alone and scared.

"Seems like I've been here for ages!" I said, glancing at the clock in disbelief. The hour was not yet up. David continued to be reassuring and encouraging as we began to pull things to a close. He had praise for my good work but I didn't really understand what he meant, and I didn't care to ask. I felt messy and exposed.

"I'm all right now, really I'm okay," I said, gathering myself to leave. "I have to hand it to you, I never believed that could happen," I remarked, moving to the door. All of a sudden I wanted to get out of there. I felt exposed. I had revealed what I saw and now I wanted to escape.

The morning had turned sunny. Getting into my old station wagon I felt eerie and unsettled. I longed for a cigarette for the first time in years. Resting my head on the steering wheel, I tried to calm down. I drove to a close friend's house and we went to a neighborhood park. "It's so weird, so strange what's just happened to me," I began. Tears and gasps interrupted my account. Making such a big deal about something that had happened so long ago, something that I thought was finished.

Barbara didn't think so. She grasped what was going on and managed to reassure me. We walked a bit and found a park bench in the noonday sun. She bought a sandwich to share, but, though I was starved, I felt sick after eating. "I'm exhausted," I sighed. "I'd better get home for a nap. Kathryn has a piano lesson this afternoon and guess who gets to drive?" I glanced at my watch and hugged my friend goodbye.

On the way home I told myself to behave like a grown woman. Once home, I collapsed on my bed, fully clothed, cold and shivering. Each time I closed my eyes, scenes of the therapy hour played in my head. "This is ridiculous!" I said aloud but my voice was unconvincing. Something had happened. I had opened my big mouth and now I was in real trouble.

I was grateful when Michael came home earlier than usual. "What's wrong?" he asked, gathering me to him in surprised concern. During sixteen years of marriage I had told him a number of polio stories, but I was still reluctant to tell him what had happened with David.

"I feel so stupid and ashamed to be behaving this way about something that happened so long ago!" He was puzzled but solicitous too. He held me and listened. He offered to drive Kathryn to her piano lesson. Somehow I got dinner on the table and made it through the evening.

Hours after we said our goodnights, I lay awake, quiet and anxious. "Are you still awake?" Michael whispered softly into the darkness.

"Yeah," I answered, "Am I bothering you? I can't settle down."

"You didn't bother me at all. I just woke up. Haven't you been asleep yet? You must be pooped. Do you feel sick or anything? Want me to get you something?" He slipped his arm around me and I snuggled into the soft hollow on top of his shoulder.

"No, I'm okay," I whispered, calmed by his kindness. But I was afraid to sleep, sure I'd dream something horrible or frightening. The hours passed until the first gray morning light when sleep claimed me for a short time.

In the morning, the world looked familiar again. While bathing, I laughed, soaping my hands, remembering Lady Macbeth. Maybe if I stayed here long enough, I could wash away everything and be safe again. But between the laughs, a palpable anxiety persisted. What the hell was wrong with me anyway? Was I going crazy? By midafternoon, feeling ashamed and failed, I broke down and called David. He got me into this, I thought grimly. Now I need to understand what's happening.

Hours later David returned my call. "Dorothea, David Willingham here. What's come up for you?" It steadied me to hear his voice, clear and calm. I felt little and foolish now asking for help. I had no idea what to ask for.

"Well, I've really been having a hard time since I saw you yesterday, and I don't know what to do."

My voice trailed off. Phones were awful things, I thought. Just voices. How could anyone say what was going on. It was Friday and my next appointment was the following Wednesday. An ocean of time. But when David asked if I could come in the following morning, I felt he had thrown me a lifeline.

The next morning I stared at him searching for answers. I was sure he knew what was wrong and I very much wanted him to fix it. He showed concern about me but not alarm. I stammered around about being shocked and confused. "How do you feel ?" he asked.

"I feel a little like glass—transparent, breakable. Why I don't even know you. And I've shown you a part of myself that even I didn't know was there," I murmured. I was embarrassed to say I felt fragile and needed someone to look out for me.

We looked at each other for a moment. David nodded his head sympathetically. "I know, it's scary. You must feel vulnerable and afraid. You've risked looking at your feelings and discovered something powerful and frightening. What you've shared is very private and personal. Partly it's the intimacy that's difficult, isn't it?" I nodded, grateful that he had said it.

"Dorothea, you can trust me," he said quietly. "I'm not going to take advantage of you. I won't hurt you. And I won't leave you alone with this. You're doing important work here. And you're a strong woman. You can do it, and I will help you. I understand what this feels like."

"What do you mean?" I said, raising my eyebrows at that last sentence. He had mentioned that he knew people who had polio, but it was obvious that he wasn't one of us. I wondered what he knew.

"I know what it's like to be afraid," he answered slowly. "And to bury it... for a very long time. When things happen to kids before adolescence they take responsibility, you know, think it's their fault." He paused and his gaze focused on something far away. "When I was about nine, I was rough-housing with my brother who was just a year older. Later that day, he seemed injured and was hospitalized. He never really got well. He died three months later. I believed it was my fault and I buried that event for almost 20 years."

"Good God," I said, awed by his tone, moved by the simple story so powerful in its consequences. I flashed on the childhood guilt I felt even when shouting at my kid brother: "I hate you! I wish you were dead, dead, dead!" Now, here was a grown man telling me he had beat up on his brother, and his brother had died. "What did you do with that?" I whispered.

"Nothing, for a long time. It waited. And finally one day it came out. But after it did, I could let it go. Then I began to heal." He paused. "I spent a lot of time before that being afraid, kind of feeling that things weren't right with me. I didn't know what it was."

"You know then, about the power, the force of the fear, I mean. David, I'm so frightened by it, feeling it physically. And then I fear that I might die!" I laughed nervously, but his laughter was warm with understanding.

"Well, it's not going to kill you. I'm sure of that. Actually, I've learned that facing your fears can't really hurt you at all. But you're right. When you're feeling fear, and it's sweeping through you, it's a powerful, scary force."

David didn't make light of my fear but it diminished as we spoke. I noticed a new sense of safety with him that I did not feel when I was alone. But when he asked me questions that made me feel uncomfortable, I hated it. I wanted him to help dispel my fears, not stir them up again. I groaned audibly when he suggested that I could get used to fear and even get over it.

Yet I was drawn to him. His honesty and openness about his brother made him a more flesh and blood person to me. I felt more comfortable about what I had revealed and more connected to David. He was no longer a stranger. Still, over the next few weeks, I often turned my head away from him, lowered my eyes and tried hard to disbelieve myself, to deny that any of this was real.

One day I challenged him. "This is some sort of aberration. What happens in this office has nothing to do with my real life. My real life goes on outside. I don't understand the power of these feelings. How can I be experiencing my childhood again?," I demanded, throwing up my hands.

David patiently explained the process by which painful memories get buried. "It's kind of like this. One day you take a mouse and you put it in the closet and close the door. Right? It stays there for years while you live in the house. It wants to come out but the door is closed. Then one day you open the door and, instead of a tiny mouse, a huge rhinoceros comes out."

He made his point. In that moment I saw the rhino at the door and my own horrified reaction. The humor of his metaphor displaced my terror—the months of being alone in the hospital, the gray walls, stiff body, hot packs, odors, salt tablets, stretching, pain, more pain. There was more to face, more that only I knew. And I did not want to look. Polio made me feel snatched away, gaunt, greedy, haunted, ashamed of my frail lifeless legs, scared with other kids dying around me. Ashamed that I wasn't good enough for God to make a miracle. All the waters of Lourdes would not wash away my lifelessness.

It was so painful to be that child again. Little. Housebound. Homebound. Chairbound. Bound up. Bound in. Bound down. Bound. I waited for years, hoping to wake up one morning, unbound. I never did.

2

DAVID

DIAGNOSING DEPRESSION

After practicing psychotherapy for 26 years, I am still challenged when I first meet a client. My first task is to clarify what is needed. While I listen, I try to figure out what is wrong and whether I am the right therapist for the person seeking help. Typically, I feel a slight sense of awe at the task because each person has lived such an enormously complex life. What do I focus on, inquire about, explore? How shall I sort through such complexity and discover the relevant information?

When I first met Dorothea, I greeted a lively looking woman, probably in her mid-forties. Like most people seeing a therapist for the first time, she was nervous. Yet her eyes twinkled and she smiled easily as she talked about herself and why she was considering psychotherapy. She seemed amused at herself and sort of sarcastically apologetic when she told me she had been feeling worn out and depressed during the past several months. Her left leg was bound in an elaborate brace made of aluminum and plastic. Forearm crutches lay on the floor beside her chair. I'd known several people who were afflicted with polio, including my sister, Nancy, but I knew little about physical handicaps. As Dorothea moved, I noticed her slow careful way of standing, walking and sitting. The process required an exquisite pattern of maneuvers and attention to both balance and surroundings. I wondered if her depressive problems were related to her polio experience.

Depressed feelings are natural and expected responses to stressful life events, but there are many kinds of depression. My task was to decide what kind of depression Dorothea was experiencing since not all depressions are treated the same way. To begin with, I had to establish whether this was a psychologically based or organically based depression. For the latter, clinical research and experience demonstrates that biochemical treatment is necessary for satisfactory recovery.

Dorothea summarized her current life in a neat package. At first glance there was nothing to explain her depression. She conveyed a feeling of closeness and security about her marriage to Michael, an attorney. And she was proud of their ten-year-old daughter, Kathryn. Dorothea taught English at a local community college where she had been on the faculty for 20 years.

She told me that her family had recently moved into their custom-built "dream house." The house-building project had been stressful. There were cost overrides and delays which finally forced them to move into the house eight months before it was completed. Thus, the last year of family life had been filled with disruption and intrusion from construction activities. I listened to determine if her depression was caused by some recent stressful change in her life. The house project had clearly been a hardship, but it didn't seem to account for the depth of sadness Dorothea reported.

I listened and waited as more of her story unfolded. She described increasing difficulty walking. Steps and curbs she previously managed easily were now harder, and she was feeling more fatigued from daily activities. A recent medical examination had suggested that Dorothea might be experiencing post-polio syndrome. As she talked about polio, I noticed that her eyes had become clouded and sometimes downcast. The humor was gone from her face and words came slowly. She seemed breathless. I had to strain to hear.

As Dorothea told her story with words, I noticed information she unknowingly provided through her facial expressions, shifts in the volume and tone of her voice, slight changes in her posture, her breathing, and her skin color. This unconscious information became very distinct. It seemed to say, "Pay attention to this. Notice how comfortable I was while talking about all the other stresses in my life and how oppressed I am now when talking about post-polio syndrome." Here was one significant change which could, perhaps, account for her depressed state.

I remembered a priest I once knew, a neighbor, who told me a story about his own struggle with polio as a young man when he spent many months in an iron lung. In that phase of his illness, he had a recurring dream. In the dream he was shipwrecked and paralyzed, floating face down in a life raft. The raft, a World War II model, had large cork frames wrapped in canvas with open webbing forming the bottom. In this recurrent dream, his genitals had slipped through the open webbing and he watched, helpless and terrified, as sharks circled below. I thought I probably needed to learn a lot about Dorothea's polio story.

"Tell me more about getting polio as a child, Dorothea, what was it like?"

She began to fill in the details. As she talked, the oppression lifted and she told a story of bravery, even bravado, in the young girl who had passed through a hellish experience. I thought of the terror of my priest friend and wondered how much worse it must have been for a small child. Yet something was different here. My ears were hearing lightness and humor now, as Dorothea talked of those terrible years. Could it be that the experience was psychologically finished so completely that now the memories were emotionally unloaded? I wondered about that, watched carefully and continued to listen.

She told a story of accomplishment, years of accomplishment. But there was a story-line quality to it, almost as if she were reciting her resume. She skipped lightly across the surface and, in several long paragraphs, she covered years of illness, pain, surgeries, and rehabilitation experiences. Telling this story sounded easy, like she had done it many times and could whip it out with simple good humor. But she was telling a story of grave suffering and loss in the midst of her childhood. I had a hunch that this was only the surface of a very deep pool.

"Tell me, Dorothea, what was done at the time to help you and the other children deal with the emotional difficulties polio must have caused? Were you able to talk about your feelings? Did anybody work with you kids to help you talk about your worries and fears?"

She seemed surprised at my question. "Oh, there was never any time for that. We were always looking at the next step, the next treatment, the next inch of progress. There was always something just ahead we had to get ready to face. You see, the focus was always on rehabilitation: learning to sit up in a wheel chair, daily physical therapy, and for some of us, getting fitted for braces and crutches and learning how to walk again. We weren't allowed to feel sorry for ourselves. There wasn't time for that."

Once again I noticed a change in Dorothea as she responded. Her shoulders slumped just a bit, her voice dropped off and she gazed down at her hands, nervously kneading them.

A hidden voice yelled out at me again. "Hey, Willingham, pay attention to this. Pay attention to this!" I felt weight on my own shoulders. My breathing was tight. I felt sadness, pain behind my eyes. Was this grief, very deep grief, buried for years, but rising now, activated by Dorothea's new losses from the post-polio syndrome? Old "forgotten" grief is never truly forgotten. But grief can be so meticulously interwoven into a person's inner psychological space that it becomes invisible, part of the deep background of the experience of self.

As she left the office I wondered if Dorothea would return for the second appointment. Sometimes, in spite of their distress, people change their minds at this point. They get a taste of what might be involved if they continue and don't want to face what they imagine lies ahead. I wondered if her discomfort and pain was strong enough to push her beyond this normal hurdle. For many people, returning to the therapeutic conversation is based on the answer to a simple question: Do I have to do it?

Dorothea returned and we spent several weeks exploring her life and getting acquainted with each other. I noticed that her sense of humor was nearly always close at hand and was a major characteristic of her personal style. While I speculated that it might be her principal method of defending against anxiety, it certainly wasn't just that. This woman had a humorous perspective about the world and enjoyed noting the daily smorgasbord of silliness and absurdity in life.

She talked at length about her life experience, past and present, filling in the details of her history. Dorothea had been a normal and active little girl until that fateful day when she woke up paralyzed, stiff and unable to move. The dreams and freedom of childhood had been ripped away. Her dreams were replaced by a nightmare filled with hospitals, treatments, equipment, doctors and nurses, painful surgeries and a seemingly endless process of rehabilitation.

I didn't directly see much of her depression during these early sessions. She talked about her fatigue and the melancholy feelings she encountered at various times during the week, but always in the past tense. This was an important diagnostic clue.

Depression is a difficult phenomenon to define. Nearly everyone knows what it is to be depressed, yet feeling depressed is not the same as having a depression. When is depression just the normal, human mood state of sadness, and when is it a condition, disorder, or illness?

The illnesses called depression are part of a diagnostic category referred to as mood disorders, meaning disorders of the emotions. Mood disorders can range from excessively high or "manic" mood states to excessively low or depressed states. Some conditions cycle between these extremes. The critical factor that separates disorders of mood from normal states of sadness and happiness is proportion—the severity and ration of the mood changes in the context of the individual's current life.

Dorothea's depression was more severe and persistent than would be explained by the development of post-polio syndrome alone. The fact that it was responsive to changes in her activities and tended to come and go led me to believe she did not have the kind of disorder called major depression. Major depression tends to be constant and unremitting and seems to persist in spite of changes in routine or behavior. Often it is unresponsive to psychotherapy without the concurrent use of anti-depressant medications. The causes of the major depressive disorders are not known precisely, but current research continues to demonstrate that there are many biological factors involved. These are sometimes referred to as chemical depressions.

My early hunch was that Dorothea was suffering a depression which was psychological rather than biochemical in origin. With psychogenic depressions, symptoms are viewed as information from the psyche (the conscious and unconscious mind), that something is unsettled within. It is as if the psychic system attempts to attract the attention of the individual by interfering with his or her ability to function in the outer world. With this in mind, I engaged Dorothea in a general review of her life, knowing that in this exploration we might trigger a reaction from her psyche which would lead us to what needed further attention.

Therapists learn to wait. I knew I must allow time for the therapeutic process to develop and watch to see what unfolded. Sometimes, of course, distress is there in the first meeting with a client—a person in acute crisis, defenses down, visible raw emotion, pain. But often, there is a lag time in the beginning period of therapy before the "spoken of" problem presents itself during a session.

With Dorothea, there was a "courtship period," a "let's check each other out" process before her unconscious mind let down its guard and revealed her inner state. Dorothea was a very independent person and I had to wait.

The day came when her depression revealed itself and Dorothea's usual humor and lightness were gone. The "other side" had arrived and she had to say very little to let me know the other presence was here with us today. I looked at her sitting on the sofa and saw the heaviness which had earlier appeared only in brief glimpses. She sat forward, slumped to one side, her face strained with tension and sadness. Again, I noticed her hands, kneading with stress.

Dorothea said she felt terrible. I said that it was quite apparent and suggested that we explore her feelings with some visualization methods. I briefly explained what I proposed to have her do. Then I simply said, "Dorothea, close your eyes now, and go inside yourself. Just breathe deeply for a few minutes and let yourself relax." She was able to do this. "Now, go right down to that heaviness you feel and ask it to show you what it wants you to know, what it wants you to look at. Let it show you pictures to let you know where this heavy feeling comes from and what it's about."

Dorothea easily followed these instructions and I watched as she began to breathe deeply and relax. She had enough trust in our relationship now to allow this direct approach to the source of her pain. She quickly went deep inside of herself, breathing normally. She appeared quite calm and comfortable. I waited and watched for cues that would tell me she was in touch with her feelings. I watched to see if she needed more direction, or a suggestion, whatever might help her to contact her inner experience.

After a few minutes, tension began to replace Dorothea's calm. Her hands, still for some minutes now, were kneading once again, and she rocked back and forth as her breathing became more labored.

"Stay with the feeling, Dorothea, let it take you where it wants you to go."

She was breathing heavily now, occasionally gasping and making small sounds of distress. It was obvious that she was in touch with some significant and very frightening inner experience. I noticed her begin to tighten up and hold her breath, fighting off the feelings.

"Keep breathing steadily, Dorothea, give yourself all the air you need and stay with the feelings. I'm right here with you."

"I'm back in the hospital and, and...." Her whispered words stopped and she seemed to be reeling with the intensity of the memory, gasping for air, her face contorted. She twisted her body as if to get away from something too horrible to look at. Suddenly, she shuddered and cried out, "Oh, God no!" and she reached out with both hands for support as if she were falling.

I sat forward and grabbed her hands in mine. "You're all right, Dorothea, just hang on and let the feelings move through you, let yourself experience them. They've been in there for such a long time."

She trembled and moaned and a cry broke from her lips. She sobbed gently. I held on to her hands and waited until the wave of emotion appeared to have passed through. After another minute or two I said, "Whenever you are ready to open your eyes, come back to the present and tell me what you've been seeing inside."

At first Dorothea could say nothing. She simply held on to my hands and rocked back and forth, still trembling from the impact of her memory. She had opened the door and discovered something that had been waiting for her to revisit after all these years. Soon she was calm enough to talk and she described the terrible experience of going through a spinal tap procedure the first day she was hospitalized as a child. She expressed amazement that the memory images were so vivid and real after such a long time.

I was relieved to see Dorothea able to regain her emotional equilibrium after such an intense encounter with her memory. The first emotional breakthrough with any new client is always experimental. One never knows just what the response will be when clients break through their defenses to an underlying feeling. At such times there are two important issues for me to assess. First, is the person able to get there, past the defenses? And second, is the person able to get back to the present and integrate the emotional experience into conscious awareness? I saw that Dorothea was able to do both.

This experience was not over, however. We talked for a while and I reassured her that what she had gone through was valuable. She listened and seemed to be relieved by it. I knew that Dorothea would feel an impact from this experience for some time following this session. Her barrier against this painful memory had been shattered and she would feel some emotional aftershock.

My diagnostic thinking narrowed to a specific conclusion. Dorothea was experiencing a form of depression which is caused by a severe delayed grief reaction, a condition which is similar to post-traumatic stress syndrome. The childhood polio had caused terrible pain and paralysis and traumatic separation from the family. This traumatization had been buried deep in Dorothea's psyche. Now, reactivated by new losses from post-polio syndrome, the old grief resurfaced and plunged her into depression.

The psyche of an individual is the entire system of brain function which we normally call the mind. It includes all of our conscious mental processes as well as the complex of memory, impressions, capacities, and knowledge bases which make up the unconscious part of the mind. As an extension of the self-regulatory system of the body, the psyche includes the ability to contain emotional charges which do not get released at the time of a disturbing event. These emotional memories go into storage, as it were. At a later time, the psyche releases these emotional charges into the conscious system. In general, the longer something has been held in unconscious memory, the more disturbing it is for the person when it surfaces. The conscious mind resists emotionally threatening memories.

I was not surprised when she called the next day and asked to see me. We arranged to meet the following day.

Dorothea was back under control, but she was confused and couldn't make sense of what had happened. She sensed that her jarring experience had been important but didn't see how it would help her. Behind everything she said were these questions: "Do I really need to do this? If I do this frightening thing and look at all these terrible feelings, how do I know I'll be safe? Can I really trust you?" Here Dorothea encountered the central issue of all psychological defenses: "If I let go of my controls, if I allow what is held deep inside to be discovered and exposed, will I be shamed, punished and rejected? Will I be overwhelmed and go crazy?"

These feelings are largely unconscious, yet they powerfully determine just how much of one's real self can ever be revealed. When we breach our defenses, break the rules and encounter memories and feelings, we feel very anxious and afraid. These fears are not to be taken lightly.

I knew about the shock Dorothea had experienced. I have accompanied many people through the struggle to discover an unfinished, painful part of their past. These memories nearly always return to consciousness in a stunning way.

I vividly remember the day it first happened in my own life when I was 29 years old. At that time I was in therapy myself, struggling to overcome a chronic, low-grade depression which had plagued me for years. My self-esteem in those early years was crippled with deep feelings of shame and it took me a long time to trust the therapy process and open up to my memories and feelings.

One Friday morning after a scheduled therapy session, I was in a very subdued mood. I didn't feel that I connected with anything useful in the session. I left and went to my office where I saw several clients, the end of a week's schedule. As the day progressed I gradually slipped deeper and deeper into a depressed state. With each passing hour my feelings seemed to become heavier and it was difficult to focus on my work. I managed to get through the day and was grateful when I was finished and could go home.

I drove to the apartment overlooking Los Angeles where my wife, Joan, and I lived. Restless, I paced the rooms and stared out at the city in the gathering dusk, wondering why I was so intensely oppressed. Joan arrived home after a while and came in full of cheer and anticipation for the weekend. She is also a therapist and it didn't take her long to realize that something was wrong with me. She began to try to find out what was going on.

By now the depressed feelings had become overwhelming. After telling Joan what I felt, my controls suddenly dissolved and I began to shudder and sob. I dropped to the floor and began to weep in a way that was completely alien to me. Sadness rose from deep inside of me and swept through in enormous waves of sobbing and crying. In my grief I was filled with the memory of my brother, John. He had been eighteen months older than me and died of cancer when I was nine years old. I never wept for John as a boy because I believed I had caused his death.

This had been my secret and I could never let anyone know. I couldn't cry then. I couldn't feel anything.

In the middle of my weeping now, 20 years later, a strange thing happened. The adult David separated from the young boy David, and I watched as if from the sidelines. Watching this weeping child, everything began to make sense. I understood what I had been searching for and why I had been haunted with shame and sadness for so many years. As I wept, and as I watched myself weep, I said to Joan, "I had forgotten what it is like to be nine years old." The memory had always been there, waiting for me to return to it.

It was in the context of this kind of personal experience that I responded to Dorothea's fear that day in my office following her breakthrough. She had to understand that what she had done was not only acceptable, it was hopeful. I explained to her that if she avoided her pain, the memories would remain buried and she would guard against them forever. But if she looked at and allowed all these hurtful memories, her pain could complete its natural cycle. Then she might discover that these same memories contained deeper, richer meanings. They might become doorways to long lost parts of herself and road maps to personal discovery and integration.

The human mind has the capacity to cope with and integrate nearly any kind of experience, even a very painful and traumatic one. It is common wisdom that adversity can be beneficial by leading an individual to a stronger and more mature sense of self. The key to this outcome is integration. This means that the adverse experience is faced squarely. The person moves through emotional reactions and galvanizes new strengths and coping skills to meet the challenges caused by the crisis. If a significant aspect of this process is left incomplete, it constitutes an unclaimed, non-integrated life experience.

3

DOROTHEA

SEPTEMBER 3, 1949

L eaning against David's comfortable floor pillow, I slid my hands beneath my legs and felt the carpet. "Sitting here, I don't worry about losing my balance or falling," I said. "There's no place but up from here, is there?" I grinned and David smiled back. "I had a close call this weekend," I added.

"Did you fall?" he asked.

"No, but I came real close. Scared the hell out of me, too. God, I was embarrassed. I was at this cocktail party with friends from work. I was using one crutch and holding a glass of champagne in the other hand. I sipped the wine but when I tried to move, I lost balance and started falling over sideways. It happened so fast. There was nothing to grab onto. The floor came up at me... fast!"

"How did you stop yourself?"

"I didn't. An act of God did it! A man walked through a doorway and caught me in his arms in mid-fall. Michael was across the room. Saw the whole thing. Said it was like one of those incredible football catches, so perfectly timed, you'd expect everyone to clap and holler. I didn't even know the guy. He set me upright and held me steady until I stopped trembling. Conversation stopped for a split second. I gasped, recovered, and flashed the stranger a big smile. 'Thanks!' I said. 'Great move! Prince Charming rarely comes along at exactly the right second!'"

"What luck! I'm glad you didn't hurt yourself," David said.

I looked down into the carpet, my legs stretched out in front of me, David's angling off in another direction. Though I was awkward about asking permission to sit on the floor, my physical unsteadiness felt perilous. Dredging up the past brought vivid memories of painful falls and broken bones. Each memory delivered a shock. Fear of falling now accompanied me everywhere, including David's office.

Sitting on the floor felt safer than sitting across from each other in the chairs. At least I knew I couldn't fall.

Just then, the sharp wail of an ambulance siren pierced the walls. The office windows facing the street rattled. I winced and felt my blood drain away. "No more sirens!" I whispered fiercely. Hearing sirens transported me to fresh images. I remembered myself sprawled on the bathroom floor, hearing the bones splinter in my leg as I fell, and, later, hearing the ambulance siren grow near. I had remained calm in front of my young daughter as the medics carted me off to Stanford Hospital.

But even now, the sound of a siren unsettled me. "I haven't always been so lucky," I whispered to David. "Falling has always been frightening—ever since I got sick. Since the first fall. It's shocking. Things shatter so fast. It's worse, too, when people see it happen. They stare. They ask, 'Are you all right?' And, of course, you say 'yes.' But it's brutally jarring. Every time I fall, I think I could have avoided it if I'd been more careful, paid more attention." My eyes burned. "I get angry when I fall—even almost fall."

David waited. "Why do you think you get angry? What's the anger about?"

"Oh, fear, terror. You know." I waved the question aside in a gesture, but couldn't say aloud what I knew.

Besides falling over backwards, I feared that if I fell, I would break apart. As a child, I had learned that falling in stiff braces was different from falling off the monkey bars and climbing back on. In rehabilitation, physical therapists had tried to teach us how to fall safely by pushing us over onto mats where we couldn't get hurt. I had hated this lesson and never got good at it. At 10, I knew walking, moving, and falling would be different forever.

I remembered standing in heavy metal braces for the first time. I swayed. A physical therapist held me secure, strapped in a canvas contraption like a baby's harness. It was my birthday and I was making my debut in brand new braces. I was excited. I was going to walk for my parents. But it was such hard work. I was vulnerable and afraid I would fall. My body felt alien and broken.

Decades of walking in braces had taught me that falling was no simple matter for me. I had broken both legs and one arm in three individual falls. Each time there was severe pain and a long recovery.

I looked over at David, but said nothing. Even thinking about those falls made me feel vulnerable. Still, sitting on the dark blue carpet in his office, I felt safe and less alone. I imagined we were in a small boat together with the sea all around us. I wasn't sure of the destination, but the boat was sturdy, no leaks.

26

"Dorothea, tell me about the first fall. Do you remember where and how it happened?" His tone was tentative, leaving me room to consider. I hesitated. No one had ever given me permission to talk about how it was, actually.

"Do you really want to know all that? I mean, the very first fall, the one that happened the morning I got polio." I watched him. This was stuff people asked about, but never directly. Curiosity was stifled by the rudeness of inquiry.

Yet, David was not everyone. This relationship had different rules. Feelings were not only allowed, they were important. Safety replaced reprimand, judgment, and shame.

"Yes, I want to know," he said. He didn't blink or hesitate. "What was it like to fall asleep one night as an ordinary 9-year-old girl and awaken unable to walk?"

"It was a very bad dream," I answered, slipping away into my story.

I'd had a violent headache for two days. Then I'd developed a sore throat and fever followed by a back ache. On September 3, 1949, I awoke in the gray half-light of morning. I heard the quiet breathing of my sister in the twin bed next to mine. I had to go to the bathroom, but my body felt like lead. It was hard to turn over and sit up. My legs dragged heavily.

Feverish and heavy-lidded, I forced myself to sit up. My legs felt like lead pipes. I half threw them out of bed. Weak and lightheaded, I set my feet on the cool linoleum floor. Hanging onto the maple bedpost, I hauled myself up and took the first step. My legs buckled. I fell so fast that I didn't feel a thing. But the early morning silence shattered.

I heard the fall, the crashing sound, and found myself sprawled out face down on the waxed linoleum floor. I smelled the wax, and saw two small clouds of dust move, felt the hard floor beneath my shoulders and hip bones. Lifting my head, I saw the slats on the underside of my sister's bed where I was wedged.

David uncrossed his legs, and his movement in my line of vision returned me to the present. My body felt stiff and rigid. I shut my eyes and pressed my palms hard against my temples. Stop going back over it, stop recalling it, Dorothea, or you'll go mad, I said to myself. You're already mad! That's what this is about, dummy, my demon whispered.

"Breathe," David said. His voice sounded as if he were directing me through a dark room. "Take deep breaths and open your eyes." I opened my eyes and looked at him. He looked absorbed and open, nodding in affirmation. "What happened to you? Tell me what you are experiencing right now," he prodded gently.

I shuddered. I had gone too far allowing myself to re-live the story. It was bad enough having lived it once. Now I saw it again, still inside me. I looked at the wall, away from David. I wanted to leave but couldn't get up and walk out. David stared at me patiently. I broke the silence.

"Right away, after I fell, I tried to scramble up from the floor. When I couldn't get up, I screamed."

My sister, Lois, snapped on her bed lamp and yelled at me to get up. By now, our whole family was roused. I sat slumped against the bed, trying not to cry. I knew I had made a mess. Then my mother was there holding my head, stroking my hair.

Dad loomed in the doorway. "What's going on here?" his gruff voice boomed. "Fell down, did you? Well, stop your crying and get up. Get a move on. Stop carrying on about it, too!" His thick black hair was rumpled. His face was heavy with sleep.

"I can't get up! I can't move!" I shouted. I was afraid of him in his cranky morning mood. "Move!" I said fiercely to myself. Now fully awake, but feeling deep in a bad dream, I ordered my legs to move. The response was a weak feathery movement, no more.

I tasted salty tears and my mouth contorted in the cry I could no longer hold back. Then Dad's arms were under mine, gathering me to him. "Can you put your arms around my neck? Can you hold on?" he said softly in my ear.

"I think so," I cried, wanting so to please him.

He half lifted, half dragged me to my feet. I felt dizzy and shaky, holding on for dear life. How I clung to him.

"Dad? I have to go pee." It sounded funny and I looked up at him. We both laughed. I was grateful for the relief.

Then my Dad and I did a strange dance down the short hallway to the white tile bathroom. He left me sitting on the toilet, the pants of my blue seersucker pajamas crumbled beneath my feet. My legs were butternut brown and healthy looking. But now they dangled like dolls' legs. I pinched one and it hurt, tickled the other and raised goose bumps. No matter what, neither leg moved beyond a tremble.

Dad carried me back to bed. While I was in the bathroom, Mom had tidied the bed and plumped up the pillows. My sister looked at me with unaccustomed sympathy. But in spite of the pampering, I felt worse. I couldn't get comfortable. My back ached and stiffness moved up my spine. I was certain the backache was from carrying my friend's doll carriage up a steep flight of stairs. A few days earlier our parents had warned us not to drag the carriage upstairs alone. We did it anyway. I was sure God was punishing me.

The household returned to its usual Saturday routine, but Dad stayed home from work to wait for the doctor, and my mother gave me special attention. She served me Sunday breakfast in bed—a scrambled egg, bacon, toast, and tea.

She tried to prop me up, but I kept sliding down the pillows. Now my shoulders and arms ached when I moved. Mom kissed my forehead and coaxed me to eat. "I'm too tired," I whined. "Can I just drink the tea?"

She smiled. "How about if I help you?" she asked. Then she picked up the fork and fed me. I felt like a little baby, but I loved having my mother all to myself. I was glad my big sister wasn't seeing this. She'd never stop teasing me.

Later that morning the doctor examined me. He moved each leg gently but even when I tried, I still couldn't move by myself. He listened to my chest, felt my feverish forehead, and reassured me. "You'll be all right," he said. He went into the kitchen with Mom and Dad. I listened to the grownups murmuring softly, but only caught a few words: signs, serious, observation. I strained to hear more.

"Did anyone say the word *polio* up to this point?" David interrupted.

"No. I was thinking it and I was sure everyone else was too. But I was afraid to ask."

Whenever the doctor came to our house, there was a reverential hush, as if a priest had come to dinner. We'd been taught to behave well. I would have gotten a good smack for speaking out of turn, so I waited.

After the doctor left, Mom said, "Dr. Aaron thinks you're going to be fine but he wants you to go to the hospital for tests to see what's wrong. Just for a few days. Grandpa is coming over with his car now. We can all go together."

She held my hand as she spoke. I searched her face. She didn't look alarmed, but I trembled. My eyes filled fast with tears and I turned away. "Don't cry, Dorothea. You're a big, brave girl. It won't be so bad," my Dad said, patting my hand. I cried anyway and felt ashamed to be afraid and babyish.

I had never been to a hospital. My Dad went once, in an ambulance, in the middle of the night. He had his stomach cut open and my mother said there was a priest there who said prayers for the dying. When he came home, he was weak and yellow with jaundice. I didn't care how sick I was. I didn't want to go to that place!

But their minds were made up. Since I couldn't run away, it was better to be brave and not act scared. As my mother washed and dressed me, I cheered up. This was a familiar "going to the Doctor" routine. She wouldn't let me leave home in faded summer pajamas.

Like Sunday breakfast there were Sunday clothes on this extraordinary Saturday. A white silk slip with lace trim, a starched pink and blue plaid dress, my favorite that summer. Mom got my limp feet into white anklets and shiny black Mary-Janes. She brushed my hair and fastened it with a blue satin ribbon. Then she handed me her silver-framed mirror.

I looked pretty, as if dressed for a party. I giggled because I felt silly dressed in these clothes, flat on my back, stiffer and achier each minute. The mirror grew heavy and slipped away.

Dad wrapped me mummy-style in a patterned summer blanket. Bending me as little as possible, he carried me from the apartment, down the elevator, and to the waiting car. My neck was stiff and I couldn't move but I saw some neighbors watching. Dad stretched me out gently on the back seat, my head in Mom's lap. Grandpa rode in the front seat with Dad but he didn't turn on the ball game. I hated listening to ball games on the radio.

I felt small and scared. What would they do to me, and would it hurt? Mom talked about doctors and nurses helping me to get better, but I worried about wetting the bed and being left alone. I wanted to ask, "Will you leave me all alone in a strange place?" But I didn't. I wondered again if I might have polio, but since no one mentioned it, I didn't want to bring it up. I wasn't really so afraid; just too sick to talk much. My mother stroked my head while I gazed out the window, watching pieces of blue sky and buildings swirl around me, topsy turvy. If I closed my eyes, I got dizzy. It was like an endless carnival ride, only the bumps and turns in the road were no fun.

At last we arrived at the hospital. A strange man lifted me onto a stretcher and rolled me down a gray corridor that echoed with unfamiliar noises. My mother's high heels clicked as she walked alongside me, holding my hand. Finally we stopped in a narrow cubicle of a room.

I held onto my mother's hand and absorbed the scene: strange equipment, low murmurs, jarring noises, occasional outbursts of crying. There was a strong odor of starch—pressed linens, bedgowns, uniforms. A starched nurse asked my mother to step outside while she "got me ready."

"For what?" I wondered, but didn't dare ask. I didn't dare cry either. The nurse was kind and reassuring as she undressed me. Still, she was a stranger. I felt frightened as each garment came off. When I lay naked, she covered me quickly with a light blanket. "Where is my mother?" I finally asked with fake boldness.

"Don't worry, dear," came her quick reply. "You'll see her after the doctor's examination." Then a jolly, curly haired man wheeled me off through a maze of corridors, farther and farther from where I had begun. I joined him in friendly chatter. It would not do to start whining like a baby.

I winced and then breathed deeply. The late morning sun spilled across the glass top of David's desk and caught my hand fiddling with the knee strap on my brace. I bent my knee and rested my head on the cushion behind me. A great weight was bearing down on me. I pushed it back mightily but it was slowing me down.

David stared at me. "It's all right to be afraid, Dorothea. Everyone gets afraid sometimes. And you certainly had plenty to fear. You must have been terrified."

"I don't remember the terror," I whispered. "I only remember the glaring white light, and being twisted in the shape of a donut. The blackness. No more waiting. No more time." I closed my eyes, exhausted. I feared getting stuck in that place again, feared getting bowed down with pain. Shrugging my shoulders, I looked at David. "You know that part, at least. About the spinal tap. I don't want to say that part again."

I had no more words. I closed my eyes and sank into blackness again, relieved to be redeemed by the end of the therapy hour.

But there was no escape. In the dark hours of the nights ahead, I drifted between sleep and wakefulness, gathering and fitting together the remaining pieces of the days following that first fall.

After the spinal tap, I awoke in a small, narrow room with gray walls. I lay stiff and still in a narrow white bed. Light glared from the tall rectangular window beyond the foot of my bed, and noise came from the open door behind and to the right of my head. My bed was wedged in a corner. To my right, I could see a white metal chair beneath the window at the foot of the bed. Ahead of me and to the left was a small porcelain sink and a white metal bedstand. The room was without color or life.

No one was there so I invented a story. My parents were lost and hadn't been able to find me in this huge hospital. I waited for them to come. I knew they would find me and take me home with them.

It grew dark outside. Soon the only light came from the corridor behind my head. I couldn't move my head. It had fallen and stiffened on my right shoulder. When I raised my eyes, I saw frightening images dancing on the ceiling. I was very hot and thirsty. I woke and slept for what felt like days. I dreamed I was next to a restaurant kitchen, hearing the clatter of dishes and other harsh noises. Then I was on a sailing ship, rocking back and forth unsteadily. Faraway noises pushed at me through a fog, muffled rhythmic pulsing of heavy machinery.

In my waking hours, the absence of my mother filled the room. Kind but hurried nurses came in often, the rustling of their uniforms announcing their approach. And one doctor kept returning and asking me if it hurt to breathe. But they were all strangers to me and I was afraid to cry. One nurse reassured me that my mother would be there in the morning. I watched her pour a chilled bottle of White Rock ginger ale into a chipped enamel cup with a spout. She cradled my head with her arm as I drank. She soothed me while I waited for my mother.

In the morning my mother finally arrived. She was dressed like a ghost in a billowy white gown and a cap which hid her lovely brown hair. She sat in the metal chair and read me the Sunday comics, but the pictures looked upside down. Then her face looked upside down, too. She looked like a monkey with her eyebrows beneath her eyes. I felt nauseous and couldn't see straight anymore. I slept again and when I awoke she was gone. The long shadows of early evening made striped patterns on my bedsheets. Then Dad came and told me stories about my little brother. I showed Dad how I could wiggle my toes on one foot. When he left, I faced another night alone.

Nights and days swam into each other. I feared the pain and cold shock of being lifted onto hard metal bedpans. I hated being fed lying flat on my back. All of it was unspeakable—the stiffness, fever, chills and agony of being moved, even touched, for a change of bed sheets or night shirt. Total paralysis was like being trapped in a nightmare where you waited to wake up. I waited to get better. I wanted to go home.

One night long after my Dad left, I heard a murmur and saw a shadowy figure at the foot of my bed. A candle flickered and my eyes focused on the familiar face of our family priest. He was reading aloud from a prayer book. I heard Latin words and saw him make the sign of the cross. He smiled."What are you doing, Father?" I asked.

"Praying for all the sick people in the world," he replied.

"Will you say a prayer for me, too?" I asked.

"Of course," he answered warmly. "Especially for you."

I closed my eyes and slid away again, this time feeling safe.

One day I awoke and my head felt clear. When my mother came, she didn't look upside down or wavering anymore. She looked happy. She said I was so much better that I was being moved to a room with other children.

My heart leaped. There had to be some mistake. I was only supposed to be here for a few days. No one had even told me what was wrong. I still couldn't move. I couldn't even turn my head I was so stiff. I knew I couldn't go home like this. I had to know what had happened to me.

As my mother gathered the personal possessions that had accumulated in the room, I asked: "Mom, will you answer one question if I ask you?"

"Sure," she said cheerfully.

"No one's said what's wrong with me." I paused and took a breath. "Mom, do I have polio?" It was out.

"Yes, you do," she said evenly. "But you're going to be just fine now." She snapped the small suitcase shut and smiled at me.

"I thought so. But no one would say it to me. I feel better being able to name it. Now I don't have to worry about what's wrong with me anymore."

Her eyes were warm and steady. She stroked my hair, kissed my forehead, smiled her dazzling smile. How I loved her for telling me. How relieved I was, finally, to know.

4

DAVID

BLOCKED EMOTION

I remember the day Dorothea first sat on the floor of my office. When I greeted her that morning, she seemed subdued and lacked her usual liveliness. She went into the office, moving very slowly, and sat on the edge of the sofa. When I asked her about the previous weekend, she answered mechanically. Her voice trailed off at the end of sentences. She sat there quietly staring down at the carpet. I could see that she was beginning to drop into the pain beneath her depression. Her head was drooping. When she did look up, her eyes were round and watery, heavy with sadness.

"Tell me what you're feeling Dorothea. What are you in touch with?"

Suddenly, she was talking about falling, telling me how she felt like she was going to lose her balance and fall. As she spoke she held onto the arm of the sofa as if to save her life. She began to talk about one of the horrors of polio, falling down. In relearning to walk, she had fallen again and again. After numerous painful falls, she became fearful, anticipating each fall with greater dread. I listened carefully. These were not normal childhood spills. Dorothea's falls were frequent, dangerous, and damaging. In the three years following the onset of polio, she had broken her right leg and her right arm in two such falls.

As she spoke, I remembered Roy, another client who had suffered polio as a young child. He, too, had been in a large hospital ward filled with other polio patients. Early in the illness his doctor said that he would never walk again. Away from the security of his home and parents, he just nodded his acceptance of this news. But inside he screamed, "No, No, No!" This defiance led to late night forays in the hospital. After the lights were dimmed, he pulled himself out of bed and forced himself to walk. His damaged legs couldn't support his weight and he fell.

Then, crawling back to the bed he tried again, and fell again. He did this over and over again to the point of exhaustion. Sometimes, staff members found him in the middle of the night curled up and sound asleep on the cold hard floor. Roy did this night after night and, years later, he remembered all the falls with intense emotion.

Here was Dorothea reporting parallel experiences with falling. As therapy moved her closer to old buried feelings, the full terror of those falls returned. Now, when she began to touch deep emotions, she felt as if she were falling again.

"Would you mind if I sat on the floor? I need to feel the solidness of the floor under me right now." She was embarrassed to ask and spoke in a hushed voice.

I said, "Okay, sure," and joined her. There was something impossible about staying in my chair, even though I really hate sitting on the floor. Since I've always hated it, I must have lied when she asked if I minded. Probably I said, "I don't mind at all." So, we sat on the floor.

I got to feeling comfortable about sitting on the floor and it was obviously right for Dorothea, perhaps essential. It was a movement to a closer, more intimate relationship. On the floor, her braced leg was displayed right out there, to be viewed, discussed, analyzed and experienced. It was, after all, what this encounter was all about.

Dorothea talked about falling incidents—the unseen wet spot on the floor of the cafeteria, crutches slipping out of control, the broken bones, the interruption of plans, the sirens. Talking about these moments, her words were often a whisper. I had to strain to catch them, and sometimes, when I did, I'd feel the breath knocked out of me in recognition of how much pain she had lived through and was reliving now. It was as if I were falling. I was hearing the bones break. I was cringing at the sound of sirens. I was seeing the world from flat on my face, sprawled out in public, and in pain.

Sitting on the floor helped Dorothea as she struggled to reconnect to her childhood experience. For several weeks our sessions began with a ritual of furniture rearrangement. I pushed an arm chair back and propped two large pillows against it on the floor. Dorothea sat on the sofa, released the knee lock mechanism of her brace, and slid to the floor. Then she leaned back against the pillows, her legs straight out in front of her. I sat in a similar manner across from her but to one side so that our legs jutted past where the other sat.

In this position, Dorothea told the story of her childhood polio. Her feelings had been so thoroughly put away that the story came in small pieces, at times nearly in gasps. As the therapy proceeded, we discovered that Dorothea couldn't connect her memories and feelings to words. There were long silences. Vivid memories came now, but the associated feelings were so intense that she became verbally paralyzed. She couldn't say the memories out loud, couldn't release the emotions which were surfacing after so many years.

This phenomenon of emotional disconnection in the face of overwhelming pain and terror is widely observed in human experience. It seems to be part of our survival wisdom. I once saw a film made in Hiroshima the day after the atomic bomb. The survivors were doing the work they needed to do to carry on and they looked as if they were in a hypnotic trance. Children disconnect in painful and frightening situations where there is insufficient security to allow them to spontaneously cry out with their feelings. These significant unexpressed emotions are not simply skipped over by the psyche. They are stored away, in the basement as it were, until we are ready to handle them.

Dorothea had regained access to the 9-year-old in her memory. But this child had given up the right to cry years ago. She had lost the words to describe her despair and terror. She recalled days of staring at the blank gray wall of her room during the most painful and terrifying early part of her hospitalization. She had emotionally disappeared into that wall and this psychological defense was still so strong that when she returned to those memories, she once again disappeared into the gray wall. That wall stood between her and the terror of the memories. When she tried to say what she felt, all that came were small whimpering sounds.

I encouraged her to breathe deeply into the feelings, allowing them to rise up and pass through her. When she struggled, I'd reach out and hold her hand. But she couldn't do it. The air caught in her throat and she thrashed her head back and forth, eyes tightly closed. I watched her disappear into an internal fortress which was tightly closed against pain.

I knew Dorothea's powerful energy had to be released for the deep wounds inside to heal. Until this healing occurred, the experience of childhood polio couldn't be integrated and the memories laid to rest. I wasn't sure what to do. I have always conceived of therapy as a fluid, experimental process requiring adaptation and creativity when the usual methods don't meet the need of a client.

My training in Gestalt therapy taught me the value of dramatic enactments of life situations as a means to help individuals break through barriers which keep them stuck psychically. I wondered what enactment would help in this situation.

As I observed Dorothea's efforts to integrate the emotional stress and pain she repressed as a young child, I imagined what it would have felt like to have been 9 years old in that hospital. What was missing for her then? What would she have needed then to allow her to experience the full cycle of feelings that illness and hospitalization would create in any child?

Emotional pain is a transitional experience. If it can be felt and expressed, the feeling is completed. But if a child has no safe place to express the pain and suffering, the emotions are held in and "forgotten."

What did Dorothea need to complete the experience now? Suddenly, I sensed that what was missing was the support of a parent. She had needed an understanding and patient adult to sit on the edge of that hospital bed, hold her hand and talk to her, encourage her questions and draw out her feelings. She needed a parent who reached out and held her in terrible moments of fear and pain, providing a safe place to release her feelings.

Once I grasped this, I no longer saw Dorothea as a 47-year-old woman. Now she was a terrified child, cringing in the face of overwhelming danger. In her desperate thrashing back and forth she was, again, that child in the hospital.

I whispered to her, "Dorothea, it's all right now. What is happening to you is horrible. You feel all alone and terrified. But I'm with you now and I will protect you. I won't allow any harm to happen to you. You feel like crying because it hurts so much and you deserve to feel sorrow for yourself. You don't have to hide this pain from anyone ever again."

When she heard these words I could see her drop to even greater depths of anguish. Her face became twisted with the desperate need to let the feelings out. The parent in me took over and I leaned forward and held her in my arms tightly and began to rock back and forth, murmuring soft sounds to this "frightened child." She began to breathe into her feelings, just a little at first.

"That's good, Dorothea. Just let the air fill your lungs, breathe it in deeply and let it all out. Let yourself make noise as you breathe out. That's good."

Her breathing slowly grew into small groaning sounds and I encouraged this by humming an old, sad lullaby. Her moaning became deeper and seemed more comfortable to her. Even though the release was partial, as if it were being squeezed out of her throat, it was obviously very relieving to Dorothea. After perhaps 10 or 15 minutes, the wave of terror passed and Dorothea sat up, somewhat stunned by the intensity of the experience.

Over the years I have occasionally held clients in moments of acute emotional unloading, a spontaneous response when someone simply needed a direct and tangible expression of acceptance and understanding. With Dorothea, this tangible support helped her feel sufficiently safe to experience her painful feelings.

In a few minutes Dorothea regained her composure and exclaimed, "Wow, that was something. That felt so safe and secure. It was just what I needed."

This experience repeated itself several times during the early phase of Dorothea's therapy. Over time her moaning evolved into another sound, not quite weeping, but closer to a full release. Relearning how to feel her emotions and release them came slowly.

I regularly interpreted for her the process she was going through and complimented her on her courage, both the courage of the child she once was and her courage now in doing this therapy work.

One day she came in feeling very sad. She recalled the close and touching relationship she had developed with an older girl, Joanne, a teenager who was confined in an iron lung. When these memories came back, she realized that when Joanne died she had never been able to grieve this loss. The feelings this memory brought up in Dorothea were even more intense than any I had seen before. She folded over into her sadness and began to weep for Joanne but she looked coiled with tension and breathed in short, rapid gasps. I could see how much her feelings needed to be released, but she was fighting them, twisting and turning, her hand tightly grasping her stomach. Taking the placement of her hand as a cue, I spontaneously reached over, placed my hand on hers and quickly pushed her in the abdomen. Suddenly, it was as if a dam burst. A wailing burst forth from Dorothea and she began to sob and cry. There was no tightness now, no constraint, and she breathed long and deep into her pain, tears streaming down her face.

The gray wall had tumbled down. Nothing stood between Dorothea and her deepest feelings. She was not afraid.

When her weeping was over she just sat back and stared off into space. She was very peaceful. There was nothing to say, no interpretation was needed.

This phase of treatment with Dorothea was quite strenuous and intense. She was breaking ground for herself in the task of deliberately looking back at the early polio experience and uncovering the unfinished emotional content. I was surprised to discover how difficult it was for her to release emotions because she is characteristically very feeling and expressive in personality style. It was only over time that we discovered there were significant limitations to her expressiveness.

Dorothea inhibited release of her emotions primarily by holding her breath. This is a common, but unconscious pattern in people who find it difficult to express feelings. Holding the breath is a powerful way to stifle feelings. I often think of the lungs and the vocal cords as the organs of emotion. When someone needs to relearn emotional release, he must learn to use the power of breath and voice.

It took many attempts before Dorothea was able to fully experience her grief. There were several times when I responded by holding her as if she were a child. Many therapists will never venture into this kind of intervention, and some consider such techniques too risky or even professionally marginal. Whenever this kind of physical contact takes place in the therapeutic relationship, there are definite risks and complications to be considered. A major risk is the possibility of creating excessively strong transference feelings in the client or counter-transference feelings in the therapist.

Transference refers to feelings from earlier relationships which become "transferred" onto the therapist; similarly, counter-transference feelings are those transferred onto the client from elsewhere in the therapist's life. Such feelings can develop in nearly all therapeutic relationships that endure beyond very brief periods, and especially in therapies which involve getting in touch with vulnerable emotional states. The presence of transferred feelings is not in itself a problem. In fact, some therapies are based on the development of transference and the treatment involves the "working through" of these feelings. My approach is to work directly with transferred feelings only when they interfere with the therapy rather than support and enhance it.

With Dorothea, I recognized that she was developing feelings in the relationship that were very much like those of a loving and trusting child towards a parent. I believe those feelings were significant in allowing her to feel safe enough to engage in the intense and painful process of reliving her earlier memories. The transference here clearly supported the therapeutic task. However, I proceeded cautiously in my work with Dorothea.

The emotional impact of such intense therapy work and the physical closeness involved required particular attention. I placed very clear and definite boundaries around the work. When each emotional unloading incident was finished, I immediately reverted to the therapeutic frame of two adults, one a client and the other a therapist, engaged in a controlled and purposeful treatment program. We talked about the experiences, interpreted what was taking place, and, through this process, shifted these experiences from the purely emotional level back to the professional context of the relationship.

Another important precaution I took was to seek regular consultation with colleagues. Consultation allowed me to step back and objectively review what was taking place in the work, to discharge the stress, and to consider whether there were implications that needed attention.

It must be emphasized that therapeutic techniques which involve physical contact do need to be applied with extremely sensitive restraint. They must never be of a sexual nature. Such behavior is a total violation of the trust of the therapeutic relationship, is emotionally destructive to clients, and is unethical and illegal.

Additionally, there are some clients whose personal issues leave them far too vulnerable for this kind of intimacy. In conducting therapy with these individuals, touch is specifically contraindicated. And, of course, there are therapists for whom such interventions would feel unnatural. Still others, because of their own personal issues, should not engage in touch. Practically speaking, this issue comes up very infrequently in my therapy work. Most therapy does not involve touch. But, occasionally, there are moments when reaching out with the hand is exactly the right human and therapeutic response.

5

DOROTHEA

IN THE CHILDREN'S WARD

I was distressed by the intensity of my emotions as therapy work continued. Once I moved beyond the initial shocking memories, I had thought the memories would subside and life would resume at a more normal, familiar pace. That was what I assumed would happen, but though I tried hard to get control of myself, I felt infantile and vulnerable. Painful flashbacks to my first weeks of polio often left me speechless. David's questions provoked fresh images. I felt overwhelmed by what might come out—fear often held me in paralyzing silence.

But memories evoked pain I could not escape. I hated the pain and feared its power. The day I talked about Joanne I felt I had opened a forbidden drawer stacked with old photographs; snapshots I wished I hadn't seen tumbled out all over.

It was a humid Indian summer day. The heat and weight of the air was palpable. My cotton shirt peeled away from my back, wet with perspiration. There in David's office, when I said Joanne's name, I heard the whooshing of her iron lung and felt the afternoon heat settling on me.

"So, you think you're lucky to be alive, huh? Is that what they said?" asked David.

"Yes, David, I am. I was lucky not to be in an iron lung. Iron lungs were monstrous breathing machines. Big yellow tin cans with an enormous black bellows at one end. Their muffled rhythms droned on, day and night. One night there was a power failure. The nurses spent half an hour hand-operating those machines!

"You bet I felt lucky not to have paralyzed lungs. People in iron lungs spent 24 hours a day there. They breathed funny, in gasps. Their voices were thin, too. It was scary."

"Had you ever known anyone who died?" David asked

43

"When I was six, I saw my great grandmother in her casket. Alive, she was an old blind woman with a booming voice. She sat in a huge rocking chair in the dim foyer of her flat on New York's lower east side. When we visited, she called me to her. 'Dorothea, veni ca!'

"I was her favorite. Her namesake. Her voice thundered in Italian. My mother urged me forward and Grandma's dry rough hands lifted me onto her lap, traced my face, touched my head, and swept down the length of my legs. I was relieved when she said I could get down.

"After she died, I peered into her casket, fascinated. I half expected her to sit up and call my name.

"That was all I knew about death when I got polio." My gaze slipped back into the ward and I heard again the familiar whooshing of the machines. "Joanne wasn't so lucky," I whispered, pressing my palms against my temples.

"Tell me about Joanne. Was she a friend of yours? Was she in an iron lung?"

"Joanne was nineteen and pretty. She had short blond hair, a big smile, and lively blue eyes. She was in the ward next to mine and I met her after I was in the hospital for several months. By then I was able to sit in a wheelchair. She always said hello to me when I wheeled past her iron lung, near the doorway of the next ward. One visiting day, I met Joanne's mother, a gray-haired woman who moved slowly as if her bones hurt. She had a warm fairy godmother smile as she hovered over her daughter, feeding her tiny, exquisite sandwiches, cut into bite sizes.

"One Sunday, Joanne asked me to feed her a sandwich her mother had brought that afternoon. My mother brought care packages too, and I felt as if I were unwrapping a treasure when I unfolded the waxed paper holding Joanne's sandwich. There it lay. Thin slices of meat and cheese towered between two thin slices of pumpernickel bread. The sandwich was evenly divided into the neatest bite-sized pieces. Feeding Joanne meant lifting one of those sections, each a perfect morsel, and delivering it, intact, to her mouth. She invited me to share equally in the feast. I salivated. I was ravenous for 'outside' food. We had a party. We talked and laughed. It was the most delicious sandwich I ever ate."

Awakened by the sharpness of the memory, I recalled struggling to care for Joanne in other, more private, ways... reaching from my old-fashioned wooden wheelchair to open the portholes of the iron lung, putting my hands through, stretching to scratch her itchy places. Sometimes I covered her chilly body. Or uncovered her heated one. Through the windows on the side of the lung, I saw her body——breast and bone, still and bare. I had never seen anyone so thin.

"I wanted to make her feel better or make her laugh more. When her birthday came in January, I asked my mother to buy Joanne some pajamas. She bought a lovely pair of Chinese red pajamas with dark blue fasteners. With effort, I slipped her arms in and arranged the top, backwards, across her chest. She liked the way the soft fabric felt and I told her she looked bright and cheerful."

I looked at David and faltered, aching at the memory of my conversations with Joanne. "I was greedy and hungry for Joanne's company as well as her sandwiches," I added. "She was full of chatter. She was delighted whenever I came, even when she wasn't delighted about much else. I was flattered. After all, she was one of the 'big girls,' almost grown up. We became good friends. She worried about her mother who took the long trip from Staten Island ferry, train, bus, and foot. She had no father, or at least he never came to see her. If friends visited, I never saw them. I mostly remember that we were company for each other."

I spoke softly and felt my tempo slowing like an old record player that needed hand cranking.

"And then?" asked David. "What happened to Joanne?" We sat looking at each other knowing exactly what I had to say. I clasped my hands and bit my lower lip.

"And then one day she was gone, moved to another ward. I wasn't there when she was moved away. We lost contact after that. I felt her absence at first. But there were so many of us. After a while she faded from memory. I only recalled that we were friends who talked and laughed and ate together. She listened to me and...we even cried a little together a few times. I wiped her tears. But I never told anyone the part about crying.

"A year later, after I had been home from the hospital for several months working on rehabilitation, I heard that Joanne had died. At first I didn't believe it. How could she be dead? I'm glad it didn't happen when I was there, I said to myself. I never talked about it after that. In a way, it was as if nothing really happened."

The room was still. I hung my head in the late afternoon shadows and searched for my voice there in the mess of my life. I could not raise my eyes. I could not move. Joanne had come alive again. My sorrow and a sense of loss pressed like a heavy stone on my chest. Tears that had waited for so long welled in my eyes. I knew I would break apart if I moved.

David broke the silence. "How awful that was for you as a child," he said, his voice heavy with emotion. I glanced in his direction, wishing he were looking someplace else. I felt exposed in laying open this story. Having shared life with Joanne, I had disregarded her after her death. Now I felt the loss of her. I quivered

45

and then, at last, I wept. Through the tears I heard David's voice soothing me. "Such an old, old soul," he murmured. I wept for a long time—for Joanne and for myself.

Painful memories came in waves, like the heat of late summer, diminishing eventually but relentless in the present. Often real pain in a therapy session came in re-living a horrible experience that I couldn't express in words. David had shown passing familiarity with polio but, like most able-bodied people, he didn't know much about various treatments for the illness. Yet he was inquisitive. One day when the heat and humidity were oppressive, he asked, "Did you say you had weeks of hot pack treatments?"

"Seven weeks," I answered, remembering my fear that they would never end. I cringed uncomfortably, anticipating his question.

"That must have seemed like forever to you. Were the treatments painful? I mean, I'd think heat would feel soothing to a stiff sore body. Was it like that for you?"

No one had ever asked before. I wondered if I could tell him in a way that would capture what it was really like? Should I compare it to a steam bath? Not really. You walked in and out of those. You didn't have that trapped, paralyzed feeling. I wondered. Could I tell David without going back? I couldn't. I had to relive the heat and near suffocation of the September when I was nine years old.

"Hot packs were horrible," I began. "I used to gag on the big salt tablets we had each morning after breakfast. All twenty kids on the ward hated those horse pills. But they previewed the treatments which came three times a day."

Just the words "hot packs" made me taste the fear again—smell the steamy wool packs, feel the heat, drenching, cooling, itching, endless waiting. Unable to move, I was a little dot in a white bed in a huge room. I saw the soot on the low window sills, the gray-white pebbly floor tiles full of cracks and crevices. I heard the rhythmic beats of the iron lungs.

I pushed on. "I hated being 'gotten ready' for the treatment, stripped of my hospital gown, embarrassed at my naked, helpless body, getting rolled over on my stomach, flat out, arms at my side. I used to arrange my dolls like that in the doll carriage. My sister always said they looked unnatural and stiff, not like babies.

"I knew the treatment was about to begin when I heard the treatment cart coming. The squeaky wheels of the white utility cart carrying two deep tubs reverberated in the hospital corridor. I was in the third bed from the door so I always heard it coming. With each breath it came closer. I dreaded it. One tub was filled with wool cloths, the packs, in boiling water. It was a literal cauldron, complete with a wooden stick for stirring. The other tub was empty but fitted with a hand-operated wringer.

"Two people were needed to give the hot pack treatment," I went on. "We kids learned fast that we were at the mercy of their moods. I tried to be brave. If you screamed in terror when you heard the treatment cart at the foot of your bed, you were called a whiner. You got scolded. If you cooperated during the treatment, you got more care. Even tenderness, occasionally, when there was time. We were told that hot packs were nothing to be afraid of. But I was afraid."

Now I felt the old fear again. I swallowed hard and shut my mouth. My mouth quivered, forming words that would not come out. David nodded in affirmation, waited, looked at me. I could not hold his gaze.

"I wanted my mother," I whispered. "But mothers weren't allowed to be there. Visitors interfered with the treatments." I scanned the blue carpet, unable to raise my eyes. "I longed for my mother to take away the terror. I just knew if she were with me, I'd feel better. She always made it better during those three short visiting hours each week."

"Three hours!" David exclaimed. He sounded at once incredulous and angry. I flinched. "There should have been hundreds of surrogate mothers with all of you, holding you all the time. It's amazing! When did you see your mother and father?"

I remembered exactly. "One to three o'clock on Sunday afternoon and two to three on Wednesday. That was all." David nodded, still looking incredulous. The details were all there but I could only retrieve them by recalling the actual experience. I tucked my hands beneath my legs and leaned into the pillow supporting my back. I was glad I had asked to sit here on the floor where it felt safer, especially, as I told this awful story.

"The cart grew closer and stopped at the foot of my bed. I watched a nurse use tongs to fish out my boiling bundle of variously sized wool squares. The pieces were wrapped in striped mattress ticking material and secured by large safety pin. The nurse dropped the boiling mass into a white porcelain basin and unpinned it. There were nine pieces in all: one for my neck, lumbar area, back, both arms, both upper legs, and both lower legs. Starting with the neck piece, the nurse lifted each Army-green piece of wool by tongs and put it through the wringer three times—fast. After the first time, it was hot and wet. After the third time, it was hot and dry. I watched with dread each time.

"One nurse worked the hot wool strips through the wringer while the other tucked each piece in place on my naked body. She covered the wool with a piece of translucent plastic, then with a dry square of wool cloth, the thickness of a medium-weight blanket. I heard the crackle of the plastic when I was covered with another blanket, secured like a mummy to sweat it out. I smelled musty, felt close."

In the warmth of David's office, I felt perspiration under my arms and at the back of my neck. I felt a trickle of moisture along my hairline. David sat across from me, still as a statue. The room was still. He looked pained to me. I thought he was hoping I'd stop. I wanted this story to be over, too.

"Go on, Dorothea," he said softly. His voice came to me from a great distance. I was turning and falling through space, tumbling over backward into darkness. I could not speak or move.

I saw the nurses and heard their distracting chatter. When they were tired, there was a grim sense of rushing. Occasionally, there was a rare luxury—a drink of cold water or ginger ale through a curved glass straw. It tasted good. I had never seen a curved straw before or ever dreamed of drinking from this strange position, flat on my stomach.

And then I was back in that bed, paralyzed once again. Time stood still. I was nine years old again. It was mid-September, 1949, in New York City. It was hot and muggy. Almost breathless, I forced out the words. "There were no cool spots in the bed. And I couldn't move. I tried chasing flies away by wiggling my tongue. But it didn't matter if I cried, or wet the bed, or got thirsty, or perspired. Everything was wet anyway."

All of a sudden I felt very weary. I couldn't say what was inside and I couldn't bear being that child again, alone. I held out my arms, trying to hold back the weight of pain pressing in on me. David leaned over, caught me in his arms and rocked me. My arms encircled him as if I had been held this way a hundred times. But it felt like no other embrace. As he held me, I leaned into him, struggling fiercely against the pain that threatened to come out. I feared losing control.

At first I held my breath. In the darkness behind my shut eyes, a light came on. Someone had come to get me, finally. I wasn't a child all alone. I felt safe. I held on more tightly, resting my head on his shoulder, listening to the sound of my own beating heart. My eyes were hot and dry. There were no tears.

In this quiet steady embrace, I felt warm and accepted just the way I was. David was there to help me unfreeze my life. He said little besides: "You're all right now. You're safe here with me. Let yourself feel whatever you're experiencing." I tried to speak but I could only make barely audible noises and breathe. Slowly my body began to let go, relax in his arms. As the moments of terror passed, I heard the sound of David's heartbeat in my ear, and it sounded very much like my own.

"Wow," I thought. "I'm here with someone who's willing to go through this mess with me, who doesn't think I'm faking it or anything. God, I'm not alone!"

Regaining my balance, I moved away and looked at him shyly, as if this closeness was accidental. His eyes glistened and he blew his nose. I felt awkward having acted out my fear so childishly. And I was awed by this man whom I had trusted to take care of me. Between us was the burden he had risked carrying for a few special moments.

We talked about what had just happened and I felt relieved, steadier, cared for. So what if I was a terrified child again. He wasn't afraid, and he was capable. I could do this work with him.

"A first-rate horror story," he remarked. "It's amazing, the resilience of the human spirit. You were so brave. And so young. You carried it alone, didn't you, for all those years."

"I know what you mean," I said. "But there really wasn't any other way. The hot packs were applied three times in the course of a one hour treatment. And the treatment was repeated three times a day. I couldn't run away. And my mother couldn't come save me. I tried to be brave and imagine that this would make me well. I thought if I had enough faith in God, prayed enough, was good enough, maybe I'd be blessed. Maybe a miracle would happen." I laughed out loud, but David did not join me.

I wanted to finish the story. "I waited for the nurse to get back for the next set of packs before the first ones got cool and itchy. It rarely happened that way. When the packs had cooled and the nurse whipped them off, the breeze on my back was wonderful. But I was plunged back into heat when the next packs were applied. To make time pass, kids shouted to one another across the ward. Often we sang. We made up a thousand choruses of *On Top of Old Smoky*.

"Three times a day. The treatments seemed endless. But then one day they were over. Gone quickly, like the snapping of fingers. We were just moved on to the next phase of treatment."

Silently I remembered how we cried together too. Some kids screamed in fierce temper, others cried in pain, some just whimpered. Screaming usually started when someone got burned, scalded by a piece of wet wool. When the nurses rushed, they got careless with a wet wool corner, lost count and only used the wringer twice. I counted when I could see, listened to the wringer when I couldn't. Soon I knew by looking if the wool was still wet. I had to believe I wouldn't get burned, but, when it happened, I sobbed out loud, wore myself out with it. The shock was as bad as the pain. I knew it could happen again. So when one kid·cried, terror was alive in the ward. Polio was catching and terror was too.

I looked at David and sighed with exhaustion. "Dorothea, where do you go when you drift away from here?" he asked. "What are you afraid of? You lived through all of this. It's over, and it can't hurt you now, any more, ever again. You're safe here with me. You know that, don't you?"

I nodded but did not trust myself to speak. I was moved by his kindness but I was guarded. I feared that speech would give these memories more power, or worse, that it would reveal a mental illness beyond help.

6

DAVID

CHILDHOOD TRAUMA

Humans have an incredible ability to adapt to changing conditions. It is one of the reasons we have been successful on the evolutionary path, survivors where many species did not survive. We are resilient. We bounce back from devastating experiences to go on with life and the pursuit of our dreams. Throughout my years of practicing psychotherapy, clients have told stories that confirm this strength. The daily news reports are replete with examples of human resilience because these stories are so hopeful and make good copy in contrast to the media's general focus on disaster.

Children are especially resilient. In crises, they do what they must to survive. They might cry for help, or withdraw, or fight, or run—whatever the circumstance and their own adaptive style dictates. But if the critical situation persists for very long, they adapt to it and set out to make it fun and adventurous. This spirit is one of the things which makes being around children so inspiring and rewarding. Their energy is contagious.

But crises often cause physical and emotional suffering in children. If a trauma occurs in circumstances where children are not able to fully express their reactions, the feelings don't just vanish. They only seem to vanish. Emotional reactions to life events are natural and necessary for physical and psychological recovery. There is a price to pay whenever suffering is put away as the cost of survival. Payment of this cost comes due sooner or later. For Dorothea, it waited almost forty years.

During the early months of therapy, exploring her memories forced Dorothea to overcome emotional blockage that prevented the release of pain. As she regained the ability to experience that emotion, Dorothea began to see how thoroughly she had learned to hold it in, to function as if painful events didn't really hurt. She had

51

stored away an enormous quantity of emotion. Each time a memory returned, Dorothea re-lived the experience and discovered the unexpressed feelings.

Dorothea had stuttered during early childhood. All of her verbal expression became filled with anxiety. This predisposition to verbal suppression became reactivated when faced with the crisis of polio. As her therapy progressed, the sheer volume of unexpressed emotion began to diminish and verbal expression became somewhat easier for her. As she became less afraid of being overwhelmed by the intensity of her emotions, she learned how to vocalize her feelings.

During one session she reported a dream that occurred the previous night:

"I was in my parents' house where I grew up in New York, in the bathroom, getting ready to take a bath. My mother came in to help me. I jumped up on the edge of the bathtub, and, holding a knife, I screamed at my mother to leave me alone. I didn't want her to see the scars from where I had been beaten."

At first this dream puzzled Dorothea. She knew she had not been beaten as a child, so the drama of the dream didn't make sense to her. But as she began to recall her actual childhood experience, the symbolic meaning of the dream began to unfold. The dream was about her childhood pain and the necessity of protecting her mother from it, even to the extreme of threatening her mother with a knife to keep her away.

The "scars from beatings" metaphor was familiar to me. It reminded me of another client, "Anna," who had suffered a crippling disease in childhood. Several years ago I saw this young woman for an acute depression which occurred just as she had fulfilled several major life goals. She, like Dorothea, walked only with great effort and the aid of Canadian crutches. She had endured innumerable surgeries and medical procedures throughout her childhood and adolescence. Anna's physical condition kept her in some pain much of the time. But now, her life was calmer and happier than ever before. She was completely confused about why she was depressed.

During the treatment of Anna's depression I did some hypnotic work with her. While in a trance state, she came upon a scene in which she saw herself as a small child lying on a sidewalk, having been beaten severely. At first she didn't understand what the child represented since she had never been beaten as a child. But as she allowed herself to identify with this small child, she came to understand that from the child's point of view, all of the years of medical treatment had been "abusive." Not intentionally, of course, but in effect her body had been "beaten" repeatedly. The beaten child became a symbol of that pain and suffering. And now it was time for her to acknowledge those sufferings and care for the child who had endured it in silence.

The parallel between Dorothea's and Anna's symbolic metaphors fascinated me. Here were two different people, coping with similar childhood sufferings, and they had registered it in the same way. Their plights had required them to be brave and courageous.

But a child's natural developmental drive is for exploration, fun and adventure—not repeated pain, surgeries, needles, and separation from home and family. The plight of severely ill children required them to be brave and courageous. In the face of such chronic illness, how do children respond? With denial. They learn not to notice or show the pain. They learn to show what is expected. If showing hurt and fear and pain results in disapproval, they quickly figure out what earns approval. If bravery and courage are required, children learn to produce that. And who would argue against bravery and courage as a good coping attitude in the face of adversity? Children find their own solutions.

But if the solution requires the suppression of their natural reactions and feelings, this results in the development of a false front or a false self, presented to the world as the "real me." Children don't do this to be deceptive. They do it to gain emotional support and avoid disapproval of important adults.

In the nature of psychological functioning, when a role is practiced repeatedly, it becomes integrated into the personality so seamlessly that, after a while, it is not a role. This is a fundamental principle of learning. It also works in developing a false self. After playing this role for a while, the false self begins to feel natural and the real self inside begins to feel like a dangerous secret that must be hidden. But the real self continues to produce thoughts and feelings and reactions to life, all of which must be held inside. When this inner life contradicts the rules or demands of the false self, it produces guilt and shame.

Dorothea talked extensively about the complex relationships that developed in the hospital environment. She described a culture of denial and suppression. No one wanted to acknowledge the pain which was omnipresent. It was too much to bear. The message spread quickly to each new patient: "Keep your pain, sadness and fear to yourself." The unwritten rules were clear, expressed by both staff and patients in such spoken injunctions as: "Don't be a baby." "This won't hurt." "Look at how lucky you are compared to so-and-so." "You should be ashamed of yourself for making such a fuss." "What? You had surgery five days ago and you're still on Demerol?"

It didn't take long for new kids to learn that if they showed too much pain, they would be ostracized as "babies" by the other kids. There were exceptions, of course. Everyone was allowed to cry out in pain during spinal taps and hot pack treatments—this was permitted. But the fundamental message to Dorothea was that she should be ashamed of herself if she expressed pain. After awhile, she even felt ashamed to have these feelings.

The other message in Dorothea's dream demonstrated her need to keep her mother from seeing her emotional "scars." She recalled an incident which took place early in her hospitalization, before she had regained mobility in the upper part of her body. On a visit, her mother brought some Life Savers candies. Dorothea proudly showed her mother how she could feed herself by picking up the candies with her tongue from the sheet where they lay. When she looked up, her mother was crying, grief stricken by her daughter's suffering.

Seeing her mother's sadness, Dorothea told her, "It's okay mom. I'll be all right."

Becoming aware of her mother's pain, Dorothea felt apologetic for the inconvenience her suffering caused. It was as if she had done something wrong that caused the polio and she felt vaguely guilty for catching it. She thought, "It's Okay Mom, I'll take care of my feelings and yours. I'm sorry for the pain I'm causing you." Each little experience like this led her young mind to adopt some more rules: "Don't make people feel bad." "Take care of it yourself." "Be optimistic and cheerful." "Don't make a mess of things."

Over time, these rules became automatic—unconscious operating procedures that played out in all of her relationships.

As Dorothea sorted through these memories and recollections, I was often reminded of my childhood and the rules I developed in coping with my brother's death. I remembered the day Johnny died. I was descending the staircase to the living room and was midway when the front door opened and my mother came in. Her face was frozen with pain and she looked up at me and said, "He's dead. Johnny's dead." I stopped and leaned against the brightly papered wall. I was terrified and did not know what I was supposed to do and what I was supposed to feel. I thought I should feel sad and heartbroken at losing my constant playmate, the brother I had looked up to for so many years. Instead, what I felt was fear and guilt, an overwhelming terror at not knowing how I was supposed to act. My grief for Johnny had to wait for 20 years before I expressed it.

Like Dorothea, I became an expert at watching the adults around me for signs of disapproval and I tried to figure out what I was supposed to do. There were rules but I didn't know what they were. At Johnny's funeral, I looked around and saw that everyone else seemed to know what to feel. But I didn't, so I felt nothing.

My parents grieved terribly for Johnny. My father was a quiet and self-contained man, so I didn't see much of his grieving. It was only years later that I understood just how severely he grieved. But my mother's grief dominated the atmosphere of the family for years. She was consumed by it and often withdrew to her bedroom, for what seemed like weeks at a time, emerging only to prepare meals before disappearing again.

During that time, being a child, I quite naturally gravitated to having fun and adventures. Life went on. I'd forget that my brother was dead. In my spontaneous enthusiasm and play, I might run excitedly through the back door into the kitchen and there encounter my mother at the sink or stove. She'd turn around with grief on her face and I'd sink into shame, ashamed that I was having fun, ashamed that I had forgotten about Johnny, ashamed at what I had done to him. I had hurt my mother. Johnny was dead and I had forgotten and here I was, having fun.

Time passed. In the hallway of our home hung a small portrait of Johnny painted by a family friend from a photograph. Each day I passed that picture and felt uncomfortable and haunted. I learned to divert my eyes from it. Johnny became a mystery to me. When he was referred to in conversation, the comments were about his sweet, gentle nature, or about how loving he was in his dying days. In my mind, he became transformed into an angelic model of childhood perfection, the exact opposite of myself. I was a "pill" and a "rascal" at the least, and "a dirty rotter" at the worst. No one knew that it was my fault Johnny got sick. This was my secret. But I knew.

When Johnny died I felt as though I lost my mother. She disappeared into her grief and I knew I had better leave her alone. It felt too dangerous and unpredictable to intrude into her private space with my needs. So I went into my own private space to handle my needs. I adapted in order to survive. It was easy to move away from the turmoil I felt inside. It was left behind, or so I thought. Time passed and the reality of Johnny's death faded into the past. I never grieved as a child, never felt the sadness of loss, never wept. Those feelings could not be felt. They were covered over with guilt and shame and they sank deeply into my unconscious.

In time, Johnny ceased to be a reality to me. I scarcely remembered that I had a brother. The years we spent playing together were completely lost from memory. The connection between my mother's suffering and my brother's death also faded with time. After awhile, she was just my mother who was often tense and unhappy and I seemed destined to disappoint her. Increasingly I lived a secret life, playing a role designed to meet family expectations, but on my own living out the destiny of the bad kid. My unconscious belief system was well established now.

These memories of my own painful childhood years attuned my ear as I listened to Dorothea's accounts of terror, suffering, and flight. Her fear of the hot pack treatments, the hospital environment, her loss of childhood—these were experiences of Gothic dimension. They were too much for a young child to feel on her own. The adult world demanded that she be brave and she did what she had to do.

And now, years later, it was time to give the young Dorothea permission to no longer be brave. It was time to defy all those rules which had kept her shut down and alone in her suffering, the rules which kept hundreds of polio kids shut down and alone in their suffering.

Dorothea had learned to deny pain, fear, and anger. She had to learn to reverse this pattern and she often felt stuck and confused while doing it. At times she was not sure what was happening to her, yet she was becoming certain that what was happening was powerful and important. What she had to learn, what is so hard to learn, is that suffering is its own cure.

Allowing the pain is the solution in the kingdom of the mind. The mind has its own methods for healing psychological wounds. What therapists must do is remove all of the barriers which block this natural process.

7

DOROTHEA

COMIC RELIEF

As the autumn passed, I recalled vibrant moments of childlike pleasure threading through my painful hospitalization. In the absence of parental visits, my dad had written me a short note every day of the year I was away from home. The four or five lines were full of teasing affection and silliness. He often enclosed cartoons from magazines or drew funny pictures that amused and entertained me. I lived for those envelopes with his funny chicken scratch handwriting. They were daily treats.

Now, with some of the hard work of therapy behind me, I sought out humor. One morning I brought David a cartoon showing a middle-aged man standing in front of a picture window, observing a single tree in his backyard. The man was sobbing as he watched the tree's last leaf flutter to the ground. A caption above read *September Song*. Below, in quotations, appeared a single word: "Waaaah!"

"Here's one for your collection," I said, chuckling.

He joined me in robust laughter. "That's great! Exactly what it feels like sometimes, huh?" He put the clipping on the mantel with his other cartoons and sat down across from me, focusing his attention. His habit of looking at me was beginning to feel familiar, even comfortable, now that some of the messy stuff was out. I felt we'd been to the "polio wars" and survived in spite of the land mines. David had been a sturdy, reliable companion so far. He was beginning to feel like a trusted friend.

"You know, something's really different today," I began. "I feel as if I've reached a milestone—the end of the beginning of this therapy business." I expected him to say something but he didn't. "I mean, I feel a little like that cartoon. You know—when the last leaf flutters down, something is over. I don't know what comes next. But I feel relief. Maybe you were right."

"Right about what?" he asked. "Of course I'm always right," he joked, "but not everyone gives me credit for that."

"Don't flatter yourself too much," I chided. "You'll get a fat head." We laughed and I felt the warm comfort of his company. "I meant, you've assured me through these weeks that I'd survive this experience. I'm beginning to see that now. I don't feel completely overwhelmed all the time. Something is changing."

"Good. It's good that you notice the changes too. They're part of the process you've been moving through very rapidly. You've been working very hard and you need to take care of yourself."

I brushed off that take care stuff and went on in my upbeat mood. "Last night I remembered some really funny things that happened when I was in the hospital. After I came home, too. Can you believe that? There were years of rehabilitation, but everything wasn't as awful as what I've told you so far. It was a little like *M.A.S.H.* Same time period too." I grinned at him, pleased to feel comfortable for a change.

"What funny things do you remember? You kids must have invented all kinds of things to keep you going through that long period of isolation and treatment. What was it like?" he asked.

"Well, in the beginning, mostly we were bored. We were just a bunch of kids together who couldn't move and couldn't get out of bed. Not sick or anything. Time dragged. We made up songs that mocked the hospital, the nurses, the physical therapists. And we mocked our bodies that no longer worked right. 'Breathe like a polio' some kid would shout. Then we'd all gasp and gulp air in a strange, labored way. Everyone laughed, even the iron lung kids!

"When I regained full arm movement, I imitated the finger crawling and floppy arm gestures of my more paralyzed friends. Walking jokes developed later when we were braced and taking our first steps between the parallel bars. My specialty became imitating the poster child for the National Foundation for Infantile Paralysis. I was very good at this—hunched over on sprawling crutches with the perfect sappy grin for begging dimes. We howled at each other for hours. With no television and no visitors, we made our own fun.

"The highlight of the spring was an outing to the Ringling Brothers' Circus. Everyone who could sit in a wheelchair got to go. We had front-row seats and the clowns gave us Slinkys for gifts. But the most fun was the trip to the circus. We went by ambulance, a half-dozen kids at a time. Once the ride was underway, we begged the driver to use the siren and speed up as he traveled through Manhattan's busy streets.

"He did. We peered out the half-frosted windows, stuck out our tongues, made devil's horns, crossed our eyes. We relished the shock effect. One woman with her arms full of grocery bags was so amazed that she dropped a parcel. A string of oranges rolled down the street in our wake. She was our best audience. We savored telling that story for days afterward. We had made our own circus.

"When I went home, I spent a full year on rehab work before I could return to school. I missed the jokes, the playful mockery of my hospital pals. Our New York apartment was across the street from a city park. In my wheelchair or on crutches, I felt the stares of gawkers—not just kids either. I saw the quick, sneaky glances of adults. At first my cheeks burned crimson and I looked away. Strangers approached me and asked how I got crippled. Can you believe that?"

David nodded in sympathetic agreement as if he could believe it all. "That's awful. How'd it make you feel? I'll bet you handled them."

"I wanted to kill them," I said. "Instead, I developed a fancy repertoire of responses. In cheerful tones I said I was playing the part of a crippled child in a local theater production. Later on, as a snotty teenager, I'd say: 'I got this way from asking people dumb questions,' or 'I got crippled from being nosey.'

"At the dinner table my family applauded the smart answers and helped me develop new ones. We kids often played reverse mockery, making fun of the pitying, hangdog expressions of the gawkers. Soon we'd go on to imitate well-meaning neighbors who were especially demonstrative in their concerns. We kind of flushed them all down the toilet together."

"Great! You couldn't have done better." David said approvingly. "Your family really banded together around you. It must have been very hard for them too. But it was so good for you to have their support."

"I know I needed them. I admired and fought with my older sister and loved and played with my younger brother. They knew that my difference didn't really make me alien from them. But most people needed my humor and high spirits to be comfortable around me. Even when I returned to my own class, I felt left behind. I couldn't run with the other seventh graders. So I entertained them and kept my loneliness at bay. Laughter felt strong and happy.

"I saw the rich mixture of threads in this tapestry. There was gentle fun and delight, often in unexpected places," I went on. "On warm summer nights, I think about the summer when I was 13 and had to return to the hospital for ankle surgery. I shared a large ward with 20 other teenagers. In spite of its gross name—Hospital for the Ruptured and Crippled—this place was airy and cheerful. Yet bones knit slowly and time hung heavily for us. Once past major pain and extensive cast autographing, we grew impatient.

"We longed to break up the boredom. One evening during a heat wave, we built an elaborate fantasy meal that sounded delicious. We dreamed of salads, a huge icy watermelon, and tons of ice cream. One bold girl suggested that the adults could produce this fantasy supper party. And they did. Regular people-food tastes wonderful when you're in the hospital. A red-headed surgical resident dissected the watermelon and passed out huge slices. We slobbered and dripped all over the starched bed sheets. We laughed and felt normal again. Even the nurses enjoyed it until we started spitting watermelon seeds at each other." I laughed softly, taking pleasure in the fun of it once again.

"Having a sense of humor is a tremendous asset for you," David pointed out. "But when you were a child, it was critical. You used it to make others comfortable, but it also shielded you from a lot of raw pain. Humor can be a powerful tool, can't it?"

"You bet. Throughout school, even in college, I honed my sense of timing and ability to see a joke in myself or others. I learned that laughter could break up tension or create ease. Turn away the knife or deliver the cut deftly. Humor became a part of my style." Laughter bubbled up as I remembered a bizarre taxi ride with two college friends.

"One spring afternoon in college, my friends Gerri and Justine cut classes and together we played hooky at the Central Park Zoo. I hailed a cab with my crutch while they rummaged for spare change. A dilapidated yellow cab screeched to a halt in front of us. It bounced and the door swung open on squeaky hinges. We piled in, a bundle of chatter, books, bodies, sweaters, purses. I boarded last since I had to sit down first, put my crutches inside, pick up each leg and move it into the cab. Only then did I have a free hand to close the door.

"Over the din of the cabbie's radio, Justine shouted our destination just as I started lifting one leg into the cab. The driver jerked the idling cab into gear and we were off. I sat speechless, legs dangling outside the open cab door, hands holding on with a death grip. We careened down Fifth Avenue for two blocks. It felt like two miles. Then a chunky man at an open-air newsstand raced to the curb and yelled, 'Godammit, Mac, ain't that lady crippled enough already?'

"Simultaneously, the cabbie and my friends saw the opened door and noticed that I wasn't inside the cab yet. The outrage of the newsstand man left us howling at the scene: Crippled girl rides down Fifth Avenue, feet dangling from taxi door."

Even retelling the story years later left me giggling and David's hearty laughter filled the room. "God, I can just see you," he exclaimed. "Maybe when you're done with therapy, you'll have another career as a stand-up comic."

"Sure," I shot back. "I could go on Comedy Tonight, you know, make the rounds of comedy clubs in San Francisco. I could plow new territory. Develop a whole slew of 'crip' jokes. Think of the great public service I'd be doing."

I enjoyed this hour. I felt relieved by my ability to move the focus from the heavy, painful events that had gripped me. When I spent my therapy time in humorous story telling, I sometimes worried that I was wasting an expensive hour, but I craved the lightness of it. Recalling the pleasant memories and sharing them reminded me of the healthy part of myself that I enjoyed.

I drove home in high spirits, charged by my own zaniness and feeling affection for David. It was important to me that I enjoyed him and he appreciated me. It was a normal kind of feeling, good in the midst of weeks of craziness. Still, I groaned aloud when I found his monthly bill in the afternoon mail. "Why have I spent an hour telling funny stories?" I thought. "I can't afford jokes at these rates."

Over the next weeks, pain and pleasure mixed indiscriminately in my recall. Both were intense and came unbidden, sometimes in my hours with David, sometimes alone or at work. Therapy sessions were no longer my "crazy" hours. All my hours were crazy now.

When I was in a zany, upbeat mood, I answered the "What was it like for you?" questions with odd-ball stories, seeing those difficult years with a little comic relief. One day I told David about how the gawkers had followed me to graduate school in Arizona.

"Once my roommate and I spent a weekend in Las Vegas. On our way there from Phoenix, we stopped for breakfast and when we returned to our car a wiry white-whiskered man stood by a beat up covered wagon. A real cardboard cowboy—scuffed, pointy boots, old straw hat shielding him from the Arizona sunshine. His dusty covered wagon reminded me of an old western roundup wagon. From across the parking lot I felt his stare. 'Hey, crip!' he boomed in a strong western twang. 'Want your picture taken? Just a dollar.' As he shouted, I read the sign on the wagon: $1/1 PHOTO. I glanced down at my brown cotton shorts, my tanned braced legs, my crutches. I grinned and shouted back, 'No thanks, Grandpa. How about you?'"

"Pretty tough, huh? A regular macho woman," David teased. "You had plenty of opportunity to get good at it, didn't you?"

"Yeah, I got real good. But never as good as Gene Seelbach. Gene's a smart, well-liked colleague, a math teacher. I was delighted when he enrolled in a writing workshop I led. Six of us used to meet in the late afternoon after classroom teaching duties were over.

"I made a real effort to run the workshop informally, encouraging people to put their feet up on the comfortable furniture and relax.

"One warm afternoon as a meeting started, I noticed Gene's furrowed brow and faraway look. He seemed unusually tired and quiet. He looked uncomfortable. 'Hey, Gene,' I said. 'Relax. Make yourself at home. Get comfortable.'

"'Do you really mean that?' he challenged.

"'Of course,' I answered, never giving it a thought. 'Everyone else is sprawled out around here. Help yourself.'

"And he did. In a flash, he pulled up his left pant leg to just below his knee, released a device, and off dropped his artificial lower leg and foot. 'That's better,' he said. And everyone in the room laughed along with him.

"I was amazed. I had no idea he wore an artificial limb because he didn't even limp. But his casual attitude among colleagues really impressed me. I envied it.

"Sure, I'm tough," I said proudly. "But I've never gotten used to people's comments. They just pop up, unexpectedly. And I always feel taken aback. Like the time I broke my leg, a few years back. After six weeks at home I could hobble around on my lightweight fiberglass cast and crutches. The cast masked the brace beneath it.

"One day, I met a friend for lunch in Palo Alto. Walking through the bar, I passed a group of Yuppie executive types who were busy impressing one another. One man caught my glance and his eyes slipped to my feet. He whistled. 'Whew! Quite an accident, huh? How'd you do it? Skiing?'

"I flashed a grin and seized the moment. 'Yeah. Really took a big spill. I'll probably have to skip next ski season too.' He nodded sympathetically. I kept walking. I laughed all the way to our table." I wondered if David could appreciate the irony of an accident making me appear less disabled than I actually was.

"Have you ever thought about skiing?" he asked. While I knew David was an avid skier, I truly thought this question was ridiculous.

"What? Are you kidding? Or have you just gone mad?" I said in disbelief.

"As a matter of fact, no. Disabled people ski. Haven't you ever read about amputees who ski or paraplegics who sit-ski? You could probably learn to sit-ski if you wanted to. Skiing is a great adventure. You might enjoy trying it sometime."

David might have been talking about going to the moon. I looked out the window and thought of the world out there, bigger than this little room, lasting longer than the safe hours we shared. There were so many things I hadn't done. I felt impatient and resented being stuck in this spot in my life.

"This isn't the real world in here," David said, emphasizing the last two words. Again, I glanced out the window at the busy world on this wind-in-the-trees autumn day. I felt irritated. He didn't know any more about my real world than I knew about his. I wondered what he understood about me anyway. My face said what my tongue didn't.

"Of course this is real all right, but it's different from ordinary life. Here, you're having your pain and going back to find the child you were when you got sick. You're a brave woman. And the wonderful humor that helped you survive those early years is healing you now." Drawing his arm in a generous arc, he said, "You're freeing energy by getting through all this pain."

Easy for you, I thought, gathering my jacket to leave. His steadiness and obvious good health made me envy him. I hated sitting there in the warm shadow of his confidence. I hated needing his help to hold together my life now, but today his words were not enough. I hated the taste of bitterness on my tongue.

I wanted to howl at him: "I know what's real, by God!"

Last summer, in Seattle, I watched hordes of salmon climbing the fish ladders. I saw their muscular bodies torn and mangled, climbing, one by one, upstream in cold rushing waters. I had leaned over the railing, absorbed, hearing the thunder of water tumbling down. I was a salmon going upstream all my life. But now I was plunging downward in the current, tumbling in darkness, spiraling deeper. I didn't always feel that way, but I knew my feelings were real.

It was the end of the hour. But visualizing the salmon frightened me. I didn't want to leave. My feet stuck to the floor. I held onto my crutches and my breath, trying to get hold of myself. Finally I said, "I don't think I can leave right now. I just can't. I need something to take with me, maybe to keep me company when I get really afraid." I looked around, unsure of what I needed.

David looked puzzled but he didn't laugh at me. He scanned the office and then walked to a low table where he kept an intriguing collection of small carved boxes and other miniature objects. He grasped something small and walked to me. "You can take this with you," he said. Then he dropped a tiny iron horse into my open palm.

"The horse is a symbol of the unconscious. I know you often feel frightened of your unconscious world, but it won't hurt you. It is your friend, and it won't show you more than you can handle. It's coming to you to help you heal. Dorothea, it is part of you. It contains everything you need."

I turned the primitive small horse in my hand, feeling its weight, shape, and warmth. "Thanks, I'll take care of it," I said, dropping it into my purse, and then I left.

The horse was an antique Chinese opium weight about one and a half inches tall. I was comforted by feeling its weight in my hand. In the weeks that followed, I held the horse whenever I felt terror or anxiety, and so it came to visit all parts of my everyday world. Sometimes I told myself I was ridiculous, a female Captain Queeg, whistling in the dark, clicking together some funny little balls. But the horse was traveling with me to connect all the parts of my world. It was reliable company.

One gray November afternoon, I sat in my own office, listening to dry leaves swirling in circles beyond my open window. I felt chilly and forlorn. Clearing my desk, I read a brochure of a new text on D. H. Lawrence. In the introductory remarks by Anatole Broyard, I read: "Nothing is enough, apparently, to prevent the kind of loneliness we have taught ourselves to feel."

Suddenly I felt icy and had difficulty breathing. It was hard enough feeling fear alone in the night, bad enough when it engulfed me in front of David and I tried to push it away. But here in my real world I was a public person frightened by words, the central tool of my trade. I reached into my purse for the iron horse and held it tight while my heart hammered away. I raised my hands to my face and inhaled the metallic aura of fear.

"Why am I afraid?" I whispered to myself. I closed my eyes to see. Many good things were happening to me. At work I was wildly creative and more confident than ever. At home my husband encouraged and supported me and bore the overflow of my pain with patience and tenderness. Occasionally I even felt okay in my therapy sessions. But I was opening up in a new way and discovering powerful feelings. I was afraid of them, afraid of myself. I felt myself careening through space and the freedom was terrifying. No maps, no boundaries, no comforting and familiar directions.

I looked at my hand clasping the horse. I was hoarding fear and hating myself for not spitting it out like nails. When I opened my fist and saw the horse, I felt young and fragile as a child. "This is ridiculous! I'm out of here," I said, beating back the fear with my voice. I packed my briefcase, shut off the light and slammed the door behind me.

Later that afternoon, I stood ironing while my daughter flipped the television channels with the remote control. Suddenly I heard a soothing adult voice, speaking to me as if I were a child again. It flowed over me like balm. Just like David, I thought. Kind, gentle, familiar. I stopped ironing and glanced up to find the face to fit the voice. There was Mr. Rogers, getting ready to leave the Neighborhood for another day.

The next day I told David what had happened. It made a funny story and we both laughed.

"Maybe I should start wearing sneakers and a cardigan sweater to work," he mused.

I waved him off with a dismissing gesture. I did not say that it had been a touching moment for me when, in my fear, I had confused him with Mr. Rogers.

8

DAVID

HUMOR AND PERSPECTIVE

In the movies, therapists are usually portrayed as stiff and strangely stilted people. Their responses are staged and predictable, very disconnected from what I think of as genuine responses. I've always hated this public image. Yet I fear it may be more accurate than I wish. To some degree, the caricature is modeled on "correct therapeutic behavior" as taught in many schools of therapy. A lot of therapists really do come across that way unfortunately.

I was never very successful at pulling off that image right from the beginning of my career, even though these were the models I thought I was supposed to imitate. New to the profession, I was nervously aware of how little I knew. Certainly I was overly serious, trying to avoid a huge mistake that would ruin, irreparably, some client's mental health. While I am essentially serious by nature, I also have a zany sense of humor. I love to laugh and enjoy the light side of even the most serious subjects.

So I was delighted when I first met Bernie, a witty teacher who integrated his sense of humor into sensitive and effective therapeutic work. It was 1968 and I was working in the psychiatric emergency clinic of the county hospital in Los Angeles. At the time, this was the central receiving clinic for most L.A. county mental health emergencies. It was an exhilarating and exhausting place for anyone, especially a young, recent graduate. Everyday we were presented with a full spectrum of human miseries.

One day I was evaluating "George," a new patient who was middle-aged, casually dressed, and soft-spoken. He sat leaning forward, elbows on his knees while his hands kneaded his temples. I asked what brought him in, a standard opening question. He looked at me anxiously and said, "My brain has turned into hot cereal." When I asked what exactly he meant by that, he repeated his complaint. I attempted to gather other information about him—where he lived, what he did, and what changes might have taken place in his life that could lead to this strange symptom.

I had been taught many evaluation approaches, and I tried them all and got nowhere. In response to everything I asked, George just kept repeating the same complaint, "My brain has turned into hot cereal." At this point my own brain began to feel like hot cereal and, feeling totally stumped and incompetent, I finally gave up.

I asked George to wait for a few minutes and went off to speak to one of the staff psychiatrists. The doc on call for consultation that day was Bernie, a part-timer who worked at the hospital for variety from his Jungian analytic practice in Beverly Hills. After describing George and my efforts to complete an evaluation, I asked for some suggestions. Bernie joined me in my office where I introduced him to George, who immediately said, "My brain has turned into hot cereal."

Bernie nodded solemnly and said, "Tell me, George, is it more like Cream of Wheat or Quaker's Oat Meal?"

George looked up suddenly and broke into laughter. Within a minute or so he was talking about what was going on in his life. The humor had snapped him out of his obsessive state. It also snapped me out of my belief that zany, funny impulses didn't belong in my profession.

I was amazed at Bernie's unconventional casualness and from then on, sought him out for conversations about therapy craft. He told many wonderful tales about responding off the top of his head and achieving successful interventions with people. His overriding belief was that all therapy was a simple encounter between people and that it should reflect what you happen to see, hear and feel in that encounter. He believed that humor was very strong medicine.

In a way, all psychological disturbances involve a loss of perspective where a person's internal experience has gotten out of proportion to his real life situation. Humor can be a powerful shortcut to a different perspective. Naturally, it's not the appropriate perspective to focus on in every situation, but when it is, humor lightens the hard work of looking at one's life and sorting it out. When a client begins to make humorous comments about his own life dilemmas, I always take special notice.

When Dorothea began recalling the funny things that happened during her polio experience, it was a signal that she had rounded a corner in the healing process. Having descended into her deepest hidden suffering, the memories of her childhood polio began to change. The memories no longer threatened to engulf her every time she looked at them. The pain had been acknowledged, felt and expressed, and the sheer volume of emotional charge in her memory was reduced. Her perspective changed and she began to see herself differently.

Dorothea never lacked humor, but in the beginning of her therapy she had used it as a way of deflecting tension and anxiety. She talked about her childhood polio in a glib, lighthearted manner. The implied message was: "That's all over now, taken care of. Leave it alone." Now that she was no longer defending against the childhood pain, her humor was different, even though it came from the same memories. Like a treasure discovered, this new comic viewpoint involved laughter at funny events that took place, not laughter at herself.

Humor is a complex phenomenon. It can reflect so many different themes and attitudes. Everyone has seen hostility disguised as a joke. That kind of humor is the mainstay of television sitcoms. Sometimes when humor is used to hide from feelings, joking becomes a way of deflecting tension in a relationship. When this is a repeated pattern, it can lead to relationships where real issues don't get addressed and alienation and distance develop.

I once counseled a married couple who sat in my office and put on a very funny show of joking and good-natured teasing during the initial interview. After moving past this relationship facade, I discovered that they were caught in a tragic cycle of mutual abuse. It was very hard for them to drop the humor because they were overwhelmed by their hurt and anger, and terrified to look at it.

Humor functions as a vehicle which transports us from a closed emotional state into a much freer one. I once read a story of soldiers in a combat unit who bolstered their courage in the midst of battles by yelling out the punch line of their favorite lewd joke about the Lone Ranger at a moment when the masked man was surrounded by hostile Indians. It worked because the humor pulled each soldier out of his solitary personal terror, reminding him of his bond with the group. This helped create the courage to fight for everyone's survival. Many of Dorothea's funny polio stories were about the ingenious ways the kids found to raise themselves above the dreadful realities they faced each day in the hospital, bolstering each other's courage with laughter and silliness.

Humor can be a defense, a psychological strategy used to overcome anxiety by diverting attention from the source of terror. In moments of fear, it is a darned good defense because humor frees our emotional energy and keeps us from being overwhelmed. It allows us to respond better than we might otherwise.

Often in therapy I find it useful to ask clients to try out new, and sometimes absurd behaviors as a way of breaking through their fears and inhibitions. For example, I might suggest that a timid person who feels underpaid on the job tell his boss he deserves a raise. When the client reacts with shock and anxiety at my suggestion, I ask him the very worst thing he can imagine might happen if he asked. He usually comes up with something like, "Well, I guess I could get fired." Then I ask him to join me in topping this fear with an even more outrageous scenario. "The boss is so shocked that he dies on the spot of a massive heart attack, and the company president not only fires you, he also sues you for everything you own, sending you into bankruptcy which leads your wife to divorce you, your parents to disown you, and your dog to refuse to come near you again." I'll end the fantasy with, "So, what's to keep you from asking for a raise, eh?"

Viewing our fears by taking them to a point of absurdity usually makes us laugh and helps us see the humorous side of our fearful behavior. It is actually very difficult to maintain conflicting emotional states simultaneously. One state or the other is going to give way. When we can laugh at a frightening situation, our fear becomes less threatening, releasing us to notice the difference between being afraid and being in actual danger. Occasionally, of course, there are times when we are afraid and actually are in danger. But most human anxiety and fearfulness seems to occur in the absence of actual danger.

One time a man came to see me, sent in by his wife who had just found he was having an affair. He was told to come to therapy to solve his problem, "or else." After a preliminary evaluation of their situation from his point of view, I called his wife and requested that she come in for an interview. She was reluctant because she saw the problem as entirely about her husband. Nevertheless, she did agree. When she arrived in my office, she sat stiffly and angrily declared, "Well, I'm here and I'm bitter."

Suddenly I blurted out, "Hey, have you ever heard of Betty Botter?"

"Who?"

"Betty Botter, remember?" I then quoted the jingle, "Betty Botter bought some butter and she put it in her batter, but the butter it was bitter and it made her batter bitter. So Betty Botter bought some better butter and put the better butter in her bitter batter and the better butter made her bitter batter better."

At this point she stared at me incredulously. I smiled and said, "So, maybe I'll have some better butter for you."

"Well, maybe, but I doubt it." A smile broke out on her face, and she began talking about the terrible feelings she had been struggling with and her serious anxiety about her husband and their marriage. So here was an intuitive, zany response that on the surface was a total non sequitur; but it had the effect of rapidly shifting the emotional tone of the encounter, paving the way for the serious work that needed to be tackled.

As Dorothea resolved the hurtful parts of her past, I noticed a gradual transformation in her use of humor. Her laughter became less protective and evolved into a genuine appreciation of the joyful side of her rich life experiences. Dorothea's wonderful story of the cowboy photographer who yelled out, "Hey, crip!" became a metaphor for us. "Hey, crip!" became a trigger to a broader and brighter perspective after hard work in the therapy. "Hey, we crips ain't so bad after all." "Nice work, crip." These became common ways to soften the intensity and bridge back to the present.

Of course, timing is important with humor. Nothing goes over quite so badly as a joke at the wrong moment. Comedians and public speakers fail dismally when they fail to notice that their audience is in a different mood than they are. This timing error occurs in therapy as well.

Once I was working with a man and made a joking comment at the wrong moment. "Michael" was an intense and serious young executive in a conservative accounting firm. He had come into therapy to learn how to relax. He faced each day with horrible anxiety about his competency. It was as if every act was a test for him. An imaginary panel of judges hovered just overhead, watching and waiting for him to make a mistake so they could reveal what he believed was a fundamental but hidden insufficiency. This had been a lifelong pattern for him.

Recently, he realized that this was not normal. He noticed that other people appeared to live successful lives without such constant stress and fear. He wanted to be able to relax and enjoy life and had no idea how to do it.

As Michael's therapy progressed, he occasionally got glimpses of what it was to "walk lightly," to simply respond without planning every step and word. He formed some inner sense of what it was like to be relaxed. He began to let go of his controls briefly and tentatively, and he discovered that relaxation was indeed a different state of being. Paradoxically, this brought up a new kind of anxiety for him. In a spontaneous daydream, he discovered that he feared letting go of his tight control because "bats would fly out of my chest."

When he described this fantasy, I instantly imagined his daydream as a New Yorker cartoon. In delight, I said, "Michael, imagine the cartoon as showing you walking down a corridor at work. Across the way are two of your partners talking.

71

As you pass by, bats are flying out of your vest, and one partner says to the other, "Look, Michael must be feeling relaxed today."

To my astonishment, instead of laughing, Michael began to weep and express his sadness and oppression. He didn't connect with my humor. I quickly dismissed my comments as irrelevant and joined Michael emotionally to help him process the sadness he felt about his painful inner life. I naturally felt bad about missing the cues so completely and, inwardly, reprimanded myself for "not being serious enough."

About four months later, Michael and I were discussing the results of an experimental assignment I had given him to practice. It required him to visualize what it would feel like to be a conceited person, to really feel superior, and then, to pretend that he was superior. He reported, with fascination, that the experience had led him to several personal discoveries. He realized that while conceit wasn't accurate, it was more accurate than was his self-deprecating inadequate attitude. He also felt more relaxed whenever he had the "conceit" fantasy and was amazed to see his feelings change when he shifted the way he thought of himself.

While reporting this, Michael suddenly stopped, looked at me and asked, "What was that New Yorker cartoon you saw?" I repeated my fantasy cartoon to him. This time he laughed uproariously. Right timing. This was an important shift for Michael. He was able to see himself from a different perspective and feel less fearful.

Much about psychotherapy is serious. We usually seek therapy because we feel bad about something in our life. Often therapy can feel challenging and threatening, or lead us to experience sadness, embarrassment, hurt, or anger. For many of us, these are unavoidable feelings if we are going to carefully and openly look at ourselves. Overcoming our fear of such a frank inward view is a significant part of the healing process.

Still, therapy shouldn't be all grim. Life is outrageously funny sometimes. When we can laugh at a new understanding of ourselves, the insight can be as significant as one achieved through sweat and tears. I think a well-rounded therapy experience should tap the full range of human emotion. It is very important to learn to hold our interpretation of "reality" lightly and to be open to viewing it through many different windows. Humor is one of the nicest windows through which to look.

9

DOROTHEA

BODIES ARE TO LIVE IN

I love to watch able-bodied people even after decades of living with my disability. I love watching them bend, dance, and run. I'm fascinated watching them climb ladders, trees, steps. Even walking styles are distinct. People bounce, saunter, skip, drag. The rhythms of footsteps, especially on bare hardwood floors, are like personal signatures to me.

My husband and daughter have the same walking rhythms. Kathryn thinks I'm a witch because I can hear her coming even from three aisles away in a supermarket.

I remember the first time I listened to the sounds of my own walking. I was working at home with some colleagues and we let a tape recorder take notes during one afternoon meeting. Reviewing the tape later, I heard the unmistakable sound of my own gait leaving and entering the room. It was weird hearing the rhythmic click of aluminum crutches, the slow deliberate step of my right foot and the slide-clunk sound of my braced left leg. I didn't know I sounded like that. I felt a little embarrassed and wondered if other people noticed.

No one ever talks about such things. But people must notice me, especially in California where external conformity to physical ideals is the rule if not the obsession. I often wonder if my own imperfect body disturbs others. Anyone would wonder this after years of walking into rooms and experiencing obvious stares. I stare at what is beautiful or satisfying to me, or sometimes what is intriguing or seductive. I never just stare for nothing.

Like watching the bicycle riders on Alpine Road. I envy their riding and often fantasize about bicycling. I actually remember what it feels like to do everything physical I ever did as a child. When I had my first massage a few years ago, I recalled how it felt to run as soon as someone moved my legs in that pattern. It felt physically free. The loss of ability to take rapid total flight is one of the great losses of polio. Sometimes immobility is stifling—like being buried on the beach, weighed down by hot sand, standing in a hole up to your neck. Maybe that's why finding my voice feels like soaring. Language catches all the currents—it flies.

But how I love the riders! In old exercise pants or sleek, bright riding outfits on their high tech bikes, they are fun. A great cyclist is very sexy to watch. There is vibrant strength in a taut body, each line and curve open, accented, symmetrical, right out there for everyone to see. I want to touch but I know I can't. I ride along the road in my car, watching with pure pleasure. Sometimes I feel that we are in two worlds that don't fit or touch at any point.

Does everyone feel this way? Or is my own vision different? Maybe I notice everything, now even more so, since I've grown less frightened and have learned to pay attention to bodies in new ways. Through my eyes I see bodily strength and beauty. Through my own body experience I know both strength and vulnerability. Being awake to both possibilities makes me want to celebrate the wonder of life. This desire seems not so urgent in other people. Most able-bodied people I know appear not to notice their gift. Neither have I always seen the gift so clearly.

I remember the day I arrived at a therapy session alive with excitement from a welcome dream. "Last night I dreamed I was doing cartwheels in circles. I ran and danced on the beach! I had no crutches at all. I could bend my leg and move freely." Dreams of wellness came occasionally but I hadn't had one in a long time.

David's smile reflected my pleasure. I was grateful for the moment of ease. Talking about my body with him was awkward. His physical grace and agility made me conscious of our differences, of my limits. I felt all the contrast.

"Do you like your body?" he asked. Dumbstruck by the naivete and intrusiveness of his question, I didn't know how to answer. "Do you love your legs?" he prodded. I drew back from his direct questions and wanted a witty line to hurl at him. I had none.

"What do you mean?" I muttered defensively. "I don't think about liking my body. It isn't important. It's just there, isn't it?"

"I'd imagine as a child you dreamed you'd awaken and this would all be gone," he said, gesturing towards my legs. "Was it like that for you?"

I remembered those years. "In the beginning, I was sure polio was a terrible mistake, a bad dream. I half expected to awake, go back to fifth grade and tell my friends about it. I hoped for a miracle. Prayed hard for years. I wore saints' relics and used holy water from Lourdes. I even had a parchment paper blessing from the

Pope, but nothing changed. I waited patiently. I was looking for a major miracle. None came. I felt unworthy, vowed greater faith. I continued to hope for the cure to come.

"Stories of cures fed my fantasies. I heard of a girl whose father refused to allow her to use crutches. One day she got up and walked. And I read a story of a boy who had a lame leg but hoisted himself up to the roof of his house where he prayed, 'so there would be nothing between his whispered wishes and heaven.' Had God delivered him too?"

"Did anything happen to make you give up the fantasies? To see that it wasn't a nightmare that would go away?"

I stared past David, searching hard for something not yet there. "Nothing happened. But it never penetrated that something wouldn't happen. After a while I felt 'chosen' for a different sort of experience. I vaguely knew that the cure would never happen. But I never said, 'forget it, Dorothea!' Cure fantasies gave me consolation. I enjoyed them." I turned away from David's gaze, aware that I had exposed something private, childish, and long forgotten.

I recalled my girlhood before the ravages of illness. How I had loved tramping through new snow, kicking the powdery flakes high with my shiny red knee-high boots. After cold sledding I'd return home to my mother's thick hot chocolate, turning the melting marshmallows in my mouth.

And then came the glory time. The summer our family spent on the beach at Manasquan, New Jersey. I savored those days. Salt baked on my skin and hair as I surfed on our canvas raft or dug for sand crabs along the shoreline. I loved the roar of the ocean, the foamy ice caps, the strong marine odors. I wanted it to go on forever. And then it was gone.

I glanced around the office and finally looked straight at David. "I don't know what else to say," I shrugged. I swallowed hard and looked down at my body. I felt confused. David seemed to assume I'd have the expectations of a normal person. But for years, other people talked as if nothing had happened to my legs or as if I were superhuman, endowed with blind courage, able to make useless legs inconsequential. Feeling that I was my body and that I counted to David in a normal way was different. I pulled back from the edge of danger.

"What just happened there?" David asked.

"I felt stupid for having believed a frog-prince story. How could I have believed the fantasy for so long?"

"Did you ever stop believing it would go away?" he ventured.

"Of course," I snapped. "It's a sick joke, watching my legs get worse, leaning more on my crutches. Walking more slowly. I hate the way I look in my new brace. Crippled!" I hated my petty vanity too.

Then I untied my shoe, tore open the velcro straps on my brace, and took the damn thing off. I flung it on the floor like an expensive piece of trash. I drew both legs close to me, bent and crossed, Indian-style. "I'm comfortable now," I announced. "This is my real body. The brace gets in my way, keeps me from moving freely." I was amazed after I took off the brace. Though I couldn't walk, I felt powerful.

While I straightened my legs, I remembered a beautiful Canadian woman I'd met in graduate school. "I wonder whatever happened to Phyllis?" I said. "Phyllis had a bad case of polio as a kid. too. But we didn't meet until grad school, in our twenties. She used forearm crutches like mine but she never wore braces."

"How'd she manage that? A miracle or something?" We both laughed.

"Not exactly. She had surgery. Her knees were fused stiff so she could walk without braces." I felt myself wince, recalling my own bone surgeries. "She said her fusions were cosmetic. Braces were out of the question. Phyllis wore expensive clothes and always looked stylish. But she was awkward and uncomfortable in any sitting position. When we were together she often told me how much she envied my flexibility."

I thought of Phyllis sometimes when I curled up in bed at night, drawing my bent knees to my chest. I thought of her in David's office when I flung down my brace. Was I exactly the same, wanting to look elegant and stylish? My style had been camouflage. I dressed the upper half of my body and disguised everything below my waist.

David had no idea of what it was like living in my body. None whatsoever. My mismatched team of frail legs was practically useless. He could talk forever about letting go of pain and moving through the experiences of the past. But all his talk couldn't heal me.

"God, that must feel awful, never to be able to bend your legs," David groaned. As he extended his own healthy legs, I counted the many problems stiff legs posed. I'd had plenty of trouble with jammed knee locks on my brace. Where do you put stiff legs? How do you sit down in a movie seat? Get in and out of cars comfortably? Once, at an important job interview, my knee lock jammed and my foot got stuck under my future employer's desk for the entire time. It was awful.

David picked up my brace and examined it as if it were a work of art. "This knee joint is incredible," he raved, releasing and securing it again and again. "The engineering, the smoothness, the light weight—remarkable. I had no idea." He laid it down next to his own leg, kicked off one shoe, and rested his heel in the plastic mold of the brace's foot. The ill fit and the juxtaposition of his healthy leg and my brace looked ridiculous. His brow furrowed. "I see what you mean by rigid. This thing really is stiff and unforgiving. I can see why you don't like wearing it or walking around in it."

That was all. The brace lay there on the floor between us. It had been wondered at and whined over. It was part of me but not my body. I was the same person with or without it. But something was different. David accepted the brace with a naturalness I admired now that I knew he was conscious of my body here, my body that wasn't as agile and attractive as his own.

I liked the simple way he did that. I left the session feeling less alone and hidden about my legs. Someone had come forward to help me feel comfortable. He hadn't stared at me as if I were a freak. He had touched me with his eyes wide open.

Leaving David's office, I closed the door firmly and balanced for a minute on the wide brick steps outside. Cars whizzed by and dry leaves crunched underfoot. I faced the sun. "I'm glad to be here, glad not to be invisible," I said aloud, pleased with myself.

I remembered other times when exposure and pain and people touching my body made me feel so vulnerable. In the hospital beside my bed there had been a dreary gray wall. I had stared at it for hours, squeezed my eyes shut and pretended I was invisible. That was my only escape from the terrible thing that had happened to me. If no one came in to move me, I could stay that way for hours. No pain. Only stillness and invisibility.

I learned darker lessons of invisibility on weekend leaves from the hospital. My older sister, Lois, often pushed me in my wheelchair across the street to our city park and playground where I played with neighborhood friends. The novelty of the wheelchair was not wasted on them and they vied for the chance to push it. Occasionally I even hoisted myself onto a park bench so they could take turns riding. I ignored the furrowed brows and disapproving glances of observing adults.

One late afternoon Lois came to get me and push my chair up the hill to the stair-free service entrance of our apartment building. The entry way was a long downward sloping concrete ramp opening onto a courtyard where you could look right into Charlie Thiele's kitchen window.

The Thieles were friends of my parents, older people who managed our 56-family apartment building. They were fond of my sister and me and, perhaps because their own children were long grown and gone, they treated us like grandchildren. At Christmas we were always invited in to see Charlie's electric trains wandering beneath the low-hanging branches of their Christmas tree. Charlie played the violin and, when I was seven and Lois was nine, he taught us to harmonize *Silent Night* while he played. We rehearsed in his basement workroom, kept our secret, and performed for our parents on Christmas Eve.

When Lois turned the wheelchair onto the sloping ramp, the courtyard looked deserted. We didn't see if the Thieles were in their kitchen. We chattered happily. Starting down the ramp, my sister mounted the back rungs of my chair, like a scooter. It was impossible to resist the ride. As the chair gained momentum, we screeched with delight and soon I felt as if I were flying, felt the rushing air as I used to when I traveled belly-down on my sled over hills of hard-packed snow.

The chair wheels vibrated, recording the speed and the rough concrete pavement beneath them. Suddenly, the small front wheels caught in the cracked pavement. Without warning, I was truly flying. Like a rag doll, I slid off the smooth leather chair seat and flew. There was barely time to raise my hands to break the fall. I landed in a heap on the hard rough ground. After a moment of silence, I heard my screaming. I was terrified. My heart pounded and I felt the burning sensation of scraped skin on palms and knees. I shook as I struggled to raise myself to a sitting position. I felt more shocked than injured. Lois ran to help me, almost in tears herself.

"Are you all right?" she shouted frantically.

"I think so," I whimpered through my tears and fright. She helped me sit up and together we looked around guiltily. The place had an eerie silence. We were grateful no one was there as we checked both my legs and the chair for damages. Though I was teary and scraped, I was okay. So was the chair.

Immediately, we concocted a story about how I fell out of the wheelchair because it hit a crack in the pavement. We left out the part about riding down the ramp together at record speed. We knew it spelled trouble for both of us, especially Lois. Our pact was our protection.

But when my mother opened our apartment door and I saw her alarmed expression, my courage melted. I couldn't help crying again. All my fear came tumbling out when I was safely in her arms. She listened to our broken bits of story and gently cleaned my stinging scrapes. She even praised Lois for "keeping her head," and getting me back in the chair alone. Although I was a small child, dead muscles made me dead weight.

My mother marveled that no one else was around at the time of the accident. After my Dad heard the story, he remarked about the same thing. Lois and I exchanged looks, relieved that no one had seen us. We kept that secret for as long as we could, but even when the truth came out, she wasn't punished for being bad. For years I didn't quite grasp why my parents' fury was directed elsewhere.

The truth came out when they told Charlie Thiele what had happened and together the adults checked the cracked pavement, trying to retrace the incident. When my dad repeated the story about the wheel catching and the chair tipping, Charlie stood and shook his head. "No, no," he said. "It didn't happen that way at all. They picked up speed and the wheel caught here because she was thrown in this direction." As he pointed this out, he revealed himself. My parents were furious. He had seen the whole accident and neither helped us nor reported it to them. They never actually repeated this discovery to us, but they must have known that their fury had resounded through the kitchen wall to our bedroom on the other side.

"So what if they were playing?" my mother's voice boomed as she banged a saucepan on the range. "To think that the man saw it all and did nothing to help those kids, our kids!" Silence. "Afraid to get involved! Afraid we'd sue! What kind of a world are we living in anyway?" She railed on. I listened but didn't understand the parts about getting involved or suing. I didn't understand why things were forever different between the adults.

For a long time, I held onto my belief that I was safe—we had gotten away with it. And I held onto another secret that I had discovered in the fall. Rides in the chair would never be the same. My legs, powerless to move, made my body feel unsafe to me. In that short flight, I first felt the terror of my body out of control, being hurled in some random way by a power not my own. Like a taste that's hard to describe, this was different from falling off the monkey bars and climbing back on. I was vulnerable now and unable to hide it. In falling, my broken body felt naked, exposed.

The shock repeated itself in a private grotesque fashion with each fall thereafter. No matter how often I fell, or how many bones I broke, I felt the shock of the event as a major jarring thrust. No matter how "grown up" I became, with each fall I secretly wondered if I would have fallen if I'd been more careful, paid more attention to whatever was right there in front of me. Falling still strikes terror in my heart.

I shuddered at this memory, still so powerful after almost forty years. Involuntarily, I let out a loud noise, one I had made as a child to shut out everything I didn't want to hear.

But today was different. I knew I had survived. Driving around all afternoon, I told myself, "This is November. You're grown up. You lived! And you're getting over the terror."

It was clear to me now that I kept going back to David because I had to discover and feel what had happened to me when I was nine. I lacked courage to face it again, alone. The personal experience of my childhood illness had been so full of loneliness.

Yet simple understanding did not overcome my fear. Driving to David's office after Thanksgiving weekend, I clenched my jaw and felt my throat constrict. My hands felt frozen to the steering wheel. I arrived early for the session. I couldn't imagine myself speaking even after arranging myself on the floor. I felt guarded and in retreat, hoping for a question from David to focus me away from the past weekend.

"You seem tired this morning, Dorothea, rather low energy."

"Yeah, it's been a long weekend. The longest time I've gone without seeing you in the past two months. I haven't felt safe since Friday, at least."

"So. What's come up for you this weekend? What happened on Friday?" I looked at him—rested, contained, contented with himself. He irritated me. I was falling apart. I wanted to flee with my messy baggage.

"Thanksgiving was okay. But on Friday, I lost my balance and almost fell in Safeway. I stumbled into my grocery cart which rammed the oatmeal display. Otherwise, I would have been flat on the floor." Incredible rage welled up inside. Tears choked me.

"That must have scared you. Were you hurt?" he asked. His straightforward concern almost undid me. I wanted to warn him that kindness would surely make me cry. I said nothing.

"It scared the hell out of me! Even telling you, my heart's hammering. After I lost balance, I hung on and straightened up, hoping no one had seen me. I felt angry for not paying enough attention to where I was going. That's all I need—another fall, another broken bone!"

"I understand your fear. I'm glad you didn't fall. Did you go on shopping or what?"

The "or what" made me flash on Carrie Shodgrass in *Diary of a Mad Housewife*. I'm going mad just like she did, I thought. Did women ever lose control in the supermarket? Fall on the floor screaming like toddlers, babbling brand names because they couldn't say they were fed up or afraid and wanted to toss themselves in the supermarket reject bin like dented cans of beans and damaged cracker boxes?

"I checked out and got back to my car as fast as I could. I was nauseous, sure I'd either throw up or cry. I had to do something," I whispered. "I needed help right there. Right away. Fear was so big."

I ran my hand across the back of my neck and wrapped both arms around my stomach. I reached out and David clasped my hand in his own warm ones. "It's okay, now. You're doing fine. Go on," he said softly. I squeezed my eyes shut and felt him there with me.

"Well, I stayed still and just breathed. My body ached with fatigue. Then I took out my journal notebook and began to write. Wanna hear it?"

"Yes, very much," he answered.

I dug into my purse for the pocket-sized notebook, and began: "Here I am in my new car, having survived shopping, trying not to throw up or cry. The day is beautiful. I am surrounded by beauty. Why do I feel like this? My legs hurt and I can't hold back the terror. Maybe if I close my eyes I can dream myself into a safer place... where my body will feel better and my mind will go away for a little while."

I looked up and David held my gaze. "Did you cry then? Scream? Beat your fits on the steering wheel?"

"In the Safeway parking lot? Are you kidding? I stopped writing but my terror grew. I blinked and looked around, but there were absolutely no safe places left. I could no longer make myself invisible. I knew my body was not going to soar like the wind in a cold December sky. Not ever. I slipped my hands beneath my skirt and touched my knees, the left one soft and still, the right one quivering when I contracted the muscle.

"Then I put the car in gear and drove home. The end." David's eyes held my own but I turned away and looked out the window. Something had happened in telling the story. I had noticed my body again, my legs struggling to do the job, my legs feeling tired and unbeautiful. But I also felt tenderness towards myself that was brand new. I was close to tears. I hadn't cried much over myself. But if I admitted how bad I felt or showed it, might David push me to accept myself or worse yet love myself as I was? That would be impossible.

He looked at me sympathetically, nodding in affirmation. "Did you tell Michael what happened when you got home?" I denied this. David shifted in his seat and angled his head to one side. "Dorothea, you don't have to protect him from this, you know. He's a grown man, he's your husband. He can handle it. Look, you went through this alone and survived it very well. But it's over. You don't have to be alone anymore. You know that, don't you?"

"I know that," I murmured. "I haven't lived my married life alone. Sometimes I've said painful stuff to Michael. Sometimes. The first time I openly broke down in front of him, he was wonderful. I'll never forget it.

"I was five months pregnant. Michael took me snorkeling at Hanelai Bay on a Kauai vacation. The color and life underwater were spectacular. I loved moving freely through it, having equal access to those treasures just as backpackers have access to virgin wilderness.

"We became so engrossed that I didn't notice how far we'd drifted. As we swam back, I grew tired and then truly weary. My arms couldn't do all the work, and my legs just floated behind me. At first I loved the sea. Then there was so much of it. I panicked.

"Treading water, I surfaced and called. 'Michael, help me. I'm tired. I can't last much longer.' He was there in a moment, grasping my head and shoulders in a strong lifesaving grip.

"'Relax. I've got you,' he said confidently. And we went forward together. In what felt like a few minutes, we were on the shallow pebble-bottomed edge of the beach. I was exhausted.

"Poor Michael was tired too. He couldn't carry me, a pregnant, wet, dead weight. I half-dragged myself and half-crawled up the white sandy beach. Peoples' stares bore into me. I felt exposed and angry. After a while I said, 'I was scared, afraid I'd die.' I touched my hard globe of a uterus where I had just felt life moving. 'I was so mad I couldn't do it. Couldn't bring myself in. Or walk up on the beach like a normal person.' Shivering, I drew the towel around me and wept.

"Michael put his arm around me. 'I know,' he said quietly. 'I felt awful that I couldn't carry you up the beach in my arms. If I were four inches taller, I could have done it.' I understood. Other people felt disabled too. They felt it and couldn't talk about it either. I was less lonely in that moment."

David beamed. "You're lucky to be married to Michael. He couldn't have done more to comfort you." His voice was full of admiration. "God knows, anyone would be moved by all you've said. You're much braver and stronger than I am. But the only way to finish these experiences is to go through them—cry, get angry, do whatever you must to fully experience the past. Then you can let it go." He was kind, but firm too.

I felt myself holding back pain. There was stiffness in my legs, soreness at the back of my neck, like the pain that signaled the onset of my illness. Therapy was a pain, I thought. "It hurts here and here," I whispered touching my heart and stomach. "It hurts so much." I longed to curl up and close off this part of me.

"The pain is telling you something," David said. "Your body feels pain in the process of healing itself. You're strong. You can stand it. That's what you're doing, you know. You're healing."

He gave me an encouraging hug as we ended the session. It had been a difficult day, but I felt uplifted. It was crazy. How could all this messy, teary, muddy stuff be uplifting?

Weeks followed and Christmas vacation arrived. I had time to consider David's words. If I listened to my body, what might I learn?

I began to pay attention to simple fatigue. The day after Christmas I spent the day in bed, reading Wallace Stegner's *Crossing to Safety*. The rich rendering of this story of friendship and love touched me. But when the narrator told the tale of a camping trip with friends, and his wife Sally's near death from polio, I felt a rush of adrenaline. Later, after Sally completed two years of rehabilitation and regained only minimal recovery of mobility, the friends met for a reunion. No effort was too great for Sally. She was happy to be there, to have her life. But in the midst of the festivities, Sally's husband said: "Sally was so joyfully there that for hours at a time we accepted her as whole."

I read the line and stopped. This is how "they" see us, I thought. Broken. Unwhole. Unacceptable. How do I see myself? I couldn't answer.

But, I reflected, I had to make changes in how I was living my life. I wasn't sure just what or how, but I knew my first "lesson" had to be accepting my wholeness as I was. I needed both courage and kindness from myself and others. I had to give up the attitude that I must overcome polio with harsh determination. Bodies are to live in.

That was the task. The wounds my legs had suffered were beyond curing. If I listened to my body, lived in it, there were other wounds to cure. On the eve of the New Year I was, quite simply, happy to be alive.

10

DAVID

OVERCOMING ALIENATION

I had to get used to Dorothea's physical handicap during the early phase of the therapy. It was a new experience to spend so much time with someone who had to cope with physical limitations. Dorothea had learned to live life methodically, carefully calculating each movement, scanning the landscape for hazards. I began to see that she could do nothing casually and I admired her deliberateness. Standing, walking, sitting and getting up again were exquisite maneuvers of exact attention to balance and surroundings. It was too costly for Dorothea to risk a mistake. Walking with crutches while wearing a rigid brace was hard work. It was nearly impossible for her to carry something while she walked.

As we worked together I learned to move at her pace and, as a result, discovered a deeper intensity of attention to experience. My mind slowed down. I noticed details overlooked before—mundane details like the texture of floor coverings, the height of thresholds and steps—all things about which I had never needed to be concerned. When walking with Dorothea, I became aware of the physical barriers created in buildings and structures designed with only fleet-footed people in mind.

Several years ago, my wife Joan and I took a sabbatical and traveled for 13 months, including seven months in Third World countries. We were astounded to discover how abnormally hyped-up and speedy we were. For example, in Afghanistan, people sauntered and strolled. There was no hurrying. Cars and trucks went 40 miles per hour on open highways. We came to realize that physically, human beings seemed to be designed to live life at about the speed of a donkey's walk. In the West, we long ago replaced donkeys with fast cars, racing bikes, and running shoes. Have we lost the natural rhythm of life?

I commented earlier that mental disorders involve a loss of perspective, a distortion in the relationship between our inner mental life and true perception of life as it is in the real world. I often wonder how much of this is caused by the speed at which we live modern life. Into a given day or week, we might condense as many experiences as our forebears lived in several days, weeks, or months. When do we sit still long enough to integrate all of this experience before we rush on to fill ourselves with even more?

Toward the end of the journey which had taken Joan and me to Afghanistan, we traveled through Pennsylvania and camped one night in a convenient field off a side road. In the morning, the farmer who owned this field dropped by to see who was breakfasting on his land. We talked for several minutes and I discovered that he was my age, owned no motor vehicle and had never traveled farther than 60 miles from this farm. We had just traveled 23,000 miles in our van through 20 different countries during the previous year. I cannot conceive the vast differences between his inner mental life and my own. I can imagine that mine would be incomprehensible to him as well.

In a way, Dorothea lives life closer to a normal pace. She is intense in her attention to her surroundings and to her encounters. She is rarely in too much of a hurry to notice the weather or flowers or the look on your face. On the other hand, a simple task like getting up and fetching something from across the room requires a lot of time and effort. It is no small thing to have forgotten something she needs. She has to plan ahead and anticipate her needs. Her slower pace facilitates this process. Like the legendary tortoise and hare, Dorothea is slower but she's very efficient. I imagine that life must seem to scurry around Dorothea as she methodically makes her way from here to there. Her pace makes for a reflective, even meditative perspective.

Most able-bodied people feel uncomfortable and self-conscious when they meet a handicapped person. Handicapped people become acutely aware of this discomfort. It reinforces their sense of being different, of not fitting in.

Dorothea often commented about how tiresome it is to always have to help people feel comfortable about her handicap so they can simply see her as an ordinary person. The cowboy street photographer who shouted out, "Hey crip, ya want your picture took?" at least gave an honest acknowledgment that her legs were different. He gave no apology for noticing that she was a "cripple." No wonder she laughed. It must have been a refreshing change.

But Dorothea never let her physical condition stop her from a robust and full participation in life. She often expressed gratitude to her parents for their insistence that she keep pushing herself in every way possible. She didn't develop a bitter or angry attitude about her life situation. Her enthusiasm for and full engagement with life showed a significant acceptance of her handicap.

Still, I sensed something as she talked about herself and her struggles. Beneath the surface there seemed to be a conflict between her acceptance of her polio damage and her attitude towards her body. It was as if she accepted the effect of the disease but rejected her body.

One day, as I listened to her talk, I suddenly asked, "Dorothea, do you love your legs?" She looked at me with an expression of incredulity and, laughing, said, "Hell no, of course not."

"Do you feel beautiful and lovely as a woman?" I pressed on.

She looked at me out of the corner of her eye like I was crazy and was asking some sort of trick question.

"Well no, I never had a chance to feel that way. Remember I'm the one for whom all those things weren't available. But I've enjoyed other aspects of being me over the years."

As I watched her respond to these questions, I felt something important was being overlooked. I knew her story well by now. After getting polio, she concentrated her attention and energy on developing her mind and learning the skills she needed to make a life for herself in spite of her body. But I sensed she was asking me to join in her attitude towards her body. I felt that challenging this attitude was risky business, but I pressed on anyway.

"When you were a young woman, did you ever notice and appreciate your feminine sensuality and attractiveness?" I knew from what she had told me about her college and young adult years that other people hadn't failed to notice it.

"Are you kidding? Look, I knew I could be cute, and sometimes when guys would see me sitting at a table and not notice my legs and crutches, they'd flirt with me as if I wasn't a cripple. But when I stood up, I knew just what the reality was. I settled this issue years ago and I don't see what you're driving at." Now she was getting a bit annoyed.

"Well, I'm not sure what I'm driving at, Dorothea, but I think there's something here so I'll just go on with it. Tell me this, do you demand for yourself the right to have full enjoyment of your body in every way possible, to love your body and feel good about it and appreciate it? Do you give your legs "permission" to be just the way they are and still validate your body? Do you claim the right to fulfillment as a woman?"

There are moments in therapy when I'm not sure where I'm going but feel pushed from inside with a sense of urgency to pursue something that is emerging. I have to push the edge and see what unfolds. This is an aspect of therapy where the intuitive part of the mind is way ahead of the logical part of the mind. This isn't magic. Intuitive perception comes from deep creative places in the mind and accesses the full measure of knowledge and experience that has accumulated in life. It's just that intuitive responses arise in a non-linear manner so that the impulse precedes conscious logical understanding.

By now, Dorothea was in a state of confusion. My questions had angered her. But her feelings suggested that she couldn't believe I had proposed such ridiculous ideas. Then I realized what was missing in her acceptance.

"Dorothea, your body didn't abandon you, it didn't fail you. It hasn't kept you from developing into a strong mature person. It hasn't prevented you from developing normal sexual feelings. Your body didn't keep you from participating in loving sexual relationships. It didn't stop you from attracting a lovely man who courted and married you. Your body didn't deprive you of the joy of pregnancy and the miracle of giving birth to your beautiful daughter."

Dorothea seemed stunned. She was very quiet and subdued. Looking down at her legs, she ran her hand over one of the attachments on her brace.

"But, I never thought I could ever feel good about this body. Ever since the polio, it has always been so different from other peoples' bodies, and living with it has been such a struggle. It seems natural to despise it."

"Of course, yes, it would feel that way. But Dorothea, now it's time to come home to your body. It's time to love it. Your body needs to be honored and respected."

Dorothea's feelings were perfectly understandable. Western culture has a narrow definition of physical beauty which is reinforced through the constant impact of media stereotypes. These stereotypes are representative of only a tiny segment of the general population, and the amount of suffering experienced by those who do not fit the pattern is incalculable. An irony not often recognized is that many of those individuals who do fit the stereotype are convinced that they do not, and they suffer the same insecurities.

People who seek psychotherapy are in some kind of distress. Nearly universally two underlying themes emerge from this distress. The first theme is a lack of self-knowledge—not knowing or acknowledging significant aspects of oneself. The second theme is the rejection and disapproval of oneself as a person.

The therapy process is based on creating a trusting and safe relationship which is objective and non-judgmental, and then guiding the individual on a tour of self-exploration. This usually uncovers many dimensions of self-illusion and self-rejection. Learning to accept oneself is not merely a technique, it is the fundamental requirement for psychological growth and maturation. We cannot change even the "bad" things about ourselves without first acknowledging and accepting them. Acceptance is basic in order to establish a mature relationship with reality.

For Dorothea, contracting polio right on the threshold of puberty meant she formed her sense of womanhood around stigmata which declared, "I'm not like everybody else. I'm not a normal woman." Every day she had to confront the reality that her legs were not like those displayed in the fashion magazines. She could never wear the shoes everyone else could wear. In order to cope with the sadness she felt as an adolescent, she used the ancient and powerful psychological defenses of denial and splitting. "My legs are not me. I am not my legs."

A quick and lively sense of humor helped Dorothea cope with people's discomfort about her legs. She made fun of her own legs, her braces, her crutches, her shoes. She gave people permission to take her physical condition lightly. This was a wonderful defense. It certainly served her better than anger, bitterness, and withdrawal. But now, in mid-life, it was time to move beyond psychological defenses.

My challenge to Dorothea came from my intuitive mind; it had flowed out of me with an intense certainty. Then along came my doubting mind. I thought: hadn't I just spent months encouraging her to feel the tragedy of her life, the sadness of her losses? Hadn't I been telling her that she has a right to feel sorry for herself? What did I know about acceptance? I'm not physically handicapped. I never experienced the kind of loss she suffered.

Where does the idea of acceptance fit when looking at irretrievable loss? Webster's dictionary defines "accept" as: "to receive, to approve, to agree to, to believe in." These are powerful words and they accurately describe what I was saying to Dorothea. "Yes, you must acknowledge the injury your body received. You must approve of the person that you have been and are now, including your legs. You must agree to the conditions that exist as a result of the polio. And you must believe in yourself, a whole person, just as you are."

The paradox is that we achieve acceptance of major losses by first loudly and vigorously rejecting our wounds, sufferings, injustices, handicaps, and limitations.

We get to acceptance by way of non-acceptance. We must give full vent to the part of ourselves that protests against things which aren't the way we want them to be.

This is natural. There exists inside every person, consciously or not, a deep wish that everything be the way we want it to be. Childhood development studies demonstrate that all of us begin life as wondrous infant beings who wake up to the world and assume we are the center of the universe. If we are fortunate, we're born into families which allow us this illusion by meeting all our needs with love and adoration for at least the first few years of life.

But eventually we have to give up this sojourn in paradise. We discover we aren't the center of the universe. We discover that our needs don't always get met, and that things are not always going to be as we want them. We have to grow up. But deep inside we retain a memory of our "rightful" omnipotence. Then later, when life brings us hurts and losses, we are touched again by that original loss of paradise, by that original rage and sadness that we don't have complete control. And we must protest, we must protest!

Then when our protest is complete, we can begin the process of accepting that we aren't the center, that life is given to us for only a little while and we don't dictate the terms. Reality does, after all, precede us. Having resolved our resistance, we then are free to learn from life, fully participate in its joys, even if it isn't just how we want it to be.

The Swiss psychiatrist Carl Jung once wrote: "There is no light without shadow and no psychic wholeness without imperfection. To round itself out, life calls not for perfection but for completeness; and for this the 'thorn in the flesh' is needed, the suffering of defects without which there is no progress and no ascent."[1]

1Psychological Reflections, Jolande Jacobi (ed.), Harper and Row, Publishers, New York, 1953, p. 281.

Dorothea and big sister Lois, Easter, 1944.

May 1947. Dorothea's first communion. Pictured with paternal grandparents Louise and Lois Grottola.

May 1948. Memorial Day Parade. Dorothea pushing her doll carriage.

August 1949. Summer at Manasquan, New Jersey, with brother Michael and Mother. About one month before Dorothea contracted polio.

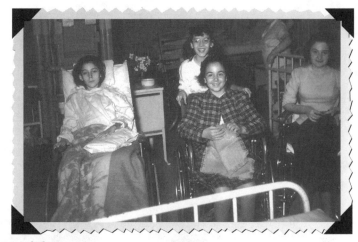

1950. Dorothea, middle, in the hospital ward she called home for about a year after contracting polio. Friend Doris Seligman is on the right in the sweater.

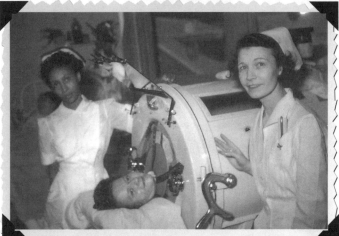

1950. Joanne, who Dorothea met in the hospital and who she writes about in chapter 5, in an iron lung. Joanne died the following year.

Spring 1950. Dorothea and her visiting parents outside the hospital.

Thanksgiving 1949. Dorothea with her sister Lois and brother Michael on her first weekend out of the hospital. Dorothea was barely able to sit up in the wheelchair, but allowed home for the holiday.

Summer 1951. Dorothea, 11-and-a-half years old, after spending one year in the hospital and one year of rehabilitation at home, returning to school.

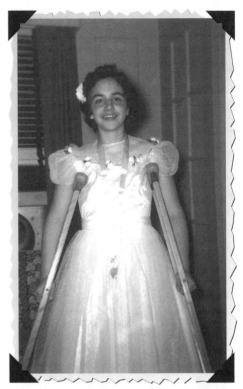

June 1953. Dorothea, 13, ready for grade school graduation.

June 1961. Dorothea's graduation from Hunter College, New York City.

Fall 1964. Dorothea's first full-time teaching position at Arizona State University. She had just finished her M.A. in English.

Spring 1987. Dorothea, just before starting therapy, at a school function with daughter Kathryn, who at nine was exactly the age Dorothea was when she contracted polio.

Therapist David Willingham

Dorothea with her husband Michael Nudelman in their new house.

11

DOROTHEA

NIGHTMARES, DREAMS, AND TREASURES

Through the bleak days of January and February, I was confused and anxious. Maybe I didn't know how to do my life anymore. Maybe I had made a mistake by letting down my defenses. I felt uncertain and unstable about going forward. Therapy seemed to lack direction and it was expensive too. I thought we should talk about it.

One day I asked, "What next? Do you think I'm wasting my time here? Vomiting out this stuff, ad infinitum? Maybe I should leave. How will I know when I'm finished? I've discovered the nightmare of the past and understand what happened. Isn't this a good time to stop?" I looked to David for an answer. I wanted him to do something, halt the chaos.

His tone was reassuring. "No, if I thought you were wasting your time, I'd tell you. This process is entirely too costly to continue unnecessarily. But I can't tell you what's coming next or when it's coming. These things take their own time. You have to trust the psyche to unfold in its own way. You just can't will it."

His sweeping answer left me nowhere. I feared asking him more, feared that he would take control and tell me something I wasn't ready to hear. Even the question about finishing he answered with a vague response. "You'll know when you're finished. You'll just know it." I left feeling irritable and covert, resenting his easy assurance.

What next? That night I had a grotesque dream. In the dream, I stood in the living room doorway of my old house, the one from which I had recently moved. In the morning sun I saw the polished oak floor surrounding our deep red oriental rug. I watched a young baby girl lying atop a blue cotton quilt in the middle of the rug. The child was naked, healthy, and happy. She was playing with her toes, looking around, squealing with pleasure, catching bright rays of sun as they bounced around the room.

While the room was familiar, I did not recognize the child. I was enjoying a peaceful moment when I glanced over my shoulder and began to feel uneasy. The baby girl continued her gurgling, but I gave a quick start when a strange man entered the room. He approached the baby slowly, talking to her in playful tones. He passed me and knelt down in front of her with his back to me. With pounding heart and trembling hands I entered the room, fearful of this stranger who had passed like a dark shadow.

I could not see his face but his hands were busy. I moved closer and to the side of him in time to see him spread her legs wide, unzip his pants, and touch his already firm penis. Its size was outrageous. Next to the child, his penis looked almost the length of her legs. I knew he was going to assault her. I was terrified, afraid I would vomit or pass out.

In the dream I was a grown woman, a wife, a mother, and a witness. I couldn't just stand still for this. I had to do something. I stamped my right foot, the good one, and shouted, "No! You cannot do that!"

He ignored me but my voice grew stronger. I shouted, "Stop it! Don't stuff that thing inside of her! You'll violate her. Damage her. Hurt her. You can't do that!" He was fondling and stroking her. I moved closer, afraid, but shouting over the fear: "Nooooooooooo!" When I got close enough to touch him, he said nothing but backed off. When he raised his head, his face was illuminated by sunlight. The man was my father. Then I woke up.

My heart pounded hard and I felt jarred by the sudden awakening. I was snuggled close to Michael under the eiderdown. He slept peacefully in the dark house. Outside a storm raged. The cracking of tree limbs and the sound of rain beating on the redwood deck made threatening noises. From our bed I saw a young plant, nestled in a protected planter box on the deck. Its wet leaves shimmered and the eerie pre-dawn light cast them in silver.

I knew my father had never molested me. I also knew that I would not sleep for the rest of the night. Even awake I was frightened. Where did this dream come from? I rolled over and curled up, pressing myself into the bed, trying to find a safe spot. This dream is a sign of my sickness, I thought. I could never repeat it to another person. I tried to picture telling Michael. We often amused ourselves exchanging bizarre or funny dreams. But this? He'd probably either laugh it off or, worse, confirm my suspicions and become alarmed. I was ashamed to have had such an awful dream.

In the morning the dream retained its power. All day I walked around with the dream demons inside. I tumbled into sleep that night, longing for respite and relief. It did not come.

Instead, I dreamed I found myself in a strange room that David had sent me to, an office adjacent to his own, connected by a door I never noticed. The room was smaller than David's office and bare except for a desk and two comfortable chairs. A woman sat in one of the chairs, someone David had said he wanted me to meet. Her long black hair and deep blue eyes were stunning. Silently she motioned to another doorway and signaled that I should go through it, alone.

A long passageway opened onto a white room with two hospital beds. Two old women were in the beds, both dressed in white operating room gowns. When a nurse came in, the old women went into a bathroom and started vomiting, one in the toilet and one in the bathtub. I closed my eyes and started screaming.

When I looked again, I was in the bathroom but the women weren't there. I looked at my face in the vanity mirror. There was a piece of loose skin on the edge of my mouth. I pulled it and the skin unraveled from my lips as easily as if I were removing a wrapper from the top of a chewing gum package. Blood started pooling on my lips. I put my hands in the blood and then touched my eyes. I looked again and saw my hands and face all bloody. It frightened me. I was a mad woman in a strange place. When I awoke, I felt ill.

The next day I called David. Common sense told me it was safe to discuss these dreams. I was certain that I needed to do so, but I feared and loathed revealing what was so disgusting and diseased in my nature. As a child I had been ridiculed for my flights of fancy, and rigorous religious training had taught me that bad thoughts—sexual, violent, destructive, even suggestive thoughts—were the work of the devil. Even though Catholics couldn't be responsible for bad dreams, surely they pointed to flaws and imperfections.

I reminded myself that I no longer believed in these sins. Still, they were my demons. They were popping out at night and I could not control them. Yet repeating them to David would mean crossing another boundary into new territory. Was this message from my dreams further proof of "certifiable madness?"

"I had to come in," I began. "I've been dreaming some weird, disgusting stuff. Really strange. It's scared the hell out of me." I took a deep breath and had no idea how to say it.

David asked, "What importance do you think dreams have?"

I laughed. "Well, I've always thought they were interesting. My dreams always have been vivid and prolific. Friends have been astonished at the fullness of detail I recall. And they're amused at my imagination. But they say things like, 'Oh, Dorothea's dreams are easy to figure out. They're so representational. It's all right there.'

"So, I've never thought too much about dreams. Except the kind that foretell something. Like when the Pope died, and I dreamed his death the night before it happened. Do you remember how I told you that the same thing happened when my Dad died? But when I talk about that, other people get quiet or tell me I'm spooky."

"What do you think about that? Do you think dreams are significant?" he asked again.

"Privately, yes. Because things just come up in dreams. You know, sometimes it's all messy or scary, or satisfying and rapturous. But I've never trusted dreams because they're not real." I paused and shuddered, wondering how I could say these dreams to him. "Since starting therapy, my dreams are so vivid and startling. The last two nights have made me want to give up going to bed."

"Dreams are real. They are from you and of you. They can be a rich source of information and understanding about yourself. Sometimes they're so chaotic or fragmented that they remain puzzles. Sometimes they send a message through humor. But they won't hurt you," he added gently.

Then we had one of those staring standoffs and I knew by now that I could never wait him out. I had to tell him the dreams, especially the one about the man and the baby. And so, I just stepped out of myself and reported it as if it were a piece I was reading from the newspaper. As I spoke, he outlined the details on his white pad. I watched him, but his face was expressionless. When I finished, I burst into tears, frightened by the words I had said and relieved to have said them.

"It was awful, just awful!" I wailed, wiping my eyes with the Kleenex he had tossed my way. I had shared other dreams with him, but nothing like this grotesque nightmare. "It's so sick! Go ahead and find something good to say about that," I challenged.

He was not shocked. "I can see why you're upset. It is a frightening dream," he said. Then we talked about it, taking the images and symbols one at a time. We exchanged questions and speculated about possible meanings. As we talked, I became less afraid. The dream felt more and more as if it existed outside of me.

Finally David said, "Threatening as the dream was, I think it was a good dream. Look at what you did. You stood up, stamped your foot, used your voice to fight off the violator. You didn't behave like a victim, and you did protect that child. You took care of her didn't you?" His voice was warm with enthusiasm.

"Well, I hadn't thought of it that way," I said slowly. "When I see it that way, I feel a little better."

Thinking about the second horrible dream, I had decided not to tell David. I feared his sending me away, kicking me out on my own, when he took me to meet the beautiful woman in the office adjacent to his own. But now that I had my nerve up, I went ahead and told it. This time I didn't cry.

I saw only what was disgusting—vomiting and bleeding. "This isn't me," I said defensively. "I mean, I don't dream about blood and guts. I have no idea where this dream came from with its barfing old ladies. Why am I dreaming about vomiting? I never vomit, not since I was a little kid and got carsick on the way to the beach. God, how I hated that! I can still see my mother cleaning up the mess."

David laughed. "Well, I told you dreams sometimes give us things in odd ways. After all, isn't what you're doing here a little like your dream? All this stuff that's coming up for you. It needs some way to get out doesn't it? And you've certainly done plenty of talking in the past five months, haven't you?"

I looked at him, speechless. How could I have failed to see it that way? I had rejected the dream out of fear, horror, and disgust. Recast, there was a touch of perverse humor. "Even the bloody part," I mused slowly. "Even there my mouth was bleeding . . . all these words . . . things I shouldn't say because they aren't nice. But I've zipped open the package and there's no sealing it up again, is there? And the blood keeps coming and pooling. God! Why am I smearing it all over and looking in the mirror? It's horrible!"

"Well, you're getting it out and looking at it, aren't you? Isn't that another way to see what's happening to you? And look, Dorothea, don't you even frighten yourself a little with what's going on in your mind? Is blood so horrible? Isn't it just another part of you, like skin? Or saliva?"

Cheap shot, I thought, resenting his casual objectivity. It isn't your body or your blood.

"It isn't your body," I repeated aloud that evening, stacking the dishwasher. Everywhere I looked the kitchen was a mess. I felt tired and irritable. How could I accept my body as it was, so slow and deliberate, often so pained. I resented Michael's obliviousness to the dinner mess, but when I called him to help me clean up I hated the irritability in my voice. I was really angry. I had this magnificent family kitchen, designed so I could create family meals all by myself, and my legs were saying they weren't going to live up to expectations again.

I was sure my bad feelings about my body came from the therapy work which had focused so much on my polio experience. Yet everywhere I looked nowadays I saw that I could no longer do things I had always done. Life was getting harder, just when I'd hoped the struggles would ease up. Last week I had stumbled twice at work when there were no obstacles underfoot. More and more I resisted walking across campus to pick up my own mail, an easy walk that had been a daily habit. And I invited colleagues to my office for meetings rather than going to theirs. These were small changes but threatening. I pulled back like a miser, hoarding my purse, even when I knew it had holes. Damn it! I had expected therapy to help me feel better, but it was beginning to make me angry.

That morning I had lifted each leg into the car as if it was a sack of groceries. I hadn't done that since I'd first gotten polio and learned to pull my legs around by yanking the cuffs of my pajamas. I bit down on my lower lip, trying to hold back the tears. "Damn!" I spit out the word in a moment of misery. I thought that years of fighting back had gotten me free of my body.

I had forgotten my embarrassment when a nun had held me up in front of my schoolmates as a "sterling example" of someone especially chosen by Christ to suffer. And I had forgotten the deep sense of shame I had felt in chapel when that same nun reprimanded me for weeping. I heard her voice in my ear: "Is life so hard, Dorothea? Don't you have anything to be grateful for?" I wondered what good remembering it again could do.

Laughter came from the family room where Michael and Kathryn bantered about unfinished homework. I walked to the doorway, drawn by the life sounds, so different from my own sadness now. Gazing at them I knew all I had to be grateful for and the gratitude gave me joyous relief. I remembered having joked all through my pregnancy that even I could produce a child whose legs worked. Didn't all her kicking prove it? Her beauty and wholeness were small, private miracles to me.

My life was vital. Yet I felt overwhelmed, confronting the loss of the past and the present ebbing of strength. Now that I could no longer go on in the old ways, denying limitations and ignoring signals for rest and help, how would my life change? Surely David couldn't tell me what to do with my discoveries or the raw feelings that came with them. Even Michael and Kathryn couldn't do anything. They lived in their own lives and their own bodies. No. I was alone, knowing I had to make my way out of this stuck place, without the foggiest notion of how to do it.

Therapy was agonizing and felt pointless during this dark muddy time. David allowed me to express my frustration and sadness and encouraged me to rest as well as ask family and friends for help whenever I needed it. The habit of asking, of expressing need, was harder to develop than I had expected. But I worked at it and was pleasantly surprised at the pleasure and ease with which people responded when they seemed to know what I needed or wanted.

Still, there were disturbing dreams at night and urgency all day. Big questions kept pushing at me. "What am I going to do? How much more ability will I lose? How will I manage now, with family, job, house? What if I have to use a wheelchair? How can I stay alive inside?" I felt David waiting with me, but he had no answers. His responses were stock, unsatisfying.

"I don't know what's going to happen next, Dorothea. We'll just have to wait and see what unfolds here. You're a strong woman. Look at how well you've handled your life so far."

I often ended sessions in a burst of impatience, but David didn't waver. "You can't force things to happen," he'd say. "Everything you need to know is in you. You've come so far, so fast. Your psyche needs time to assimilate all this. You'll just have to wait like the rest of us."

He spoke with warm good humor and there was simple truth in his words. I forged ahead ambivalently, grateful that he hadn't thrown me out, fearful that I might be chained to therapy forever.

At the end of January my psyche delivered a vivid dream, vastly different from all the terrifying earlier ones. In the dream, I found myself swimming in dark, cold water, full of whitecaps. I heard a voice within me saying I must dive through this sinister black sea. I felt fuzzy-headed and tired. Still, I tried to fight the voice. I lost.

I dove in and began the descent through the inky water. It was dark and cold. As I went down, the water became easier to permeate and I saw dim light. I kept my eyes open and soon I began to see all kinds of sea life, many rocks and fish, all colors. Even under water I could breathe freely and I soon came to the bottom of the ocean. There were rays of light coming from everywhere. Mammoth caves and twisted crags were all around. The bottom of the sea felt like velvet beneath me. I sensed that this was mine. I was totally at ease—mobile, engrossed, happy, childlike.

Exploring a cave, I spied a huge pirate chest bulging with treasures. When I opened it, I was almost blinded by sparkling jewels, big chunks of emeralds, sapphires, rubies, diamonds, everywhere encrusted in yellow gold. I had never seen anything like it.

The voice within directed me to go home, get my silver soup ladle, and return to retrieve the jewels. I argued that the ladle was not large enough. The voice insisted, urged me on. When I returned with the ladle, the voice told me to fill it, pour the jewels on all the people I love, and witness their reactions. First I went to Michael who was sleeping in our bed. He sighed contentedly and said he felt good. Then I visited Kathryn, asleep in her bed. She purred and curled up like a cat. I went to my mother and Michael's, in their kitchens. They didn't seem to be aware of me at all, but after I sprinkled them, they were lighter and moved more quickly.

I enjoyed sprinkling the jewels. They bounced and danced down the bodies of people and left light wherever they touched. I noticed that the ladle was always full but never heavy. I sprinkled my few best friends and they were delighted, uplifted by it. Then I sprinkled David. In the dream he appeared in a picture, a vignette enclosed in a small gold frame. When the jewels fell across his face, he came alive, smiled, closed his eyes and said nothing. He just glowed.

Then the voice told me to pour the jewels on myself, and I did. It felt wonderful. "Oh! This is what it's like to be loved by me," I sighed. "How nice. I should love myself again sometime."

The scene shifted abruptly to a beach where I found myself washed ashore. I awakened in the dream feeling suffused with warmth and peace. I stayed still and reflected. I knew I had been to a very special place for the first time. I knew that I needed to remember the dream.

At my next session with David I didn't control my excitement when I recounted the dream. I felt as if jewels were tumbling out of me, tumbling over us both, filling the room with great beauty and the promise of what was to come. My hands flew expressively, and I often grasped David's hands to tug him along with me. He had shared so much of the pain and fear and loneliness. He had to have the joy too. I had to give him joy as the true return payment.

"Isn't it incredible?" I asked. I felt the grin on my face and a surge of vitality. "It came out of nowhere, like a gift to me. I think I should take it as a sign, don't you? I mean, I know I'm not done yet or anything. But if I persist, who knows? Maybe there's more to come after all the pain. I've never had a dream like this in my life."

David smiled broadly and I knew that he, too, was pleased. "It didn't come out of nowhere, Dorothea. It came out of you. It is all your dream and it is a wonderful one. I think it's prophetic."

We looked at each other and this time I did not need to look away. Everything was still, relaxed, safe. There was a new presence in the room with us. I tingled as if I had sprinkled the jewels again. David glowed as he had in the dream. Having told the dream, I saw myself alive at the center of it. I was brave, willing to take risks to discover things. I was powerful, able to go to faraway places freely. And I possessed a magic ladle, capable of giving love freely without emptying itself. I was worthy of giving and receiving love.

12

DAVID

THE UNCONSCIOUS MIND

E very therapy has its plateau. There comes a time when a clear sense of direction disappears and the therapy meanders. In the early years of my work as a therapist these plateaus bothered me. I struggled against them, assuming that I was failing in my responsibility. Gradually, I developed a more relaxed attitude about my role and learned to have a greater faith in the wisdom of the unconscious mind. Often, vigorous change takes place in the unconscious during periods of surface meandering.

The brain is incredibly complex. Our knowledge of how the brain function called "mind" works is relatively primitive, even though there are many theories and ideas about psychological functioning. We don't actually know exactly what makes the mind get well, but we do know that the whole body is a system with built-in, self-correcting functions. Psychotherapy is designed to engage these healing functions.

I used to have a German car which, unfortunately, broke down quite regularly and expensively. I know quite a bit about how cars work, but my mechanic always impressed me with the exquisite detail of his understanding. No matter what part of the car was malfunctioning, he always seemed to know what needed to be done.

In contrast, take a problem to psychotherapists and notice just how general, varied, and sometimes contradictory the opinions are about what needs to be done. It's not that psychological services don't work—they often work quite well. But we therapists are at a marked disadvantage in comparison to expert mechanics. We can't take the brain apart and locate the mind. There are no windows, no access ports. There are no road maps which spell out a solution. We watch and experiment with the information a client reveals. We interpret and make inferences. But nonetheless, psychotherapists have discovered many important and useful things to do that help the mind to cope.

In Dorothea's early therapy work, the re-living of her childhood polio was very specific and focused. There was little doubt about the meaning of these experiences relative to her therapy goals. As time passed, Dorothea moved into a different phase of her psychological work. She was less focused and clear and was often confronted with intense and confusing experiences. She began having upsetting dreams which left her shaken emotionally.

She once dreamed of an infant threatened with rape by her father. In our explorations of her family history and her relationship with her father, there had never been any hint of sexual abuse and she did not show the kinds of anxiety and grief usually experienced by victims of childhood abuse. In another dream she encountered a beautiful woman who took her to a hospital room and left her with two vomiting old women.

These were powerful dream symbols. Important struggles were taking place in her unconscious mind and Dorothea was beginning to feel overwhelmed by emotional states. Each day she felt frightened in ordinary situations where she had never felt afraid before. She needed more time to allow integration of the changes that were occurring. We were intrigued by the symbolic meaning of these dreams, but I decided to direct her attention away from them. I gave brief, encouraging interpretations of the dreams to help her manage the anxiety they often caused, but focused our therapy on daily work and family issues.

The outpouring from Dorothea's unconscious mind was like the flow from a fire hydrant. It was all very rich and meaningful, but the volume was far more than she could work with. This happens at times in therapy. Sometimes the internal processes become so activated that external life becomes overwhelming. There isn't enough energy to cope with ordinary daily needs. Dorothea needed to temper the work, to slow it down. She needed to pay less attention to the outpouring. I told her, "Take time off from inner work, Dorothea. Don't record dreams for a while. Let them come and go. Don't ponder them."

Not everyone who enters therapy works with dreams. Many successful therapies occur without any attention to dreams. But for some, dreams are an important, central aspect of the change process. Many people assume that the value of a dream is contained in the meaning of its message. Therefore, if one doesn't understand the dream, if one cannot interpret the message, it is not useful. This is a misunderstanding. I believe the central value of a dream comes from grappling with it. When we notice a dream, think about it, write it down, or tell it to someone, we are being affected and changed by it. This change occurs whether or not we understand its "meaning."

Throughout childhood we are taught to ignore and be wary of the unconscious part of our mind. This training is part of the normal process of socializing that nearly all of us receive from our parents and teachers. We repeatedly encounter responses which warn us not to pay much attention to our unconscious process: "It's just your imagination, be serious." "You're just a dreamer." "It's only a dream, it doesn't matter." "Stop daydreaming." The implied but clear meaning of these messages is that the important mental experience is conscious and rational, and what comes from the unconscious is nonsense.

We are thoroughly indoctrinated by mid-adolescence or early adulthood. Our conscious mind has become alienated from our unconscious mind. We function as if we have two minds, one that is good and sensible and another which we don't understand. When we have a frightening fantasy or a nightmare, we shudder, shake our head, and say to ourselves, "Thank goodness, that was just a dream." Then we try to get it out of our memory as fast as possible so we can feel normal again.

But we don't have two minds. We have one mind, and it is a wonderfully complex and integrated system of many functions. There is an ecological balance in the psyche when it's healthy. When the balance is upset, some parts may be overactive or underactive or may function in ways that conflict with the system as a whole. Therapy is designed to restore the balance. One aspect of therapy is to pay attention to our fantasies, our fears, and our dreams. In doing so, we reverse our normal alienation and we learn again to value the unconscious side of our mind.

Acknowledging a dream creates a connection between the conscious and unconscious mind. The power of this connection may be a healing force. Acknowledgment activates the integrating function of the unconscious mind, signaling that the conscious mind is now open and ready to deal with incomplete emotional experiences from the past. Emotionally significant memories held at an unconscious level of mental function are resolved when the individual consciously remembers and integrates those experiences into her sense of self.

Sometimes the responsiveness of the unconscious is so specific and dramatic that the effect is startling. Several years ago a man who was not in crisis requested therapy because he had recently recognized that he seldom was aware of his own or others' emotions—particularly negative emotions. Whenever angry or sad feelings occurred, he responded as if they were problems to fix rather than emotions to express. He was reasonable and logical to a fault. He felt successful and happy in most aspects of his life, but his absence of feeling affected his relationships.

As we began our work together, I suggested that he notice his dreams and jot them down. During his third session, he reported a dream from the previous evening. It seemed silly, strange, and without meaning to him. I asked him to tell the dream as if it were happening right now. This was his dream:

"I'm walking down the street. A small dog is coming up to me from behind and it begins nipping at my Achilles tendon. I shoo it away, but it just keeps coming and biting at me."

He was embarrassed and apologetic and declared that he didn't have any idea what the dream could mean or even whether it had any meaning.

I thought for a moment and then said, "Tell me about the dogs in your life."

He began to tell me about the two dogs he had owned and loved as a boy. Within a few minutes he was weeping with sadness. He had tragically lost both of his dogs. Each had caused some minor problem and had been destroyed by his parents. He had not even been told in advance and there had been no consideration or concern for his feelings. On two separate occasions, he had returned from school and learned his dog had been put to sleep. Now, years later, his dream simply reminded him of those experiences and the intense sadness it caused him. He also remembered that, after the second incident, he had defiantly declared to himself in his grief and bitterness: "I'm never going to care about anything again."

In a similar manner, Dorothea's unconscious was responding to her conscious mind. It reminded her of the full range of terror which she had held in check during childhood. What a panoply of terror it was: infants threatened with incestuous rape, desolate old women vomiting out their despair, lips oozing blood. Parallel to these nightmares, she bore daily fears and grief.

Was this the mental health psychotherapy promised? What kind of reward was this for hard and courageous therapy work? If her therapy investment had been evaluated at this point by a bystander, he probably would have assessed it to be a poor one.

Yet it was a reward. Dorothea was intensely alive and dynamic. There was an enormous amount of action taking place, a dramatic contrast to the shut-down, stagnant, and depressed state she had been in for so many months. Here was real action, very personal and subjective, but real. It was like a thorough spring cleaning was taking place.

This cleaning out takes place at a literal level for some people who enter therapy. After a few weeks or months of opening themselves up to their inner disorder, they report that they get inspired to put their houses, garages, offices, and files in order after years of procrastination.

104

Dorothea's dark side was being revealed. Having pushed through her fear, she was saying, "Let me see it all." And here they were, her forbidden thoughts and fantasies, repressed feelings and impulses. Her dreams and emotions were laying out the agenda of work yet to be done. A beautiful woman made her appearance in the dream of the old women. In the dream, Dorothea had come for a therapy session and I sent her to an adjoining room to meet someone. Her unconscious mind used me as a symbol, the "voice of authority" in her dream, to give her direct advice: "Go see this woman and see what she wants to show you."

What did this beautiful woman show Dorothea? Horrors! Two old crones in a hospital room dressed in operating gowns. I thought to myself, what a collection of feminine figures. A beautiful woman and two vomiting old women. Since all elements of a dream represent parts of the dreamer, what could be the message in this bizarre scene? It was a wonderful message. Dorothea's ideal feminine sends her in to look at the distorted feminine identity she developed about herself as a young girl. "You are over the hill, Dorothea. Sexuality is not for you. Polio made you unacceptable. Fast-forward to old age and decline."

Carl Jung believed the unconscious contains a profound wisdom that is more intelligent than the conscious part of the mind. This intelligence often comes as advice, telling us what we need to do. What does Dorothea's dream tell her to do? The message is clear. "Get rid of this, puke it up. And do it in the bathtub and in the toilet." The bathtub is where we clean the impurities on the outside of ourselves, and the toilet is where we get rid of the impurities on the inside. A very thorough cleaning. "Get rid of the old women, Dorothea! Get rid of the old feminine identity and make ready for the new."

In the dream she screams and the scene fades. A scream comes from the center of a person, expressing an essential truth in that moment of time. When we break through to hard-won truth, it punches us right in the stomach. The scream declares our recognition. Years ago in my own therapy work, when I recognized my childhood belief that I killed my brother, the truth didn't come with a gentle, "Oh, I see." It knocked me off my feet and my weeping "screamed" from deep inside.

In Dorothea's dream, she screamed in recognition and moved on to the next action. She looked in the mirror, a great symbol of literal self-reflection, and what did she see? A wonderful, though gruesome, symbolic picture of what she was doing in life right then. She had "unzipped" her lips and broken the taboo against speaking forbidden truths. Her lips were "pooled" in blood, the vital fluid of life.

The unconscious mind often expresses itself in strange, forbidding images. This is the language of symbols and metaphors: graphic, dramatic, exaggerated—very much like the imagination of the child. Because of this, we often have anxious feelings about the surface appearance of dreams, particularly when they are intense or bizarre.

The richness of the unconscious does not always bring us frightening dreams. Dorothea's next dream was a lovely fantasy. She was swimming in "a sinister dark sea." A dream voice told Dorothea to dive down to the bottom of this dark, watery place. She was afraid, "tired and fuzzy-headed," but she dove anyway. The sea is definitely not human territory. It symbolizes a place other than the territory of the conscious mind. It is the realm of the unconscious. We instinctively feel afraid to dive down into a dark sea, the hidden places beneath the surface, the unknown depths.

Her dream took her through murkiness and darkness. She emerged in a place of light, "inside my own treasure," and she gained mobility and felt "as happy as a child." There she found a cave hidden at the bottom of the sea (her unconscious mind), and came upon pirates' treasure, the riches of life which had been stolen from her. They weren't lost after all, merely stored in a safe place until she was ready to claim them.

The treasure was hers to give to all the people she loved. To do this, she had a magic ladle which never emptied. She tapped into a source within, full of precious jewels. The unconscious mind gave her a fairy tale of wonder and delight, promise and hope. It said, "Go down into your dark and fearful places and uncover your hidden treasure. Claim everything that was put away and denied, all the pain and terror, all that was left behind. It is all hidden treasure."

The foremost purpose of psychotherapy is to relieve the suffering of the patient by eliminating the painful symptoms and restoring psychological equilibrium. But there is something else that can be accomplished in carrying out this task. The nature of the symptoms may contain information vital to helping the individual achieve a higher state of personal maturation and psychological development. This is the transformational possibility in psychotherapy. I viewed Dorothea's dream as symbolic of this potential for personal growth.

As we move forward in this story, we will discover just what the buried treasure turned out to be in Dorothea's life.

13

DOROTHEA

THE BEAUTIFUL WOMAN

As therapy work progressed, my dreams became road signs along an otherwise unnavigable route. For weeks I dreamed about the women in my family. In one dream I traveled to my great-grandmother Dorothea's home in New York. I was with my mother, grandmother, sister, and daughter—five generations of family women. In the dream I attended great-grandma Dorothea's funeral, but I was an adult, not the child I had been when she died.

My sister Lois came out of her bedroom. She wore a white sheer cotton dress with delicately woven lace around a deep collar and a low cut front. It outlined her breasts. The dress was lovely; she was lovely. I touched the dress, longed to try it on and feel its prettiness. My mother gave me a "that dress is not for you" look and left the room. Then my daughter, Kathryn, came to show me how much her breasts had grown. She was proud. I embraced her with fierce energy. I was happy to see her growing up.

Later in the dream, a large package arrived for me. It was ratty looking, beaten up from the mail, but I was curious opening it. Inside there was a box and a scrap of paper that said, "I'm there if you need me. Mike." I remembered Mike, this guy I'd recently met. I reread the note and wondered if I needed him. Too soon, I thought, and turned my attention to the package.

I opened the box and found a small round mirror that I set on a table. Undoing crumpled tissue paper I found trinkets—a small angel with wings and harp, a painted bird, a handful of small colored stones—childlike things. I set them all on the mirror and thought of the man who sent them. Peter Pan, I said to myself. Playtime.

I touched my sister's dress again just as my mother returned and saw me. "You want all that body stuff, don't you?" Her voice was bitter.

"You're damn right I do. But I want *all* of it. Unless he wants all of me for always and he's not going to go away and leave me, I don't want any of it," I shouted. I rose up and left the room, my eyes burning with tears.

The dreams did not always feature family women. The strange, beautiful woman I had dreamed of in the earlier nightmare about two old ladies re-emerged. I recognized her immediately. Her loveliness made my heart turn over. She had cut her hair. It was still jet black, but now it was short and curly. Light shone through it. Her eyes were warm and intense. We met in Amsterdam, by a canal, in front of the house where I had first made love. I did cartwheels for her, on a sunny patch of lawn beside the canal. I wanted to ask this mysterious woman some personal questions, but I was afraid of "muddying the waters" between us, afraid she might slip away. "Who are you and how did you get started in your business?" I asked.

She laughed. "You know who I am. You have always known. Just look to yourself." Her voice was resonant and rich.

In another dream, again in Amsterdam, I sat in a large comfortable chair in the front room of one of the canal houses. The beautiful woman tucked pillows all around me while I protested. "Why are you doing all this?" I asked, overwhelmed by her attention.

"I'm here to make you comfortable," she said lightly. She had a quiet joy and grace that was deeply moving and erotic.

I don't need comfort, I thought. But I sank down into the comfort she offered and I enjoyed it. "I'm so new at this," I said in wonder.

"Yes, I can see that," she smiled. She kept smiling at me as if she knew a whole warehouse of stuff that I had yet to discover.

I tried to understand what these dreams were telling me. Were they signs? Pointers? To what or where? The focus on women, the erotic and sensual suggestions aroused a shadowy part of me I didn't wholly trust. My Catholic upbringing as well as my illness had taught me to think of my body as housing for my soul, not as a source of erotic pleasure. While my passions sent contradictory messages, I didn't trust them as much as I trusted my mind. At home I became irritable and angry. I was bitchy with my husband and often felt unappreciated.

With David I felt remote, embarrassed and adolescent. I told him about the dreams, but I felt ridiculous saying, "Look, there's this beautiful woman who keeps coming to me." This just wasn't the way we had worked together when we talked about the past. For a while I wondered if it would be easier to talk about erotic feelings with a woman therapist, then I dismissed the idea. David and I worked well together and I felt too far along in my work to face making a change.

But the past was gone. Here and now I felt unlikable and stuck. Anything nice David had to say to or about me was psychotherapeutic etiquette material. If he knew how lost I was in all this female crap, he'd be disgusted.

After therapy sessions, I began to seek out distractions. One day I went to my hair stylist to have my hair trimmed. While I waited, I leafed through a professional styling magazine amusing myself with far-out haircuts. As I looked, amusement became excitement when I saw a photo of a very attractive woman whose face and hair length resembled my own.

It would be fun to look like that, I thought. My father would kill me! My father, who had recently died, had been a professional hair stylist. When I was nine, he had lopped off my waist-length thick braids just before the family went to the beach. There remained a shiny mass of hair that fell just below my ears. I never grew it out again. At fifteen I asked him what he'd do if I bleached my hair. He didn't even lower his newspaper. He just said, "I'd shave your head." Of course I didn't bleach it. I never curled it either.

But the photo on my lap was striking. The woman was spirited and saucy but not too young. Her hair was short, done in soft curls, that rang out like bells. On impulse I signed up for a permanent. Afterwards I felt exotic and transformed. Michael said "Wow!" when he saw the change. I was relieved, at last, to have something tangible to show my difference. At my next visit, even David looked twice, not sure at first what had happened.

After another session I walked down University Avenue in Palo Alto. Then I saw her! In the window of Shady Lane, a local artists' cooperative, was an antique brooch, fashioned in many metals, a vignette of a woman in profile, her copper hair blowing in the wind, her raised hands holding wild flowers. I stared. This was the beautiful woman of my dreams. Her face was carved from ivory, but all her features were made of various metals and were shown in relief on a tarnished pewter base.

I could not let this treasure go. But how could I spend fifty dollars on something for myself just because it was beautiful? I resolved to buy it for my sister's 50th birthday, a few weeks away. I showed the brooch to everyone I loved. I knew it would be hard to give away, even to my sister. I wanted to keep it. I needed to give it away. It was proof that beauty was in the world, that I could find it, have it, give it. I bought it.

Five days later, for my own birthday, my closest friend gave me the same beautiful woman brooch as a gift. It wasn't exactly the same as the one I'd admired, but very close to it. There was one remaining brooch in the shop. But that woman's face looked unhappy and unbeautiful to me. There were no more, ever again.

I enjoyed the antique brooch and the new hair style, but they felt like only outward signs of enormous inner changes. I didn't yet feel at ease with the inner changes. "It all feels crunched together," I told David.

"I don't understand what you mean. Is it that you're moving so fast?"

"No," I snapped impatiently. "I mean the chaos. Look, I'm having trouble walking, and you're talking to me about accepting my body as it is. And my husband loves me, but he doesn't want to face this loss either. Then I go to sleep at night and I'm still working. Lots of weird dreams, peopled mostly by women. Then this beautiful woman. I dream about her a lot. Sometimes I think—well, I know this sounds crazy, but..."

"Skip the preliminaries and apologies. Just say it. What do you think?"

His irritation pushed me forward. "I feel like I missed a lot of that stuff. I mean, it wasn't just what the polio did that I'm seeing now. The dreams are like fragments, bringing parts of me to put together." I struggled against admitting the impact of loss. I had always dwarfed my losses against the background of such good luck and the many blessings of life. Admitting loss might admit pity as well. That was unthinkable.

"I always told myself that I had gotten over the illness. And I did. I escaped. I got over, got past, got by, you know, like narrowly missing a fall over the edge of the cliff. God, here I am, alive, aren't I?"

"You certainly are," he said emphatically. "And you've got the whole rest of your life to enjoy. It's coming together for you now, in the healing. Isn't it?" He paused. "You really don't have to be doing anything with a lot of this stuff. Just let it come. Let it pass through you."

"You make it sound so easy," I answered, shifting uncomfortably. "It's shocking just to notice how big chunks of your life never happened or, worse, happened and you didn't notice them." I was annoyed that he didn't understand what I meant.

"And now, now these dreams about a beautiful woman. I have no idea who she is. But she comes and goes, and I love her when she's here. Then she disappears. It's weird. I know I'm a woman. Sometimes I feel so girlish. Unfinished. I mean, I've had a full life—what am I doing having girl dreams? I can't go back to get..."

"Get what, Dorothea? What did you leave behind?"

"Why, the broken parts, of course. All the broken parts. When my body hurt and I couldn't get rid of the pain, I left my body, mentally. Even when I was a teenager, I wasn't like other kids. I needed to do different things from what I wanted to do. In summer, the high school girls in their rolled-up jeans ran around singing 'Dungaree Doll' or went to Rockaway Beach for a day of fun. I always imagined the fun I was missing."

I sat up straight. "The summer I was 16, I was old enough to wear lipstick and date. But I spent that time in the hospital having an ankle fusion because my bones were mature enough for corrective surgery. The hospital was like summer camp for polios. Surgeries were planned. You booked a spot in advance."

David groaned.

"Oh, I could handle it. After all, it was my second surgery. I had the first one at age 13. I had hospitals down cold by then. I was tanned, slim, and pretty that summer. And Dr. Hass, the senior resident on the orthopedic team, was what teenage girls called cute. Curly reddish blond hair, blue eyes, great smile.

"The night before the surgery he sat across from me in my cheerful four-bed ward overlooking the East River in Manhattan. Step by step he explained the operation. At one point he scanned the floor and picked up my right shoe. Watching me he said, 'Is this the kind of heel you want to wear for the rest of your life?' He held the ordinary brown oxford between us.

"'What do you mean?' I asked, and he shifted in his seat.

"'Well, we fuse your ankle at a precise angle. That means you can never wear any other heel again. Your foot won't bend any which way anymore.' His eyes shifted to the shoe again, then back to me. 'No going back, you know.' His careful tone had just the hint of a question.

"And that's what I mean, David. In a split second I saw all those dream shoes I longed to grow into—the dancing slippers, the high heels, the summer sandals. One June night, before the operation, I sat on the closet floor and tried on my sister Lois' shoes. When she was out, of course. For years, I felt if I could wear regular pretty shoes, I would look okay, even if I couldn't walk or make the natural shoe wrinkles other people made.

"There was a feast of shoes! I remember slipping a looped string around my toes to keep them from curling under. Then I worked on the shoes and straightened my legs to see how they looked. I tried four or five pairs of shoes before I knew it wouldn't make a difference. My feet just drooped.

"So, when Dr. Hass held my ugly shoe between us, I knew it was mine for the rest of my life. A big swallow for a girl with pretty dreams."

"I'll bet it was," David said softly. "Did you and the other kids ever talk about those moments, with each other I mean?"

"Oh, we laughed about our shoes and casts and braces. We made jokes about ourselves. Sometimes we bitched. Once in a while, someone threw a fit. It wasn't popular, but since we all felt that way, we understood.

"There were worse things. Once I was put in a room with a girl named Lynn who'd had surgery the day her mother died, and they didn't tell her. Not for two days. Finally they had to tell her. I wasn't there then. I came a week later. The privacy curtains were drawn around her. She smoked and cried. I finally got her to talk to me one night when I couldn't sleep. I remember her voice. I had never heard a person sound so sad and hopeless."

"God, how awful. I see what you mean, how your summers were different from the other kids."

"The worst part, though, was going into the hospital feeling healthy and pretty and then experiencing pain and bodily violation in a way that was totally debilitating. It was like losing it all over again, only this time I wasn't a little kid anymore.

"From the start, the ankle fusion was a rough surgery with severe unremitting pain. After three days of Demerol, I was too weak to hold a paper cup of water. I felt disoriented too. I kept expecting the pain to subside, but a week passed with little relief. Unable to eat solid food, I weakened. Drugs weren't helping and now I was ashamed to beg for relief when people told me I shouldn't need it anymore.

"One night about an hour after a shot of Demerol, the pain was so severe that the drug wore off. When I asked for more, I got lectured about having to wait at least two hours. At the mercy of the nursing staff, I raged, got hysterical with pain and exhaustion. Magically, the resident on duty ordered another shot. I floated into oblivion.

"But the next day I was feverish and thirsty. Every sound in the room penetrated the thick cast encasing my right leg. When my mother touched the sheet or smoothed the pillow to comfort me, I cried out.

"On the evening of the eighth day after surgery, Doctor Hass came in and, holding my hand in both of his, asked how I felt.

"I turned away from him and gazed out at the few tugboats on the East River. 'The pain is terrible. It shouldn't hurt like this, still, should it?'

"'Of course not,' he agreed. Holding my hand firmly, he went on. 'We have to take a look at what's going on there. Make sure there's no infection.'

"My fingers fluttered inside his hands. I asked, 'What are you going to do?' trying to remain calm.

"'We'll have to drill open the cast, the foot and ankle part,' he said, drawing imaginary lines up both sides of the cast. 'Then we'll lift off the top, remove the dressing, and have a look.'

"I felt like a Thanksgiving turkey about to be undone. My insides trembled. 'Don't be afraid,' he said. 'I'll be fast. And gentle. It won't take long. I promise. It will relieve your pain and help the healing.'

"I fought to find my voice. 'Will it hurt a lot? Can I have something for pain? Can you put me to sleep?' I blurted it all out like a ten-year-old.

"'We'll give you something afterwards,' he said, and then he left. For a few seconds I watched the boats and felt serene. But when I saw the metal cart carrying cast-cutting equipment and fresh dressings, I sucked in my breath, curled my fists, and got ready to be strong."

I looked at David in that still moment, glad that we were here together watching that girl from afar. It had been terrible being there when the cast was drilled open and the wound exposed.

"Doctor Hass worked quickly with his young assistant. Above the whining drill he called out to me, cheered me on. He held my leg at the knee, under his arm as if it were a football. He faced away from me as he worked, passing things back and forth to his assistant. But the heat and the vibrations of the drill were painful. As the blade approached my ankle, I shouted 'No! I can't!' He went on working.

"I caught snippets of remarks—dressing too tight, calculate space for post-op swelling—but the staccato remarks were mostly medical jargon.

"From far away I heard the assistant's voice. 'Only a little longer, only a little more, Dorothea. You're doing fine. The wound is clean, no infection. I'm just putting on a loose dressing now. The first one got too tight from the swelling. Cut right into you. That was the culprit.'

"From the open window I heard the wail of a fire engine siren. Then many of them growing closer. 'Hear those sirens, those fire engines? Can you see them from there?' the young assistant asked as I dug my fists into the bed trying to hold back noise. Tears came but he persisted. 'Don't cry, Dorothea. Watch the fire engines,' he said, pointing out the window.

"I was enraged. And then the sirens were upon me, full force, their clear shattering sounds passing through and over me. I fell back, wrapping a pillow around my face, and cried out, hearing my own voice mingling with that big sound in the world beyond my window. Before that long moment was over I shook, cried, and wet the bed.

"Later there was Demerol and much kindness before I floated off into sleep. When the medical staff cleared out, it was dark. My roommate, her head and back rigid in a scoliosis cast, whispered, 'Was it awful? Really awful? God, don't you hate what they do to you?'

"'Yeah,' I answered. I knew she knew. She was comforting. I wished my mother had been there to hold my head in her arms until the aching went away, maybe until I fell asleep. I wanted to be touched in a tender way by someone who loved me. But the cool night air, the relief from pain, that was enough, really. That was all there was."

It had been some time since I had recalled a polio memory so vivid and complete. My general good health had allowed me to ignore the ongoing struggle of those years. But in telling David what I had been doing while the other girls were at the beach, I saw that large chunks of normal life pleasures had been replaced with struggle and endurance. It had happened over and over.

David asked one day if I had, perhaps, assumed an "embattled" stance toward life.

"I don't know if I'd call it embattled," I said. "But often I've feared pushing myself too far—as if the little bit more I ask of myself will injure me. Am I asking too much? Wanting too much? Will I lose it all? I fear personal violence—like when I almost fall, or hear screaming sirens. I know this is crazy, but I've become terrified by violence and bodily harm. Like someone's poised with an ax at the back of my neck. A cold steel blade, set to drop at any moment."

I flushed and lowered my eyes, ashamed to see myself living on the edge of peril. The words and pictures in my head had power to frighten me.

David interrupted my long silence. "Dorothea, look at me," he said, in a cool direct voice. When I looked up and saw him, he was bright in the morning sun, not at all soft around the edges, the way I wanted him to be. I was slow and fuzzy, struggling through my mire of fear.

"I'd like to teach you a way to move through those fears more easily."

"What do you mean? I'm saying them, aren't I? Having the feelings instead of burying them? There's so much fear to get out. Isn't that what I'm supposed to be doing? Feeling my feelings?"

"You're much better able to get to your feelings than you were a few months ago. But I've noticed that you get overwhelmed by emotions, so much emotion that you get bogged down by it. Is that right?" Yes, I nodded. "Well, I want to teach you some methods for gaining better control over your emotional experience. Let's look at how the mind works, how some of our emotions are caused by how we think about things."

I shifted stiffly. The therapy office had taken on the aura of the classroom. David threatened to become preachy. I put up my guard. "You mean I should deny the intensity or reality of my emotions?" I challenged. "Feelings are a powerful part of who I am."

"Of course they are," David agreed. "But you are more than your feelings. You are more than feelings. Yet when you are having a strong emotion, that feeling often seems as if it is the whole of who you are. Emotions are like that. They can dominate our experience. You have a mind. And a body. But you are not either of them alone. All of you, as you are, existing here and now, that is the whole experience."

What was he driving at? I felt growing resistance in my gut. "But when I'm having my feelings here and now, isn't that my truth? My experience? I don't see your point?"

"Okay, look. See that blue ceramic cup on the mantel?" In two steps he had it in his hand and held it toward me. I took it, felt its weight, saw its delicate design. "Now set it down," he said. "Close your eyes and visualize the cup." He waited a moment. "Can you see it in your mind?" he asked.

"Of course," I said, feeling impatient. "I can see it exactly."

"Now, tell me what you see."

"The blue cup," I said, feeling stupid.

"But the cups aren't the same. Open your eyes now. This cup," he said, holding the literal blue cup, "has a physical reality different from what's in your mind. The image in your mind appears to duplicate the cup, but you know it isn't the cup itself, don't you." I nodded. "The cup exists outside of you whether you notice or think about it or not. Objectively, it exists.

"Human experience is like that too, Dorothea. An experience occurs and we mentally record it. But, once it is over, the event no longer exists. What remains is a memory. The memory of a powerful experience is not, objectively, the same thing as the experience itself. Right?"

"So, are you telling me, that when I'm feeling fear, for example, I'm not feeling it or there's nothing to be afraid of? That sounds like denial."

"Those feelings are real all right. But the events your memories are about are not real—they no longer exist. They once were real. But now, only the feelings are real. And those kinds of feelings are different from emotions about an event happening in the present. It is very helpful to be able to recognize when your emotion is being triggered by a thought or memory."

"I understand the difference between viewpoints, if that's what you mean. But emotions are subjective. If you objectify them, isn't that just another way to intellectualize feelings?"

"Not really," he said. "If you're afraid, and you can observe your fear, you can step back, ask yourself what the fear is a response to. Without denying the feeling, you can bring your mind into play in a very useful way."

"You mean, find out if you're afraid because your car is really hanging off a cliff? Or if you're afraid of something existing in your mind, like a memory or the possibility of something that's not actually happening?"

"That's what I mean. With the car, fear is appropriate, a primitive signal to make you pay attention. The connection is important, literally, in a lifesaving way. But when the fear is of something in your imagination alone, it's real in a different way. Maybe it's asking you to see something or understand something or even finish something.

"But the emotion itself can't hurt you. When you begin to notice this, it gets to be a habit. Your observer becomes strong. After a while, you see the fear looming up and you say, 'Ah Ha! That's the old fear again. Let me look and see what it's about.'"

It seemed so simple that I was surprised I had never seen it before.

"I think we did something very important here today," I said. "I've analyzed and used my mind to work things out all my life. But I haven't known how to bring the thinking dimension to my intense feelings. I mean, as a way to solve personal dilemmas. I've listened to everything you've said. I think it's really going to be useful to me."

David watched me as I spoke. "Well, time will tell, won't it?" he said. I wondered why he seemed so skeptical.

Even so, something was new. I visualized massive entanglements of feelings warring with each other. I knew that anger and hurt drove out the erotic, beautiful woman in me. I had used my mind to save me from the overwhelming terror of my illness. It was time to begin a conversation between my mind and all of my feelings so they could live together in my body, not in flight from the past or in fear of the future. The challenge was enormous.

It had been weeks since I'd dreamed of my beautiful woman. It was time, as David said, to go inside and find her. Now I knew that the habit of fear was the great crippler. It froze everything.

To be beautiful I had to fall in love again with myself and the miracle of life. I began with simple physical indulgences, pampering my body with vibrant silk shirts in colors of wine, purple and cobalt. I bought a cashmere sweater and expensive perfume. I purchased five wonderful compact disks instead of one or maybe none.

At first the choices were spontaneous and unconscious. But after a while, I knew that I was learning to give myself pleasure and enjoy the immediacy and indulgence of it all. I deserved it. The trip to consciousness was painful, but it had its pleasures.

Spring rains had drenched our garden and produced a profusion of Iceland Poppies, long-stemmed, papery-petalled, delicate beauties in pink, crimson, and sunshine yellow. One morning I picked at least three dozen and brought them to David's office. I thrust them toward him. They were still shimmering wet, bright, lovely. "We need to have this beauty in your office. I need to give something back to you, for all I've taken away. Having the pain requires having the joy too."

He smiled, thanked me, and arranged the flowers in a vase. It wasn't a bad way to begin our work for the day.

14

DAVID

BREAKING OLD PATTERNS

It is a wonderful experience to work with people in the special atmosphere of the therapeutic encounter. I am repeatedly humbled by the magic that occurs when people are able to lay down their fears and open themselves to the healing forces that are unleashed in a trusting relationship. A peculiar bonus of the therapy profession is that trust is a transformative process for both the therapist and the client.

Each new client presents an unknown and unpredictable situation. I always feel a certain level of tension when I meet someone new. Who is this person? What will he or she present? Will I be adequate to meet his need? Will I be able to connect with him and he with me? What will I discover?

Every new therapy session is unpredictable. I wonder what will happen. Was the last session useful? Are we making progress? Do I really understand this person? Will I be fully present? Will I recognize what is important and what isn't? Am I good enough? Will I be able to respond in a useful way?

Therapy is a dance of trust. I say to my client, "Trust me." I say to myself, "Set aside everything else and be fully present." One of a therapist's most crucial duties is being emotionally and psychologically present. He must let go of his preoccupations, focus on being with the client, and respond to whatever emerges in the session. In spite of extensive professional training and experience, he cannot know in advance what to do.

A unique aspect of the work with Dorothea was the sheer density of psychological material that emerged throughout the therapy. There was no way that I could take in, remember, and process everything she presented in each session. Using my earlier analogy, it was like trying to take a drink from a fire hydrant. She

119

was in the middle phase of her treatment now and this psychic intensity persisted. Her daily life and nightly dreams were emotional and challenging. The work on childhood experiences was mostly done. Now her memories began to focus on later stages of development; specifically, on unfinished material from her adolescence.

One day Dorothea dreamed she was at a gathering of five generations of women in her family. In the dream she is an adult, even though the dream was about her struggle as a maturing young woman. The dream theme asks the question, "Who am I as a female and sexual person?" She envies her sister's beautiful dress, and feels tension with her mother because she wants sexuality and beauty for herself. Mike, the new boyfriend, is off in the wings sending her messages, a mirror, and trinkets. Here is the family crucible revisited. Dorothea goes back to it with her adult self and reviews the family dynamic during her adolescence. She goes toe to toe with the forces of repression, represented by her mother, and declares: "I want all of it!" Her newly found sense of feminine beauty is expressed with the conviction that she has full rights to wholeness.

Dreams can be an accurate gauge of therapy progress. The content of therapy sessions becomes reflected in dream life and themes brought up in dreams affect what is done in therapy. The therapist can observe the inner process of integration taking place. The dreams create a tangible sense of the active relationship between the conscious and unconscious sides of the mind.

The unconscious mind sometimes gives very specific messages that pertain to the therapy work. I worked with a woman who was in therapy to heal a physically and psychologically abusive childhood. When she got to the bottom of her inner fear and terror, she became overwhelmed with strong suicidal thoughts and feelings. In the midst of this psychic struggle, she came in with a magical dream, the kind of dream Jung referred to as "archetypal," meaning that it comes from regions of the psyche which are beyond the purely personal. Her dream is bathed with golden light and in the dream, she herself is pure gold. A loving dream voice tells her powerful affirmations about herself, notes that she is going through "the darkness before dawn" and instructs her to "remember this message."

Repeatedly, I was reassured by Dorothea's dreams. In any therapy there are multiple issues one can focus on, directions one can go in the exploration. And every therapist knows that sometimes we pursue "red herrings," we go off on tangents, only to have to find our way back to the most relevant issue for the healing task. The dream messages from Dorothea's unconscious mind seemed to confirm the direction of our work. She was increasingly giving full attention to her feelings, thoughts, and impulses, accepting them without censorship, and learning to trust that everything from her psyche had value and meaning.

During a relaxed and reflective session, we discussed the meaning of the dreams which dealt with Dorothea's identity as a woman. She sat on the sofa and I noticed she was wearing one of her favorite outfits, a denim skirt and a soft work shirt type of blouse. She often wore this or a similar combination and I mused to myself about how different this style was from the dramatic flare of her "inner beautiful woman."

I commented, "Dorothea, I was thinking about your choice of clothing. Your style appears sort of 'college coed' to me. Did you adopt this when you were a student?"

She laughed and said, "My whole wardrobe is for comfort and I've always looked for clothes which hide my body. Who would want to look at this?" She gestured to her body. "I don't pay much attention to clothes and only shop for myself out of necessity."

Clothing is often very reflective of an individual's inner state. Our style is seldom without some specific psychological consideration. I once knew a woman who purchased nearly all her clothes on trips to another state to visit her family. She was always very well dressed in expensive and tailored outfits, but they were of a design which was more typical of her mother's generation than her own. In her therapy, one of the issues was her incomplete emotional emancipation from the control of her family.

I told Dorothea my thoughts about her beautiful woman, and wondered whether there was something for her to discover about her studied casual style.

She was provoked by my inquiries about her feminine self image. She didn't like it. This was touchy material. After all, she had worked long and hard to convince herself that these things didn't matter. And in the largest perspective, her "style" didn't matter. What mattered was that she grapple with the question of free choice in style and beauty of appearance. This is what her dreams kept demanding. It was as if her unconscious mind was yelling at her, "Hey Dorothea! You are not settled about this stuff." What mattered was that her choices should truly be choices, not compromises she made out of her personal and cultural conditioning in order to avoid conflict or disapproval.

Her experience with buying the beautiful woman brooch exemplifies this kind of self-limiting compromise. Dorothea showed me the brooch. It was very beautiful and, at $50, an incredible bargain. So what were her feelings when she first saw the brooch? "I can't let this go, I want it. But how can I spend $50 on something for myself just because it's beautiful?" In her own mind, such self-denial seemed like common sense and obvious truth. So Dorothea bought the brooch for her sister, but I knew that if Dorothea had been in a bookstore and had come across books she wanted, she wouldn't have hesitated to write a check for $50. There would be no debate about it. I knew that if she had come across something that would delight her husband or daughter, buying it would be no problem. I didn't accept her rationalization.

It was important for Dorothea to get provoked by something as superficial as clothing and style. It was another facet of her larger journey to full membership in womanhood. I challenged her to entertain her dream images and discover how they applied to everyday decisions. Therefore, it was psychologically significant when she went to the hair stylist and on impulse decided to get a permanent. This was a breakthrough, not merely an ordinary decision. She was smashing down her inner barriers against free choice. Over time, these kinds of small changes create an accumulation of inner strength that overcomes the power of one's old inhibiting conditioning.

One of the joys of practicing psychotherapy is being able to witness these kinds of breakthroughs, seeing clients make decisions which reflect inner freeing up. People quit jobs, change careers, get married, buy treats for themselves or others, buy art, return to school, etc. These kinds of exciting changes symbolize some inner change.

I once worked with "Barbara," a young woman artist, talented in both music and dance. She had a cheerful and lighthearted personality and appearance, yet she had struggled with recurring depressive episodes for years. These episodes always included strong suicidal thoughts. After several months of difficult therapy work, her suicidal feelings reappeared and she plunged into deep despair. She came for her appointment one day in this state, and I sensed that it was the right time for her to challenge this destructive part of herself. I asked her to visualize it as a separate person sitting in an empty chair in my office. I coached her on how to have a direct dialog with this suicidal part by switching back and forth between the two chairs, thereby switching between the two parts of herself. A tremendous battle ensued. It became clear that the suicidal part was powerful and aggressive. In angry demeaning terms, it told Barbara she was worthless and stupid and deserved to die. Barbara trembled and wept in the face of such hatred. She was a gentle soul, the kind of person who seldom expressed anger, who was never mean or nasty to anyone. She was terrified of the murderous rage that came out of her and at herself.

Weeping with despair, she turned away from the empty chair and said she felt helpless.

There are moments in therapy which scare the hell out of me. At times, the most terrifying psychological dramas unfold right there in the consulting room. Nothing is theoretical anymore. We're no longer having discussions about life "out there." It is as if Darth Vader, the agent of death, has entered the room and is sitting there thumbing his nose at both me and my client. Here is the dark side personified. I sometimes feel like running away, yet I know I must stand firm.

I reached out, took Barbara's hand and held it tightly. I asked her to look at me and breathe deeply. She struggled hard with her feelings but finally got control of her breathing, opened her eyes, and looked at me. "Now listen very closely to me, Barbara. This is very scary stuff, but it is also an incredibly important moment for you. This suicidal part of you has terrorized you for years and it has made your life miserable, hasn't it?" She nodded and I went on. "You've held her off or you wouldn't be alive today. But, you have been afraid of her and she has stayed in control, lurking just beneath the surface, and you have never known when she's going to appear again. Isn't that right?" Again she nodded, listening intensely. "She seems very powerful to you, doesn't she?"

Sniffing back her tears, Barbara asked, "What did I do, why does she hate me so much?"

"We don't know all the reasons but someday you probably will. The important thing for you to realize, right now, is that this suicidal part is part of you. That incredibly powerful and aggressive woman is you. It's not someone else. It's you, a part of you that is turned against you. You have to get that power back. Remember this. As many times as she has come to you and told you that you should die, that you should kill yourself, you have always prevailed. The truth is, you have always been the stronger one. Now it's time for you to confront her directly and end this struggle. Let her know how you feel about her. Don't let her keep torturing you this way. Look her in the eye and take back that power."

Barbara turned to the empty chair and stared at it for a few moments. Then she began telling her suicidal part how miserable it had been for her all the past years. As she spoke, her energy began to build and her voice got louder. She was finally in touch with the full intensity of how much she hated this suicidal struggle. She began yelling until she was screaming at the top of her voice, tears streaming down her face.

Finally she screamed out, "I don't care what you say to me, God dammit! You are never going to win. I am never going to kill myself. Never. Never. Never!"

There was a stunned silence in the room. Barbara leaned back in her chair, trembling and sobbing quietly to herself. I waited. I felt privileged to witness this incredible event and had tears in my eyes. I vaguely wondered how much of the loud screaming had penetrated the only partly soundproof walls and intruded into the sessions of my neighboring colleagues.

Suddenly Barbara sat forward and turned to me with a radiant smile. She reached out her hand in a strong handshake and declared, "Put 'er there, partner. I'm alive, damn it, I'm alive!" I roared with laughter and congratulated her on her powerful new self.

So what happened next in the life of this frugal and conservative young woman? She decided to buy a new car and arrived at one of our next sessions driving a bright red convertible with the most powerful V-8 engine available. Empowerment by psychotherapy and Detroit!

This was the kind of relationship between inner and outer change that I was presenting to Dorothea in looking at clothing, style, and self-expression. Nothing is too major or too minor to look at and ponder. What is on the surface of our lives is never unrelated to what is taking place inside.

Dorothea's therapy continued to focus on her adolescence and the painful surgeries that ruined her summer vacations as a teenager. More pain, more loss to go through. More cleaning out of the closet.

Therapy often proceeds in a sequential order from childhood experiences, through puberty and adolescent struggles, and eventually to the present. It is amazing to watch this orderly unfolding.

Sometimes people ask if therapy requires them to go through every hurtful and unfinished event in their lives. Absolutely not. The healing process only requires that we settle those items which have such significance that they block psychological growth and the development of important functions. Nearly everyone's childhood and adolescence has countless difficult moments and hurtful experiences. Therapy touches on a mere fraction of them. Ordinary daily life and loving relationships heal the rest.

Dorothea remembered being hospitalized during summer vacations. Imagine how terrible this was for all of those young polio patients. How intense it must have been for the staff, having to deal with the surgeries, treatments and medical needs of these teenagers who wanted to be anywhere else but there. Not to mention having to deal with the normal energy, bravado, and rebellion of a bunch of teenagers.

When Dorothea revisited memories of these years, she again descended into old pain and hurt. I noticed that dealing with pain was easier for her now. She had learned that even painful memories have an end point and that she changed by her journey through them. Even so, her therapy was spilling over into her everyday life. I noticed that she tended to emotionalize too many of her ordinary experiences. She had developed a "hair trigger." Daily events were overwhelming her and making normal life difficult to manage.

One day I asked her to look at the emotional responses she was having that had nothing to do with the past. I pointed out where she experienced negative emotional states when other responses were possible. She needed to learn how to observe her own psychological behavior to discover that there are numerous possible responses to events. Without this understanding, excessive emotion would continue to dominate her life, creating unpleasant experiences in circumstances which weren't negative.

The creation of an internal observer is a powerful tool for bringing about personal change. Our normal mode of mental life is that we live, as it were, inside of our minds, taking our perceptions, thoughts, and feelings for granted, and therefore assuming that our decisions and actions always make logical sense. It is possible to develop the mental ability to watch ourselves from a detached position and observe the way our minds work from within. When we do this, it usually becomes obvious to us that we don't function rationally in all circumstances.

Dorothea felt sensitive about this subject. I remember how tense she was when I began exploring these concepts with her. She listened closely, but was subdued. She reacted as if I were telling her she was bad for having her particular emotional experience. The sensitive issue here was that I had been saying, in essence, that her depressive and anxious experience was the result of intolerable and painful past events. Now I was telling her that there was more to the task of healing than resolving past issues. She had to change how she approached life now, in the present, because she was caught in a pattern of repeatedly feeling hurt and mistreated by life. More work to do.

Therapy doesn't always involve both of these tasks. Not everyone has a traumatic past. Many people simply encounter difficulties in the transition to adult life, or have problems in relationships or work. But these are not necessarily the result of wounds from the past. For some people, certain skills learned in their family were limited or prove dysfunctional in their present life situation. For them, therapy might focus on reviewing the problem areas they encounter, identifying where their coping style is ineffective, and learning better approaches. I usually find a review of personal history useful in discovering the dysfunctional pattern.

In contrast to Dorothea's case, when there is not trauma in the past, such history taking can be enjoyable and interesting, rather than emotionally stressful.

Dorothea is by nature an intensely feeling person. Her repeated exposure to painful experiences in childhood created heightened sensitivity to hurt. Under stress, she tightened up and her emotional tension escalated. She also had developed a fierce sense of independence and prided herself in not asking for help. This was admirable, but sometimes it meant that her needs went unmet and she pushed herself to the edge of fatigue and frustration, felt overwhelmed, and got depressed. These basic patterns were ineffective for her.

In addition to these patterns, she still obeyed the unconscious rule that she should always be nice, brave, and cheerful. But it's hard to be nice when you're afraid, hurt, or exhausted. Most people feel like asking for some tender loving care in those moments. Dorothea couldn't allow this. She held in her feelings. Her emotional stress escalated until she reached a breaking point, then her feelings spilled out in bitchy complaints at her family. But this was a violation of her unconscious "niceness" rule, so she felt guilty and unlovable as a result of expressing her complaints.

I was shifting our work to what is known as cognitive therapy. In this therapeutic approach, attention is not on the "contents," but on the underlying "structure of mental activity." For example, consider a person who feels afraid in an encounter with another individual. The "content" focuses on who was there and what behaviors occurred. The "structure" focuses on the internal cognitive behavior of the fearful person—his perceptions, thoughts, memories and other related associations. Thus, his fear may not be a simple response to the encounter. The fear might be a response to an elaborate interpretation of the meaning of the encounter. How people structure their cognitive experience determines how they feel and behave.

It is hard to interrupt these patterns. Emotions have a seductive quality. When they get triggered in us, they feel justified by our experience, and we have strong impulses to express them. Understanding our emotions is confusing because sometimes, our emotional reactions are natural and appropriate responses to life events. Yet at other times, they arise from distorted perception and thinking.

How do we distinguish between these correct emotional responses and the ones which are internally generated? It is my observation that, for many people, as much as 80% to 90% of their negative emotions result from faulty cognitive patterns. This creates enormous, unnecessary emotional suffering. There is a certain amount of truth to the old saw, "you are what you think."

Subjectively, it often seems as if our mood determines what we think. It works both ways. How we think affects our mood and our mood affects how we think. In applying cognitive principles to depression, it is important to discover and change the automatic thought patterns which create and support a despairing way of perceiving life. For example, depression is usually accompanied by gloomy memories of the past and pessimistic projections about the future.

A man attending a class I taught told a story about himself which poignantly demonstrates this process. At work one morning, a secretary called and told him to schedule a meeting with his manager for 2 o'clock that afternoon. This was unexpected. During the following hours, John became anxious and fearful. He repeatedly thought that he must have made some serious error or caused some terrible problem, and he had anxious fantasies about meeting with his boss. Finally, at the appointed hour, he nervously walked into the manager's office. His boss looked up from his desk and said, "Hi John, great news! You were granted stock options."

John's five hours of anguish perfectly demonstrates an internally generated experience. His anxiety was not a response to his actual life situation. It was a response to his cognitive process, to his imagination run amuck. He projected his negative interpretations onto an unknown future event and terrorized himself with his fantasy. Is there anyone reading this who doesn't recognize some variation of this experience? It seems to be a universal pattern of the mind to struggle with the unknown, and often, in a negative direction.

In James Clavell's novel *Shogun*, there is some advice which conveys this dilemma in an Eastern, metaphorical way: "... always remember, child, that to think bad thoughts is really the easiest thing in the world. If you leave your mind to itself, it will spiral you down into ever increasing unhappiness. To think good thoughts, however, requires effort. This is one of the things that discipline, training, is about. So, train your mind to dwell on sweet perfumes, the touch of this silk, tender raindrops against the shoji, the curve of this flower arrangement, the tranquillity of dawn. Then, at length, you won't have to make such a great effort and you will be of value to yourself."

Cognitive therapists look at this negative tendency as a mental process to be corrected so that one can live free of unnecessary, noxious emotional symptoms—a very worthy goal. Eastern philosophy views this as the essential struggle for consciousness: how to create a state of being where one experiences life with clear perception, undistorted by the confusing contents of the untrained mind.

127

Usually we grow up and grapple with the world, taking our inner mental activity for granted. Our thinking process achieves a seamless connection to our perception of external reality so that we often come to function as if thought is real. The thinking process is real; it is a brain function. But the content of thought is never real. It is always an artificial representation of reality. Nevertheless, thought can be very powerful. It can help us comprehend possibilities in actual reality that are beyond our ability to perceive directly. Thought has led to the creation of science, technology, art—the whole of civilization as we know it.

Thoughts can be powerful in a specifically personal way also. If we do not learn to regard our thinking process carefully, it can distort our perception of external reality, create irrelevant and strong feelings, and impel us to act in unhealthy and ineffective ways. Our feelings and actions are real, regardless of whether they are based on accurate or inaccurate perception and thinking. Our thoughts powerfully impact our reality.

Dorothea understood the importance of learning to sidestep her emotional reactions. It wasn't easy. Cognitive process is automatic and unconscious. Learning to observe perceptions, thoughts and feelings is a complex experience. Our emotional patterns are literally embedded in our natural experience of life. They seem invisible, but we can learn to see them.

One day I said, "Feeling afraid is not the same as being in danger, Dorothea. Think about your typical week. How often are you actually in danger? How often are you in a situation where there is an actual threat to your well being?"

"Well, not very often I guess. Once in a while when I'm driving my car. Or sometimes I stumble or slip and almost fall. But I really am very careful."

"Now think, how often are you afraid in a typical day or week? How often are you anxious, tense and on guard?"

She laughed when she got it. "Wow, sometimes it seems like I'm afraid most of the time. What am I, paranoid or something?"

It often is amusing when we discover our own patterns of distorted perception, thinking and feeling. And it is important to do so, because they can color our life experience in ways we wouldn't choose if given the choice. For some people, fear creates an excessively dangerous world. My own distortion was fear, and also a belief that I was bad. Thus I kept myself hidden and distant so that other people wouldn't see the truth about me. Some people have a sense of fragility, so they frequently feel hurt. Others are chronically angry. They are constantly finding unfairness and injustice in the world. Each person has his or her own style.

Dorothea's task was to develop an inner observer, and she was a fast learner. Her lively emotional style gave her lots of opportunity to observe. Once she had learned her pattern, she was able to catch herself in the middle of an exaggerated reaction. This allowed her to check her perceptions and thoughts and find new and creative responses to situations. For example, when she began to feel annoyed at Michael or Kathryn for not helping around the house, on reflection she often discovered that she hadn't told them she needed help.

The process of mastering one's emotional life is gradual. Each time we interrupt an old reactive pattern, new choices become possible. When we respond creatively, we immediately notice different feelings. We stop feeling pushed around by our emotions and by life. We begin to understand that every moment presents a broad array of possibilities and we are free to choose. When we are no longer simply reacting to life, we generally choose effective ways to get our needs met. We feel good and our enjoyment of life grows.

15

DOROTHEA

THE VOICE OF ANGER

Music had comforted me during the early months of therapy when I struggled to uncover buried feelings. All through autumn I had listened to a haunting, poignant recording of the Pachelbel Canon and a few Bach pieces which gave me refuge, a place to be alone and at rest. Music was blessedly free from words. But in springtime, Michael brought home a new tape with the Pachelbel Canon played by the Canadian Brass, entirely on trumpets.

The horns were at first piercing and delicate, then evolved into something glorious and celebratory. About midway through, I heard the faint sound of the motif, expressed in the distant voice of a single trumpet rising in the background. As the leading trumpets carried the weight of the melody, the background thread grew stronger and took shape. Finally, the full strong sound of the single instrument joined the others, merging into powerful wholeness. Privately, I played the music over and over and it filled me with joy. When I drove my car I listened and then sang each of the parts. As time passed, I wanted the glorious music to spill over into all of my world.

I didn't want to become a musician. I wanted to make beautiful music outside of myself, in the world outside David's office. What was keeping me from celebrating life in the clear sharp tones of the trumpets? I had learned to look at many dark feelings and had felt primitive satisfaction in releasing them. I had begun to think about finding a finishing place in therapy. Michael had said, soon after I'd started therapy, that he thought I'd be done by spring. But it was June. He laughed when I reminded him and quipped, "I didn't say which spring." I was feeling much better, happier, stronger—but something was holding me back.

While therapy was progressing, my home life was tense. I felt more irritable with my family because they seemed insensitive to the practical challenges I faced. When I wanted help around the house and Michael or Kathryn seemed oblivious, I growled—made demands instead of requests. Sometimes I thought I was living with Hansel and Gretel, facing tell-tale trails of shoes, socks, papers, pens, and books. How could I do less work if they remained blind? Doing less meant yelling more. The atmosphere grew unpleasant and sometimes explosive.

The knot of irritability grew into a tight little wad of anger. I hoarded it and it grew larger and harder. I tried to ignore this petty smallness, but it wouldn't go away. I knew expressing anger was out of the question. It just created more anger and escalated bad feelings. Being aware of it was enough. Saying it was bound to get me into trouble.

Observing my bad feelings never came easily to me. My parents had been very clear about bad feelings. As a toddler, my temper tantrums evoked scolding and spanking from my father. My mother sent me off to the bathroom until I was ready to behave again. I was told to think about my rude behavior and look in the mirror to see my ugly face. Sometimes my father teased me and his barbs were humiliating. Then I always flared to greater heights of fury.

At four years old, I started to stutter. Dad was impatient and furious. He'd yell "Stop that! Start over again!" I was angry for not being able to get the words out. When he yelled, I became afraid to speak.

One day I told David, "As long as I can remember, I have felt there was this person I was supposed to be—and then there was this person I was. It got worse after I got sick. Talking became harder for me. Not only was my voice often literally stopped at home, but when I returned to school after the two year absence, my stuttering became worse. There had been some school instruction in the hospital and regular home instruction during the year at home, but two years away from the classroom and friends was a long time.

"At first the school principal hesitated to return me to my old classroom with my friends who were starting seventh grade. My parents argued that I could do the work and it would be good for me to rejoin old friends. I was devastated by the idea of being held back. Luckily there was no room for me in sixth grade, so I entered seventh grade on a trial basis. I was so eager to start school again, so eager to prove that I could do it. I worked hard. In June, I won the General Excellence Award for the highest grades in the class. By then, I stuttered whenever I confronted formidable adult authority or felt afraid.

"I never knew when I'd stutter. It was hard to tell. One minute I'd be questioning or defying someone; the next, gagging on my own words. By the time I was 13 and starting my freshman year in high school, I couldn't say my own name out loud to an adult. And I couldn't read aloud from printed text, even from a paper I had written. I remember one time in a college freshman sociology course, being asked to read aloud from my straight-A exam. I was so frightened that I left the room."

It was hard to say these things to David, hard to admit that I had walked out on many opportunities to use my voice. I had disguised what was unacceptable to others so that my pain was hidden. It was hard work, but it made living a "normal" life possible. By the time I left home for graduate school, I had proven that I'd won my way with my brains, my pen, and my sense of humor. Proven it well enough to feel some personal confidence and actually use my voice more freely.

It remained a private agony that I had never regained the full range of my voice sufficiently to say my name with ease and assurance. Three days before my wedding I had gone to my priest with an attack of stage fright. "Are you rethinking your commitment?" he asked. "No," I said. "Just terrified about all those people looking at me. About saying ALOUD the vows I had written." What I did not say was that I was afraid my voice would be stopped or lost. That possibility made me want to flee my own wedding, this central celebration of my life. When I did not stutter, I was grateful for the blessing of a perfect day.

A very close friend had her wedding three weeks after my own. She had honored me by inviting me to read aloud a poem for the occasion. I told her something about being nervous reciting at formal occasions, about not wanting to spoil the perfect aesthetics of her ceremony. Privately I agonized over rejecting the honor. But I just couldn't take the risk. I felt damaged.

Remembering these moments made my blood boil. Everywhere I looked, I saw struggles and tough choices. I knew I had made costly mistakes. In my marriage, I behaved as if I could do everything. I was passionate about being a genuine companion and helpmate to Michael. I welcomed motherhood into the deepest part of my life, held a responsible job, ran the household, even planned our social life and vacations. Somehow I'd make up for the parts I couldn't do.

My eyes grew hot with tears and I felt my nails digging into the palms of my hands.

"What is it?" asked David softly. "What are you feeling now?"

"I'm afraid again, full of fear. I really don't think I can talk about this."

"Why don't you try to step back from it and just look at what you're afraid of? You can do that. You've done it before."

"I know. But this fear is closer, more present. And I don't know how to say anger, spit it out like nails." I moved my hand to my heart and felt the wild beating inside. "It's anger. I'm afraid if I let it out, I'll lose everything. Just shatter. Blow apart. It is the old fear that keeps anger lodged like an ancient brick in the middle of my chest." I paused. "I don't see that saying it is going to change anything at all. It will only cause more pain and ugliness."

I had seen this as a child when my parents argued. My dad often exploded in anger and my mother shielded us from his rage. I had grown accustomed to her pain, then her depression. It finally wore her out. While I had much in common with Michael and our relationship was well-balanced in most ways, he, too, expressed anger explosively. I dreaded anger and hated the cost. Even when I became angry, Michael was better at it than I was and I often withdrew, feeling overwhelmed by his rage.

It seemed less painful to set anger aside, withdraw from it or transcend it. My parents had humiliated me when I was angry. And Michael outstripped me at it. Honestly, I preferred not to get angry at all.

"I don't believe that's true," David said. "Just like the pain and grief of your illness, sooner or later it needs to come out; to make room for fresh life. You have to begin someplace."

"I already have begun. What do you think I've been doing these past nine months?" I snapped. "But this is different. It's one thing to admit my disability to myself, but haven't I already caused plenty of pain and adapting in my family? Who needs more?"

"You do. You need to change the way you live to enjoy your life. You've got a wonderful family. You have a right to expect cooperation from them. So what if it causes them pain and discomfort at times. You don't need to worry about them. Or try to protect them. They'll change. They'll get used to it in time. You have to make clear to them just what changes are needed."

He was decisive and I knew he was right. But I was also glad it was the end of the hour.

When I reached home, early summer brightness flooded the kitchen. I lowered the light blue pleated shades to shield the room from sunlight, poured a glass of chilled white wine, and sat down for some respite before starting the evening meal. With Michael still at work and Kathryn at her music lesson, I breathed deeply into the silence. I saw at once the fear of seeing and saying my anger. But staring at the blue shades I had just lowered, I saw something vivid as a dream.

Wide awake, I felt transported to a small thatch-roofed hut in Africa. I sat alone in the middle of a barren room on a crudely made three-legged stool. Beneath my bare feet was an uneven dirt floor. The room was in semi-darkness. Ahead of me, about ten feet away, was one window covered by a woven bamboo shade. The room was quiet but there were noises outside. When I lifted the shade, I was treated to a wonderfully exciting sight. Out there, wandering freely across the Serengeti Plain, were wild animals of every size, shape, and color. They ran and romped and hid in the tall grasses, very much like children at play, knowing what they were up to, enjoying every minute.

Their vitality excited me, but I also felt frightened by their power. I imagined them with me inside the hut, but the space was too small to contain them. An impulse pushed me to join them on the plain, but the hut had no door I could find, and there was no way to get out of the window. The vibrant colors and activity were irresistible to me. When I could no longer bear this visit from afar, I dropped the shade and shut them out. Alone in the hut again, I wondered how I could live in this world with the variety and intensity of feelings I had without feeling a sense of danger, a fear of loss.

Long shadows stretched across the kitchen floor when I returned from my reverie. Fear pervades everything, I thought. But giving into fear means shutting out a whole range of good feelings. I don't want to live alone with fear, locked away in a room with no door. I want my spirit to be free. I want to live well with all of my feelings, including anger and rage.

"Tell me what you're angry about," David challenged, toward the end of the next therapy session.

I didn't stay silent. "Okay," I said. "I don't know what I'm angry about. Everything, I guess. Angry that all the grownups lied and told me everything was going to be all right. Angry at myself for believing them. I don't even know if I believe myself now! Maybe I just made this up." I shrugged. This was going to be impossible, ridiculous.

Taking a deep breath, I tried again. "Well, right now, I'm angry at my house, really. I hate my house—a lovely place we've designed and built for ourselves. Most people would kill for such a place. I hate it!" I was amazed to hear my own rage.

"No, that's not really true," I countered quickly. "I don't hate it. I hate that I don't feel comfortable there. It's not my house yet. I have to make peace with it to live there. And I don't know how." Silence.

"I'm angry at the house. And I don't know why. It's big, and beautiful, and new. This is so stupid!" I was cross and irritable, ashamed to be so petty and ungrateful.

I hated, too, that this therapy session closed on a tense note. But I was also relieved. I had started something and now felt in retreat. The clock was on my side.

David stood up. "Dorothea, I'd like you to try something this week. Take your pen and make a list of the specific things you don't like about your house. Don't censor yourself. Just walk around in each room. Notice everything you don't like. Write everything down. Even the shape of a knot-hole that annoys you. Make the list specific. Name everything in the place that's driving you crazy."

By this time David had gotten up some steam, and I laughed. "Homework yet? And I'm paying for this?" But in the following days I was surprised to find that it was hard to do. Each time I thought about making the list, I found a good reason to put it off. David didn't ask about it the following week, but it haunted me until one night I dreamed I had hidden my anger and turned it into depression so no one, not even I, could recognize it.

I awoke knowing that hiding anger was a lie—useless and self-defeating. Alone in the house that morning I wondered, what would happen if I showed my anger, my hate, to anyone? To David? I trembled but picked up my pen and wrote:

"I hate that the house doesn't have dark, safe, cozy hiding places. It's too big around me, too far to walk everywhere, too hard to push my wheelchair over the thick carpet.

"I hate that I can't walk around outside because the ground is too uneven. I hate that the house overwhelms me. The dust is unending. The place takes chunks of time just to maintain.

"I hate that I haven't finished unpacking after a year.

"I hate that my legs have hurt since the day I got here.

"I don't feel grateful for the house. It costs too much.

"I hate that the house is new, young, strong, and beautiful—and I'm not. I'm angry at my legs now, this house NOW, both tangible, mortal, needing attention and care. The house stares at me with a thousand eyes: the enemy. I am angry at feeling noisy, demanding, needy, and bitchy. I am afraid my needs won't be answered. I fear more pain.

"Man, you bet I'm angry!"

I finished and felt exhausted. I folded the yellow lined pages and shoved them in my purse. Not much there about knot holes, I thought.

For two weeks the list sat in my purse while I mulled it over. I imagined myself saying it aloud, pictured David listening and, worse, saying anything after this ugly litany. "Can there be anything too terrible to say? Certainly," I told myself. "It's enough to write this down. Now stop it! Just shut your mouth."

But summer was unfolding. My old fears were wearing thin. I carried my angry list, peeked at it, got more angry, added items:

"I'm angry at losing more physical ability. It's not fair! Images of further losses scare the hell out of me.

"I'm angry that I feel a sense of ingratitude for all I do have.

"I'm angry that Michael wants me to be brave, and I want to be myself who is sometimes brave and sometimes downright useless."

On and on I went, railing at myself, the house, the universe. The list in my purse grew longer. My purse grew heavier. It felt like it was full of stones. It weighed me down.

Still I resisted. In therapy sessions I hid my anger because I didn't want to say it and feel it. So other issues emerged. I got side-tracked and muddled. New doubts about going on with therapy plagued me. Should I quit? Was I telling the truth or making this up? Was I really strong enough to live through this crap? And if I did, would it be worth it? The challenges had changed over ten months, but they didn't seem easier most of the time.

David enlarged my perspective by reminding me that change took time, that I was making progress, that consciousness couldn't be forced. His encouragement and willingness to wait with me helped, but it also made it harder for me to get angry in his presence.

I didn't believe that saying the anger aloud was different from writing it. Wasn't it enough to say it to myself? Saying anger sounded awful and shameful—like tattling on myself and others. I couldn't understand why the ugly feelings needed to be expressed and shared with someone they couldn't hurt. I had already made enough messes, filled enough Kleenex with tears and snot. It didn't make sense that acting out anger could get me beyond it.

Even as I argued, I knew I would lose. Everything I had said and done so far was opening me to new sounds that I liked and had never heard before. Suddenly I was hearing the whole orchestra for the first time. I was animated and passionate. I couldn't permit my lack of courage to halt the angry sounds. I had to release anger to get to my joy.

Years ago, in the first month home after my return from the hospital, each step I took had required energy and attention. My parents discussed removing all the inch-high wood thresholds in our Manhattan apartment because they were such obstacles. They decided to leave them there because the world is full of thresholds.

My body still remembers standing there, crutches planted for balance, trying to lift one braced leg high enough to clear that one inch obstacle. Again and again I tried. The beads of perspiration gathered above my upper lip and forehead. My palms strained against the cushioned rubber handles of the wood crutches.

I got angry when I thought I couldn't do it. I yelled and beat my crutch against the door of the bedroom I shared with Lois. I wanted to get out of there. Screaming with temper I tried once more, and in that noisy moment came a small miracle. I did it. Somehow my foot moved forward and I was free. The joy tasted sweet.

It was time to do it again. One day late in June I told David I had made my list of anger. "Want to hear it?" I ventured, flashing him a challenging grin.

"Sure," he said, rubbing his palms together in mock anticipation.

"I'll have to sit on the floor for this one," I shot back, making fun of my awkward movement to the floor where it felt safe enough to say this awful stuff. Sitting on the dark blue carpet in the late morning sunshine, I dug into my purse and dragged out the yellow pages for their first read aloud.

David rearranged himself in his chair but did not move to join me on the floor. I was glad. I wasn't keen on looking him in the eye while reading that list. When he crossed his legs and looked over at me, I took it as a signal to begin.

My voice sounded strangely high and thin. My throat ached. It was hard to keep saying "I hate" and "I'm angry." I tried to keep my voice steady and clear through the list that now seemed endless. Whenever I looked over the top of the page, David's face, though attentive, was otherwise expressionless. After the final angry line, I cast aside the papers with defiance. I folded my arms across my stomach and stared at him.

"Quite a list you've got," David mused, and then he rose. From the floor he loomed large as he crossed in front of me, bent down and collected the scattered pages. Sitting on the sofa, he glanced at the writing, then at me. After about a minute he asked, "How'd it feel? Reading this, I mean."

"Oh, okay I guess. Even though I wrote those words, it was very hard to say them aloud. But I did it. Got through the whole list, didn't I?" My smugness surprised me.

"Yes, you read it all right." He paused. "Do you think you could read it again? This time a little louder?" he asked. That last page—page three—your voice kind of dropped off. I'm not sure I heard it all."

He handed me the pages and I snatched them up. "Of course I can read them again. Do you only want page three or do you want to hear the whole thing again?" I snarled. I couldn't believe it. This guy was asking me to read it over. Jesus!

"Go ahead and read it all," he answered, as if he were asking someone to please pass the potatoes. "And remember, nice and loud," he added, actually smiling. He stretched his legs out on the sofa and looked at me squarely. I wanted to hit him.

I began at the top of my stride, in a strong angry voice. "I hate that the house doesn't have dark, safe, cozy hiding places..." With each line I spoke louder and then found myself glaring at David. You want it? You got it! I shouted out the final line, "Man, you bet I'm angry!"

Tossing the list aside, I burst into tears. I wailed and heard the harsh rasping noises pouring out of my throat. I shook with anger and tasted the hot salty flavor of sorrow. There were tears everywhere, in my hair, my mouth, on my clothes. Old tears, and so many of them. I curled up into myself and cried on. When the tears finally subsided, I was exhausted.

I heard David's assurances through my tears. "It's good to see you cry," he said. "You've really learned how to cry again. Look at how well you do it. See how far you've come. You've come so far, Dorothea."

When I was done, all messy and spent, I uncurled. David came and held me for a moment. "You survived, didn't you? Did you notice that? Nothing happened. You're still here and you didn't blow up or go crazy, did you?"

"Why did you do it? Why did you make me say my anger again?" I whispered.

He laughed gently. "Because anger should come out of you like a lion. Big and powerful. Because you are a powerful, intense, feeling woman." After a pause he added, "You've done hard work here today. And you've done it well. I'm proud of you, Dorothea."

I believed him. I felt I had moved a mountain. His words fell like a mantle on my shoulders and the back of my neck as I left the office. I hadn't cried so much in years, nor dumped such rage since I was a kid throwing tantrums and getting sent out of the room. But this time I wasn't sent away. I felt a tingling warm sensation, new and different from what had been there before.

Often I left therapy sessions feeling unburdened, sometimes reflective, pleased, even happy. But today when I turned the ignition key and heard the engine kick in, I felt power. Still tingling and a bit stunned, I drove to a nearby country bakery where I had ordered a fresh apricot pie for that evening's dessert. The pie wasn't ready, so I sat in the cozy window seat and inhaled the warm scent of fresh bread and baking cookies. I stretched my arms and breathed deeply, like a snake in the sun, just having shed a layer of old skin.

In that moment I felt pure relief and profound quiet inside. I noticed each busy noise in the bakery. No noise felt harsh or dissonant. Like the sweet bakery scents, all noises belonged there and I belonged there, too. An enormous sense of pride welled up inside. I did it, I shouted to myself. I really did say my anger. I said it aloud to someone. To myself. To you, too, David. And I didn't break. I only felt this bare, strong, shining plane across the top of my chest, near my throat.

When I heard my name called, I rose to collect my pie. I was happy to be a member of the human species, content to be alive in that moment.

Driving home, I reflected on the new pride that announced itself so boldly. It came from a tremendous sense of power in me. Something new was coming into life, growing out of my unleashed passion. I glanced in my rear view mirror and saw that I was flushed and quite beautiful. How strange, I mused, that anger expressed can feel like love. It is a blessing.

16

DAVID

EXPRESSING THE NATURAL SELF

Dorothea had been in therapy for nearly a year now, and she had moved through a wide range of issues. At this point she was very alert to her daily functioning, thought about herself a lot, and observed her own reactions to events and reflected on them. She often remembered her dreams. Occasionally she was so self-aware that it was bothersome to her. An abnormal self-preoccupation is often a temporary side effect of the therapy process.

Sometimes she felt strong and optimistic. At other times, she felt oppressed and bothered by feelings that lowered her general mood level. The therapy was working, she was changing, but she was often discontented.

I like people to feel good. It's hard for me to be the therapist during these parts of the process when people just can't feel good. There is a stage where it seems as if patients are caught halfway between their old way of being and the new emerging self. This stage is unpleasant, sort of semi-disoriented so that it is hard to relax. I fantasize that there is an electronic technician in the brain frantically rewiring the system, and nothing works smoothly until the job is done.

Sometimes Dorothea sat in my office, obviously feeling lousy, and I'd want to have some magic words to make her feel good. But often, there were no appropriate words to say. It was necessary for her to muck through issue after issue, feeling after feeling, until the underlying theme emerged.

During times like these, I listen with two minds as people talk about their struggles. One part of me is there in the chair, listening, sensing, feeling and responding. And then there is this shadowy, intuitive part of me which hovers around, sometimes in my head, sometimes in my gut. Sometimes it appears to float around the room, off to the side. I'm only vaguely aware of this other intuitive self, sometimes not aware of it at all.

This shadowy self is like a scout, poking around at the edges of things, watching all the signals I don't notice in my focused attention, making connections to past sessions and other experiences and knowledge. I notice myself nodding unconsciously as I listen, almost as if the nodding is some kind of energizing mechanism for this intuitive function. It's like I am putting out sensors and weaving them back and forth to see what I might discover.

During my early teen years, I used to skin-dive along the coast of Southern California and Baja. None of us kids could afford scuba equipment, so we did free diving. In the 1950s, the shallow waters of many areas of the Southern coast were still rich with sea life. We sought out places where there were reefs and underwater rock formations, where fish, abalone, and lobsters thrived.

Diving was adventuresome for me because I was always scared. The ocean was clearly not my territory, but it was endlessly fascinating. I learned to hold my breath for long periods of time as I poked and prodded into every nook and cranny before desperation drove me back to the surface for more air. I can remember feeling my way along submerged ledges and reefs, peering into the dark recesses, afraid of what I might encounter—maybe a Moray eel—but hoping for an abalone or some unknown treasure. I felt like the first human to have ever peered into these places.

Finding a lobster was always the biggest thrill for me. Making my way along a ledge, suddenly I'd see the tips of slender tentacles barely showing at the entrance to a hole. The tentacles were usually black with a blush of reddish orange on the edges. They swept back and forth, gently and feelingly. On spotting them, my heart quickened and I felt a surge of excitement. I had to be careful not to touch the ledge or make any noise, or the lobster would withdraw deeply into the hole. After moving away to fix in my mind the location of the hole, I'd rise to the surface for more air, plotting how best to approach the task of getting the lobster out of its lair. If I accidentally touched one of those tentacles, it would immediately jump back and wedge itself into the hole so tightly that I could never pull it out.

With lungs full of fresh air, I dove back to the hole and maneuvered my body and hands into just the right position. Peering into the hole and seeing the shadowy outline of the lobster's body, I watched the tentacles carefully. At precisely the moment the tentacles were out of the way, I thrust my hand deeply into the hole and grabbed the hard, scratchy body of the lobster. It exploded into a frantic fight, twisting and flipping, straining to get free. When my grip was sure, I could overwhelm its resistance and pull it out of the hole into the light. All the way to the surface that lobster kept fighting, flipping, and twisting, trying to get free. It was always a thrill. A lobster was the best catch of all.

Waiting with Dorothea as she looked into all of the crevices of her life was a little like those diving trips. We didn't know what we were looking for much of the time, but knew that if we were watchful, her psyche would lead us to the treasure.

One day Dorothea talked about a wonderful daydream; a spontaneous, unconscious reverie that had transported her to the Serengeti Plain in Africa. In the daydream, she finds herself in a hut and looks through a small window where she sees the Plain. She is transfixed by the beauty of the wild animals in their natural environment. Excited by their vitality but frightened of their power, she wants to bring them into her hut. But there is not enough room and she can't join them outside because there is no doorway out of her hut. She is trapped.

This metaphor describes the dilemma of humankind. We began as free and wild animals participating in the daily organic drama of nature, part of the integrated whole of life on the planet. But we left the Garden of Eden and became civilized. Now, living in huts and shelters, buildings and cities, we can only look back at the natural world through windows. We feel we cannot return. There seem to be no doorways through which we can regain our original form, our "wildness."

Dorothea's daydream describes her personal exile from the Garden. The wild animals on the Plain symbolize her natural wild forces. She glimpses them through the window and yearns to join them. But these forces won't fit in the bound-up, closed space of her psyche, and she cannot get out of the hut to rejoin them. There are strong and powerful forces awakening in Dorothea, but she has no means of expressing them. As I listened, I wondered if this was the source of the gnawing discontent which marked her daily experience.

Just like the animals on the Plain, we humans are born wild, untamed and untrained. We must cling to our parents for a long time in order to survive. Our parents respond to us, but gradually tame our demands to fit their needs and the needs of the wider community and culture. This reciprocal process transforms us into civilized persons. Yet deep in the heart of each of us, the simple wildness remains. Our developmental process is a journey from this organic wildness to the discovery of individual and unique selfhood.

In the earliest stage of childhood, developing our natural self is mainly an expression of inborn temperament and potential. As we grow, we watch and imitate the behavior of other people, especially our parents, and eventually our own unique version of "self" emerges. We express our self freely, venturing out in activity to explore the world. If we are fortunate, the essential nature of this emerging self is respected and nurtured, even while our behavior is being shaped and molded by the surrounding culture.

Not all children are so fortunate. Their natural, real self is not supported by life circumstances. Some children must discover that it is unsafe to be spontaneous. They learn to be cautious about what thoughts, fantasies, or feelings can be expressed. They create a false self which they present to the world to protect them from rejection and punishment. Survival is always the fundamental requirement of life: physical, psychological, and emotional survival.

When a child must guard against her natural mode of action and expression, the real self goes underground. The adapted, learned, false version of self is carefully practiced until she finds just the right formula. It is a compromise which satisfies some of her own needs while assuring love and protection from the important people in her life. Meanwhile, the real self remains hidden, perhaps forgotten, but it never goes away. The wild-animal self remains, like buried grief or pain, waiting to be found again.

A woman once described this process in her childhood in a most striking way. Whenever she was behaving in a way that displeased her mother, her mother said, "Where's my Mary? This isn't my Mary. What happened to my Mary?" Mary learned to become very careful about what she allowed herself to express. In part, her adult depression was an outgrowth of forgetting her real self, the real Mary.

Dorothea's daydream suggested that we begin looking for the wildness that was shut down and locked out. What wild animal needed to be released? This daydream occurred during the period when Dorothea was full of complaints and discontent. She felt grouchy and irritable and then felt guilty about her discontent. Her anger turned against herself, and she felt like an ungrateful and undeserving malcontent.

Her pattern began to emerge. Whenever Dorothea's anger slipped past her censor and came out her mouth, she stifled it as badness. Yet she was complaining about very real difficulties in her life. She squelched her spontaneous feelings, denied her voice. I thought to myself that if the eyes are the window into the soul, then certainly the voice must be the doorway to the natural self. Without a voice, there is no free expression of vital and wild inner experience. Dorothea had no voice with which to roar her discontent. Her false self allowed no wildness.

As a young child, Dorothea learned that it was dangerous to open her mouth and blurt out her thoughts and feelings. She began to hesitate and stammer and, eventually, became unable to speak without stuttering. She became so self-conscious that she couldn't even form words. What she had to say was unacceptable, and even the way she spoke was unacceptable. She had felt ashamed, and her voice had become an enemy to guard against.

Dorothea once exclaimed to me, "As long as I can remember, I have felt there was this person I was supposed to be, and then there was this person I was." Here was an eloquent contrast between the false self and the real self. Managing this kind of inner division becomes so automatic that it seems natural and correct to deny real needs and feelings. Hiding real feelings becomes a pervasive style of interpersonal relationship for many people.

This lack of voice manifests itself in people in different ways. One of my clients, "Susan," was a professionally competent and culturally refined young woman who was successful in nearly every aspect of life except intimate relationships. In 12 years of adult life, she had repeatedly fallen in love with inferior men who were destructive and hurtful to her. Her self-esteem was devastated by repeated physical and sexual abuse, financial exploitation, and emotional humiliation.

As Susan's therapy progressed, she saw that she was unable to express angry, negative, or aggressive feelings. Her false self would not allow such impulses, and worse, didn't recognize hostility in her male friends. She rationalized away the abuse she received, excused it as not important, because she "knew" her partner was actually a positive and loving person. Susan was unconsciously attracted to the anger, the missing part of herself which was present in the men. Being unable to have assertive feelings towards men, she couldn't establish boundaries and prevent the mistreatment. She responded with "sweetness and light" when she should have been saying: "Knock it off!"

In direct contrast to Susan was a man named "Gene." I treated him years ago, in a maximum security hospital for violent mental patients. Gene had been committed to the hospital for homicide, and he presented a protective front of ominous threat and unapproachable danger. I had taken his life history and realized that he was filled with overwhelming vulnerability and fear, sadness and despair. He had suffered a tragically deprived life. Having no means for experiencing vulnerable feelings, he projected them onto other people and saw them as being dangerous to him. He was always on guard and defended himself against others with anger and rage. His provocative behavior drew reactions against him and he lashed out in violent attacks.

Susan and Gene were opposites in their relationship to anger. Susan had no voice for anger. She could not sense when her essential self and integrity were being violated, so she was vulnerable to untrustworthy men. Gene only had an angry

145

voice. He was unable to recognize when he felt sad or hurt. When something stirred inside, he looked for someone to blame. In many respects, Susan's and Gene's treatment needs were quite different, yet there was a similar pattern. Both needed to overcome powerful inhibitions against basic human emotions and learn to express them.

In Susan's therapy, she had to become comfortable with feeling angry and learn that saying "no" was not an unloving thing to do. She reviewed her past relationships and saw the anger and rage she had never felt before. In her current relationships, she saw how she became powerless by trying to please other people. She discovered that people liked her even when she asserted her own needs and feelings. She didn't have to try to be a lovable person.

Gene had to learn the opposite. He had to learn not to be constantly on guard, to learn that anger was an ineffective way to deal with sad and vulnerable feelings. There was one incident that marked a shift for Gene, where he learned that it was possible to switch from one perspective to another, from one feeling to another.

I had just returned to the hospital ward after lunch and was in a particularly jolly mood. However the hospital atmosphere was tense; I discovered that the attendant staff were bracing themselves to move in on Gene with restraining straps. He was barricaded down a side hallway, screaming invectives at the staff, holding a chair as a weapon and threatening to kill anyone who came near him. He stood just across the hall from my office door.

I edged by the attendant staff and out of my jolly mood, began talking loudly. "Hey Gene, you look terrific, you look fantastic! I wish you could see yourself right now. You are the most terrifying person I've ever seen! You are amazing!" By this time I was nearing my office door, holding my keys ready to enter, a big smile on my face.

Gene was disarmed by my cheerful manner and by what I had just said. He looked at me and said, "You're not afraid of me, Willingham."

Still smiling, I looked at him with mock surprise. "Are you kidding? I'm terrified of you! You should see yourself right now. You are fantastic. You are the most terrifying man I have ever seen. You should see yourself from here. You look great!"

Suddenly his anger was gone. He began to giggle, smiled sheepishly and put the chair down. As soon as that happened, the attendant staff relaxed and walked away, clearly relieved that this incident was over. Gene followed me into my office, sat down and began to talk about what happened. In this spontaneous moment of rapport, he was able to see past his defenses and identify the feelings he had deep inside. Being able to snap out of rage and into humor helped Gene see how much he overused anger and how limiting that was in his relationships with people.

Anger is a very complex emotion. It can be terribly destructive in peoples' lives if they are stuck in a pattern of repeatedly experiencing life as threatening, unjust or unfair. But anger is not inherently bad. It is a natural emotion and serves a critical function in healthy living. Anger lets us know when we are feeling intruded upon, threatened, or misused. It helps us define our personal boundaries, those critically important values that uniquely reflect who we are. Healthy anger is incredibly important in defining personal identity. It motivates us to take effective action when we are being violated in some way. Healthy anger springs from clear perception and is proportionate to the present situation.

As I listened to Dorothea during those weeks of discontent, it gradually became clear that she needed to learn to identify angry feelings and express them without such excessive concern for whether they were justified or reasonable. She was an eminently reasonable person. In her case, what was needed was less reasonableness.

One day, when she was complaining "unreasonably" about her beautiful new house, I asked her to deliberately focus on what she disliked about the house. I told her to write down these complaints as "hatreds" and to bring this list to a session.

Dorothea procrastinated on this assignment. She didn't want to do it. But I knew this dutiful Catholic girl would eventually feel guilty for her procrastination. I waited and, of course, she finally got around to making the list and bringing it up in a therapy session.

She took out her list and read it, rather like a rebellious student presenting her homework with an edge of resentment and smugness. Her expression said, "So there, smarty pants?" But I watched her closely. It was obviously very uncomfortable for her to say these hatreds out loud. She hurried through her list, never looking up from the pages. When she was done, she defiantly threw them onto the floor.

Her list of angers and hatreds lay there. It was a good job, a thorough list. She had paid attention to her feelings and allowed herself to acknowledge them. In the writing exercise she had set aside her censor and validated her complaints. But there was something missing. When she read her list, there was no passion. There was no voice of anger, no rage, and no wildness. There was no messiness, no noisiness, no nastiness. Who really gets angry without being messy, noisy, and nasty? Certainly not me. And, I suspected, certainly not this "wild" Italian girl from New York City.

I looked her in the eye. "Read it again Dorothea. Don't be so genteel. Let's hear your real voice. Be loud! ROAR!"

Now there is a door in Dorothea's hut. She can go out onto the Serengeti Plain and join with her own natural wildness.

Psychologically based depression often involves a loss of the ability to release strong negative emotions like anger and rage, hurt, sorrow and grief. When these emotions are not allowed to be expressed, the self-regulating function of the body is blocked and disease results. This blockage can lead to emotional disorders in some people and to psychosomatic disorders in others.

Often, animal symbols appear in fantasies and dreams to call attention to our basic instinctual nature. Animals function naturally; they don't try to be anything other than what they are. This is not always so with humans. For myriad reasons, we do try to be something other than what we are. Psychological maturation often requires us to discover important aspects of our basic nature which are either inhibited or inflated out of proportion. To become healthy, we must become whole and balanced in all of our psychophysical functions.

17

DOROTHEA

ACCEPTANCE

Six euphoric weeks followed my angry outburst. During that time I was filled with a sense of certainty and direction. I wore power like an invisible cloak which heightened my zest for life. The horrors were behind me; I knew I had survived the last scary rapids on the river. Soon I would no longer need David's support or guidance. While there were loose ends to tie up, and adjustments to be made in my everyday life, I had control again. I wanted to finish therapy.

I anticipated summer vacation with relish. The separation from David was timely and the break in the academic year had relieved me from my duties at the college. I welcomed the respite from all responsibilities, including therapy work.

Late in June, with our daughter at summer camp, Michael and I set out on a two-week trip to Sunriver, Oregon. We were ready for fun and excited about visiting a new place. The trip was upbeat from the beginning.

We liked the leisure of traveling slowly through northern California, the way we had on our honeymoon years ago. We explored Mount Shasta and the McCloud river, areas we'd visited before. We stopped to smell wild flowers and do a little fishing along the way. The years and burdens fell away, almost by the hour. The further we got from home, the more free I was. Anticipation and excitement pervaded the atmosphere. It was contagious.

On the eve of our seventeenth wedding anniversary, we arrived at Sunriver. There was cold champagne in our room, and Michael built a fire in the rugged stone fireplace. We drank champagne and made love with leisurely abandon. We drank more. Laughed at our wonderful silliness. Made love more. We never ate dinner that night. Neither of us noticed.

When I awoke the next morning, I felt happy to be alive. In the chilly morning air, I snuggled closer to Michael and giggled softly. "Aren't you glad we're here together?" Michael hugged me and smiled.

What a way to start the day! It wasn't as if we'd never made love before. But it was better. I was alive and excited in a way that I had never been before. I was thrilled that my body remembered all that it liked and could do, just as fully as it had remembered past pain. It was good to taste the pleasures of renewal in marriage, surprising to feel the pure animal lust of a 20-year-old when I was 48.

And lust it was! I had never felt such pure sexual desire, quickening, aching, longing, all the time—not ever. I couldn't get enough. I attacked Michael and he loved it, roared with laughter and enjoyed his own healthy appetite. "Is this what happens to you when you do therapy?" he mocked. "Do more then. What's gotten into you? I love it when you're like this!"

My whole body broke out of an incredible, vice-like grip. I had slain my dragon and now I was a powerful woman—exquisite, erotic, passionate. All flesh, blood, nerve endings, movement, heat, desire. No mysterious searching for the beautiful woman of my dreams now. She was here. Being me was a pleasure from the top of my shining brown hair to the bottom of my feet. No exceptions.

Each day of our vacation continued that way—like many pieces of a patchwork quilt, each unique in design with occasional muted moments in which we caught our breath. But mostly there were vibrant and intense moments, colored by lovemaking and playing. We played golf on at least three different courses, Michael driving the balls and me driving the cart playing the "inner game." One afternoon we took a ski lift to the top of Mt. Bachelor. I loved dangling out there over the steep slopes, carrying my crutches like ski poles. The vista was breathtaking and special because it was a road I could not have taken otherwise.

We explored the old parts of Bend, Oregon, and the nearby small towns. We'd always enjoyed snooping but lately this pastime was turning into a physical challenge for me. To our delight, central Oregon was so sparsely populated that parking was easy. The accessibility left more energy for walking.

One day, in the quaint town of Sisters, Oregon, we visited a local gem and mineral show. There Michael found a fist-sized ball of azurite that looked very much like the pictures of earth taken from outer space. Rich deep cobalt blue and emerald green mottled the smooth shining ball. There were signs of fissures and hints of white and tan scattered about that made it look even more like an image of the real world. That afternoon when we got in the car to leave, he gave it to me. "Here," he said, thrusting it forward in a crudely made box. "I've always wanted to give you the world, and now I've done it," he said, looking like the cat who swallowed the canary.

I kissed him and laughed. It was a little like being a kid and getting the very best toy in the world. But it was more. It was the world and we had the very best of it there, together.

After we returned home, I set the glistening treasure on the white kitchen counter next to the telephone. From there I could see it all the time and hold its smooth solid weight in my hand whenever I wanted. It was an irresistible beauty—everyone touched and held it.

I looked forward to my next meeting with David in the spirit of reunion with an old friend. There was much to recount, much laughter, even some strutting. I felt so good, so normal and together again, that I planned to discuss ending our sessions within a few weeks.

"Well, how was it?" he asked, relaxed and refreshed looking after his own vacation.

I plunged right in. "We had a great time! Couldn't have been better. I felt so alive! Can't remember a time when I had more fun."

"Oh, yeah?" David said, catching my bubbling enthusiasm. "Let's hear about it."

"For starters, my libido has returned—and made up for lost time, too!" I felt my face flush with pleasure. "I mean, it's not as if we haven't enjoyed each other before. But this last year has been full of struggle and I've felt so...well, exhausted...and depressed too."

"Had you been depressed for a long time?"

"No, not really. But I've been afraid a lot. So much fear and so many bad dreams. So much going on inside my everyday life. All this absorption in myself. Not exactly an upbeat atmosphere for lovemaking. Would you say?"

David gave an understanding nod. "You've had volumes of fear and hard living this year. And it's been difficult for Michael, too—dealing with the changes that are taking place. You know, what's happening to you isn't happening alone. It affects the relationship between you. But in the intimacy of marriage, making love is one of the simplest, most direct ways two people can give immediate enjoyment and satisfaction. I'm happy for both of you that you've had such pleasure."

"With my blue azurite 'planet' sitting in the kitchen, I'm hoping some of that magic will rub off on the house. Maybe we should make love in every room so I won't be mad at it anymore!"

"Not a bad idea. You've been back now almost a week. How are things since your steamy vacation?"

He asked the question with casual good humor, but the shift in focus registered in my gut. "Pretty good. Although I caught myself regarding the house as the enemy the other day. I expected to feel settled about the house after I got angry at it. You know, I thought I'd get over it."

"What is it about you and that house anyway? Is it some kind of sacred shrine?" His tone was mocking and irreverent. I shrugged.

I glanced at the tiny clock on the bookshelf across from me. I had spent the hour rattling on about my vacation as if I were socializing. I had wanted to begin wrapping up my therapy work. But the house had interrupted my agenda. We agreed to pick up the topic the following week. I left annoyed at myself for having failed to get to the point.

Two days later in the mid-afternoon, I made a cup of tea and sat down in our family room. I faced a soaring trapezoidal window that framed the valley and Windy Hill beyond. I often sat there to enjoy the magnificent sweeping view. Gazing out the window, in a peaceful reverie, I felt like I had x-ray vision, as if for a minute I could see through the walls.

I heard my voice whispering to me: "This is a man's creation: steel bars, concrete, towering beams, yards of wire, tons of wood. See the guts intertwined, holding it up, making it strong. See the double-pane glass dividing inside and outside. See the men on the high beams, driving nails, raising the roof, covering it over, making it safe, trying to make it whole, to finish it so we can live here."

My God, I thought. What I wanted, what my body wanted, was new life. Another baby! I'm nuts!

For a moment I felt vulnerable, then robbed. Finally, just bewildered. I put it out of my mind.

"What's come up for you about the house?" David prompted at our next meeting. I had resolved to tell him what had happened and see if he could make sense of it. Then I wanted to address getting out of there. A year of intense therapy was enough for anyone, and I knew I was as good as done.

After I recounted the story, I was amazed. A peculiar sadness over my other baby, the one I hadn't had, overcame me. "Did you hear the story about the baby born on the United Airlines flight, the one born and abandoned in the rest room?" I asked. I ached as I said the words.

David said, "So the house was Michael's baby, not yours?"

"Right. But of course all of this is ridiculous. Hypothetical. There couldn't be another baby. My body could never have supported another pregnancy. I knew that before I had the C-section."

"What happened? Did you have a complicated pregnancy?"

"Not really. I didn't have any problem getting pregnant. But my obstetrician warned me not to gain more than 20 pounds. Otherwise I might need a wheelchair because my legs couldn't bear extra weight. His warning sounded like a prison sentence to me.

"Aside from that, the nine months were heaven. My body led me, totally. The only time I can remember in my adult life. It wanted only the nutrition it needed. No booze. No rich foods. No junk. I only gained about 20 pounds. Kathryn was small but entirely healthy. Afterwards the obstacles came."

"What happened after Kathryn was born?" David prodded. My eyes swam through dizzying images.

"I was immobile after the surgery. I had a cold and I developed bronchitis. I had inhalation therapy. The therapists forced me to cough. My incision felt like it would rip open. But I had to get well for Kathryn, this exquisite new life. A beautiful tiny person.

"I was too weak to hold her. When the second bed in my hospital room stayed empty, I was grateful. It was December. Seeing other new mothers leave in two days, their babies neatly tucked into bright red Christmas stockings, would have been agony.

"I was in the hospital for 12 days. After five days in bed, three nurses got me on my feet. I hemorrhaged all over the floor. I was terrified at my own blood, afraid I'd die and not be a mother for Kathryn. It was a month before I was strong enough to pick her up and hold her by myself.

"In the beginning there was fear and silence. And fierce love. How I loved her, and how afraid I was to fail her."

I sat quietly, absorbed in that long-ago memory. David nodded with gentle understanding. "A lot of new mothers feel that way, Dorothea. Do you know that?"

"Yes, I've heard it. But I felt a difference between normal difficulties of new parenthood and what I was experiencing. I was afraid I was in over my head. I was physically overwhelmed and shocked, and I didn't know how to talk about it, especially when everyone else was so excited about the birth. I expected sleepless nights, soreness, totally upset schedules. I expected anxiety from not knowing how to bathe her, or understanding what her crying meant, or whether I had enough milk. I had read a lot. But I expected to be able to enjoy her too."

"And did enjoy her? Your pleasure in her always seems to bubble over."

"Oh yes! Kathryn is the bright joy in my life. After she was born I held her and sang to her and knew that this time, when I left the hospital, I'd take something precious with me. Not like all the other times.

"We went home a new little family, with one exception. I needed special help. I wasn't part of a disabled people's community and I didn't grasp precisely how to get what I needed. I couldn't do simple things like pick up a crying baby and walk the floor. Michael had to do that, and he did. He walked the floor at night when he was tired. He did it when he was cranky. He did it when he had to be in court early the next morning. I remember especially well because it was January. The house was cold at night and he got up anyway. He had to because I couldn't.

"One night I got up because he was so tired. At that time I didn't even own a wheelchair. I strapped on the cold metal brace, put Kathryn in the stroller with some warm blankets, and took her to the living room. I nursed her and sang her to sleep. It was cold and quiet. I felt as if I were the only person awake in the world."

"Did you have anyone help you during that time? Or were you alone?"

"Even among friends, it was hard to ask for help. I had learned how to be self-reliant. Then a former student named Rae who had become a good friend offered to come help. Rae had already reared a family of daughters and all through my pregnancy, she told me that kids were the neatest thing that ever came down the pike. She arrived at 8 o'clock, the morning after I got home from the hospital. She stayed all day, every day Michael worked. She was my friend, but she mothered me as well as Kathryn really. I nicknamed Rae "BTB"—Better Than Blood—because she extended my own family. She remains one of God's gifts in my life."

"Good for her," David exclaimed. "You're right. She was a blessing. What would you have done without her?"

"I shiver thinking about it. Two-and-a-half years elapsed before my first trip out alone with Kathryn."

"Two-and-a-half years?" David asked, astonished.

"Well, look at me! I couldn't stand, balance, and lift her at the same time. She had to climb in the car on her own steam. And she had to understand about not running away. We really had to communicate.

"I remember our first outing. We went to a little market near here. She just knew what to do. With my hands wrapped around the crutch handles, we linked our fingers together. I never had to tell her to walk at my pace. We did well together."

"I can see you two. And even now, you'd like another baby?"

"Sure," I said. "It defies logic. It's not about logic." I was tired and felt sad. "I don't know why I want one. Maybe I don't even want another one. Maybe it's about some joy that was lost."

I was comforted that David seemed to understand my longing and didn't think I was outlandish. On the way home, I chafed at the thought of still needing him, still depending on him to help me sort out the puzzles of my life. I wanted to open all the secret doors, and I knew I had the courage to do it. But my legs were shaky. His were much stronger. I needed him for the journey. Maybe it was not yet time to give up therapy.

For the next few weeks we talked more about the past. I reflected on what was lost, and what might have been. All my thinking returned to the incredible wealth I had. Did I have to look over my shoulder before I let the past go? Was that the cure that would wipe clean the palette of my life? Something was happening but I had no idea what it was. I continued feeling unsettled and impatient.

In August, Michael and I took a brief trip, this time to Ashland, Oregon, for a week at the Shakespearean Festival. We had honeymooned in Ashland. We so liked the small scale and beauty of the town that we had considered buying property there. Over the years, we had often stopped for a play or two on our travels north, but we hadn't returned for an extensive stay. We both hoped that the magical abandon of Sunriver would repeat itself. It didn't happen.

Everything went wrong from the start. Our downtown accommodations were poor and there was an incredible heat wave which made exploring the town an ordeal. The lightweight plastic shell of my brace stuck to me and I felt wet and irritated. The long blocks were difficult to walk—I could not help noticing how deliberate and labored walking had become.

Still, I wanted to poke around, determined to see and do what I could, even if I could only walk two blocks at a time. Michael balked. He was disappointed in the place, annoyed by the crowds, worn out from the heat and, after a while, just sullen. Tension grew between us. He looked at me, noticed when I stopped to rest or rub the sore palms of my hands.

"I don't like this," he said. "It's boring. And it's too damn hot. Why don't we just go back to the hotel and cool off? The walking is too much effort for you. This was a bad idea."

But I was stubborn. "I'm hungry. Let's stop somewhere to eat. That's not a hassle, is it?" I snarled, defying his downer mood. We stopped at a place called Gepetto's Workshop for lunch. On the way in, Michael grabbed a real estate throw-away. We ate in awkward silence—he read, I steamed. I was cross and disagreeable. He was remote. I couldn't get him to talk. If I challenged him, I knew things would get nasty.

In the tense atmosphere following lunch, Michael repeated the offer. "Wanna go back to the hotel for a nap? I'm into a good mystery. And we've got theater tickets for later. I don't want to spend the afternoon out here."

I snapped at him. "I didn't travel all this way to lie around napping or reading. Why don't you go ahead; I'll stay out a while." I was relieved he was leaving. I resented his glum mood and wanted to hiss "good riddance." After he left, I assessed the blocks ahead and mentally divided them, deciding just how far I could go and still get back. People often tease me about always planning ahead, but planning is my survival.

I returned to the room in better spirits. Michael had read and napped so we got ready for dinner and the theater. When he groused about making dinner reservations on vacation, I wished the tension would go away. After dinner, I could not climb the steep hill to the theater and when he dropped me off, he cursed when he missed out on a great parking place. Tears welled up as I walked away from him.

This wasn't working. I knew I was feeling sorry for myself and sorry for Michael too. What a pain in the ass this was for him, I thought. But as I made my way through the crowd, I had to pay attention to what was in front of me. No time for the luxury of self-pity.

For three days we continued drifting further from each other. Occasionally we were angry and remote, sometimes covering the dark feelings with banal talk. We often read or spent time by ourselves. We never talked about our disappointment. I amused myself in bookstores and crafts shops. Whenever we separated, my oppressive feeling lightened up.

But I knew we were both angry. I hated confronting a difficult physical situation, and Michael hated watching me struggle to stay on my feet. He said as much, and I sympathized. I even agreed. It was shitty. But if I couldn't make polio go away for myself, I certainly couldn't do it for him. He refused to discuss it. I grew discouraged, infantile, and self-indulgent. Then just plain mean. I wanted to kill him. What did he want to do anyway? Flush 17 years down the toilet because I was crippled? God dammit, it wasn't fair!

One afternoon I returned to the hotel, hot and exhausted. Michael nodded hello as I headed for the bathroom. After washing my sore hands and sunburned face, I caught myself in the mirror. In the second before recognition, I looked exhausted. I was shocked.

156

I returned to our room and in a clear, flat voice said, "Michael, I think I want a divorce."

He lowered his book and looked at me coldly. In a distant tone he answered, "All right, if that's what you want, it's okay with me."

I burst into tears. The noisy, wet release felt so good. I didn't care that Michael hated it when I cried. I cried on, even as I heard him ranting: "God dammit, what are you crying about?"

"Because, because...I just can't do it anymore. Because I'm exhausted. I've worked so hard to come to grips with myself, but I can't really change anything. I have to learn to live with myself, my legs, just the way they are. But you don't."

"That's right. But what does that have to do with anything? I knew that when we got married. What'd you expect to change?"

Sobbing I went on, hating my whining tone. "Well, I didn't expect to become more disabled after we married. Maybe a little slower in old age, but not all this crap before 50 even. And now that I've done all this therapy, I feel the loss and the struggle of coping with it."

"So maybe you've had too much therapy. I don't like some of the way you act now. It's damned uncomfortable around here. You and your damned psyche," he hissed.

"Shut up!" I shouted. "I don't see you trying to make it easier between us. You've been locked up all week, reading mysteries. Acting like you can't even stand walking around with me! It's been hard enough getting around out there, not having someone I love and enjoy. But I've managed. And I can go on, alone if I have to. It's just something I wouldn't choose for myself," I said. My voice softened.

I looked away and then faced him again. His voice was gentle. "Then why do you want a divorce? You know I love you. That hasn't changed."

"But the way we are together, that's changed. A barrier's between us. You're so shut down and cold. All week you've been mad at something. I can't stand having to cope with my limits and yours too. What happened to the fun we had at Sunriver?" He flinched. Pain passed over his face like a shadow. He sighed. "What are you angry about, Michael?"

"I know I've been a bastard all week. But I hate watching you struggle to do things we used to do together easily. You're so feisty—you just keep going for it. I hate seeing you like this, knowing it's not going to get better. There's so much I thought..."

"We would do together? Me too. There still can be. Maybe different from what we thought. But I can't stand it this way, both of us tearing at each other, full of disappointment and resentment."

"The pits, huh?" he said, flashing the grin that made me love him. "I'm sorry," he added. "What do you want to do?"

"I'm miserable here," I admitted. "I'd really like to go home tomorrow. Even if it's a day early. I want to be comfortable. Staying isn't worth it. I want to feel better."

"Me too. I'll vote for that," he said with relief I understood. We took the journey home in one long sweep. The trip was quiet but not hostile. We talked about the impact of my loss on him, but we knew neither of us could make it all right for the other. We were isolated in separate downward spirals. It was mid-August and David was on vacation. My next scheduled appointment was August 30. Talking with anyone else was out of the question; I had to wait.

Before David returned, I drove to Half Moon Bay for an afternoon at the beach with a trusted friend. Georgia and I met as young teaching colleagues in the English department more than 20 years ago. We had become fast friends during my first year there when she had undergone great personal adversity. We enjoyed the good times and tried to "be there" when life got rough. We shared a passion for literature that grew richer as our personal relationship matured.

Georgia never turned down even the remote possibility of a trip to the beach. After lunch she managed to find an accessible promontory overlooking the surf. I sat cross-legged with her on the blanket, watching the gray-green ocean, thinking about Virginia Woolf.

"Did you ever wonder how Virginia Woolf actually got herself to walk into the River Ouse? You know, fill her pockets with stones and just walk right in?" I asked.

"No, but I can imagine. The world must have looked bleak and hopeless to her. It was 1941, in England, after all. Why'd you ask?" She knew my reference to Woolf's suicide wasn't simply a literary topic. I had already confided in her, shared the progress of my therapy, and a slim account of the devastating trip to Ashland. She waited.

"Oh, sometimes when I see the breakers on gray days, and hear the pounding surf—it sounds like it's bringing in stories. You know, not just Virginia Woolf's. Others' too. People we never heard of. Or only half know." I felt muddled.

Something pushed out from inside me. "Actually that's not entirely true. I've been feeling some despair about going on with it?"

"What do you mean, *it*?" she asked.

"All of it," I answered flatly. "The therapy, the marriage, the whole nine yards. I feel so alone. One other time in my life, in grad school, when I was alone, I felt this bad. And then I thought about just doing myself in. Of course, I couldn't even walk into the water like Woolf," I said with deliberate sarcasm. "But it's too hard. I get tired of trying. This week, I wish I didn't have to try anymore."

"I know what you mean," she said softly, covering my cold hands with her warm ones. She was quiet for a while and then added, "Have you told David about feeling this way?"

"No. He's out of town. He doesn't know anything. Besides, I can't imagine how I could tell him something like this."

"Why not? Isn't that what you're paying him for? What he's there for? Why not tell him?"

"After all the work we've done together? How can I tell him I feel beaten? Admit defeat? It would be awful. I'm mad anyway. I should be done with therapy. I'm fed up with this crap."

"Dorothea, I think you should tell him. It's something he'd want to know. You need to share this with someone who understands. You deserve that. And it will make you feel better. I'm sure of it."

A week later I sat in David's office. For the first time in many months, I couldn't speak without feeling as if someone were choking me. I felt ashamed struggling to find a place to begin, and David looked troubled watching me. Finally I held my head with both hands and sobbed.

When I stopped, David asked, "Dorothea, what's happened to you? Tell me. You can tell me."

Incoherently, I pieced together the story of the past three weeks—the pain, the isolation, the despair. Finally I told him about the suicidal thoughts. I had thought about trying to "slip it in" with the rest of the litany, the way we used to do in Confession, but I knew he'd pick up on it.

"You've really had a rough time, huh? I can understand why you're feeling so much pain and sadness. The changes you've made this year are bound to place strain on the relationship, on the whole family as well. It's inevitable. How's Michael doing?"

"Okay, I guess. I can't help him with this. It's hard for him. He's hurting, too. We're not fighting or anything, but he's angry about post-polio syndrome and he doesn't want to talk about it. He's been entirely supportive so long as it was my problem. But Ashland brought home reality—we're both going to have to face changes. It's no fun, David. I've worked hard. I want the fun part *now*. Not the burdens of love."

I banged my fist down on the table beside me. "What's going on here? What'd I do all this hard work for anyway? Therapy goes on without end. I know people who have had shrinks for years. But I'm not going on with this forever. Maybe I was better off not knowing anything. Unconsciousness is hell, but consciousness ain't no picnic either, you know." I glared at him.

"Well, that's a sign of your good health. You're no pain junkie, are you?" We laughed and I felt relieved. I was grateful for the humor. Then the hard question came. "Tell me, are you still thinking about taking your life?" He went right to the point in his quiet and low-key manner.

"A part of me is. Yes, I am. I have to relearn so many lessons to go on differently. It's a pain in the neck for everyone. Thinking of what's ahead is overwhelming. I lack confidence. I just don't know if I can—"

David interrupted. "Have you made any plan? Given any thought to how you might do it?" he asked.

"Well, no. I hadn't gotten that far actually. The only other time I felt bad enough to think about suicide was in graduate school, when I was overwhelmed—single, scared, young. Then I thought about driving my car into a wall.... This sounds sick!"

"Dorothea, it's not unusual for people who have had pain, struggle, and trauma to have suicidal thoughts. Anyone would long for release. You've spent the last year processing a great deal of pain. But there's a big difference between thinking about suicide and doing it."

"I know that," I blurted out in a rush, tears filling my eyes. "I don't think I'd do it—actually kill myself. Leave Kathryn behind. Or Michael. Or the whole rest of my life."

"Have you promised yourself that? Actually talked it over with yourself? Made a pact? You know, it's okay to have these thoughts and feelings. Life can seem cruel at times. You need to remember that the thoughts and the feelings in you are not the act itself. Don't be afraid or ashamed of them. They exist in your mind. Distinguish them from reality. If you make an agreement with yourself not to act on the signals sent by your mind, you won't do it."

I saw David twice in the following week. He reminded me that I'd come to him deeply depressed and had worked out of that depression by discovering its source. He characterized my current despair as another depression, one that sometimes occurs late in therapy, when someone sees and feels the weight of the pain and struggle that has been processed.

"Look at the year you've had," he said. "You've moved so fast it's dizzying. You've done good work, difficult work. So much rapid change often results in unstable feelings. You have to give yourself a chance to catch up and assimilate so much fresh material." His hands rested in his lap, palms up, open and empty.

"This never should have happened to me," I said, gesturing at my legs. "Never."

There was silence. After a moment David asked, "When are you going to forgive yourself, Dorothea?"

"Oh, I think I have. For the illness long ago. But now, when I feel so alive in spirit, in passion...now, when I long for joy and celebration...and...and I see all of it attached to this body that is slipping away. It's hard to accept.

"My life demands a new way of seeing things. I'm struggling to get beyond my *stuckness*. I keep trying on new hats, slipping into new skins, looking for a comfortable fit. The right one. You know?" I wanted to ask him again to wait for me, not to leave me alone out here. It was too hard alone.

"Of course I know," he answered softly. "That's the challenge. And it takes time, doesn't it. You can't control what happens. You have to go with it and trust that life will give you what you need."

I listened hard. What he said made sense when I was with him in the daylight. Like a speeded-up movie, the past was racing by. It was dense and intense. David had listened for a year. Now I had to stand aside and just let it pass. I had to focus energy on the challenge at hand, on physical losses which would change my life still more.

My despair subsided but depression lingered like the remnants of an illness that had lost its power. My dreams were dark and troubled. One night I dreamed I was a one-member firing squad. An older woman told me to shoot four little girls who were standing in white coffin-like cartons, open at the top. You could see their heads. The woman handed me a transparent plastic gun with a long narrow barrel filled with tiny gray metal bullets. Aim for the head and shoot, she said.

The first kid turned away, asking me not to shoot. I didn't shoot her. The second girl, about 8 years old, had thick, brown braided hair and blue eyes. She looked right at me. I aimed and shot her twice in the face, but the bullets deflected, bounced off her. She flinched. The woman said to try again and I aimed at her mouth. The woman said aim higher, the mouth is too bloody and messy. I saw the blood. The girl's eyes were heavy with pain. I shot wildly to put her out of pain. Finally she died, a horrible sight.

I emptied the remaining bullets and handed the gun to the woman. "I won't do the other two," I said. "Here. The gun can't hurt anyone, anymore."

I awoke terrified by the violence in my dream. The 8-year-old looked very much like me before polio, except that her eyes were blue. Several nights later I dreamed about shooting the children again. This time I recognized the blue eyes. They were the eyes of my beautiful woman. While the dream felt perverse, there was much to consider. For starters, I needed to stop shooting myself.

One day in late September, I went to the ocean alone. On an overcast afternoon I watched the tide ebb, leaving glistening wet sand in its wake. It is always the same and always different, I thought. We each have this little space in life and we are being swept away all together, out to sea.

If I let the tide take my last illusion, what might that be? That life would be different for me now that I had accepted what had happened to me physically. How different? That somehow there would be magic. Not a little-kid cure of the sort I'd hoped for as a child, but a change so profound and so apparent that the fact of the polio wouldn't matter. That all the work of therapy would wipe away the effects of polio and I'd be a new person.

I had wanted David to be able to make that happen even when I knew he couldn't, even when he told me he didn't have answers. I had wanted to be able to make the miracle happen through my own acceptance of the facts as they were. My story had been hard to tell; the acceptance lessons hard won. I wanted to simply transcend that past, escape the edge undamaged, and go ahead with life.

It grew late. I was startled from my thoughts by a strong autumnal wind and the cries of sea gulls. In a flash I saw that I was looking for a miracle in therapy. I wanted acceptance of my polio *to make the loss not count*. I wanted to be delivered. This was the magic I hoped for.

In that moment, I saw that nothing I did, or David did, or Michael did, would make polio not count. I had to embrace my personal reality, including the unknown, just like everyone else. If I wanted to walk, I would strap on the ugly brace each morning. I would not awaken uncrippled. I had to deal with myself now on a day-to-day basis again and again and again. Some days would be better than others. Clearly, these were the conditions of my life. I had to move to a more active acceptance, practice acceptance on a daily basis until it became part of the fabric of my life.

I saw that this was the challenge of all people who awakened to the miracle of their own lives. I was no different.

18

DAVID

COMING TO TERMS

D orothea was rewarded with several weeks of euphoric feelings after she reclaimed her angry voice. This elated response followed her release of great emotional energy. Instead of devoting her energy to holding in her feelings, she was learning how to flow with emotional responses that came to her, thus making energy available for excitement in ordinary living. As she learned to control her negative thinking patterns, she created less negative emotion and was able to allow the natural feelings as they occurred.

Emotions play a critical role in human life. We connect to our basic instinctual nature through our emotions. They arise from centers in the brain which existed long before the evolution of the cortex and our abstract mental abilities. We were "feeling" animals long before we became "thinking" animals. The basic function of emotion is, simply, to motivate us to action. The word emotion comes from the Latin, *emovere*, which means "to move out, to stir up, and excite." If an individual has a fully developed capacity for emotional experience, his or her life will reflect a rich liveliness and fullness.

When our emotion gets excited, we experience what we interpret as tangible energy flowing in our body. This is true of all emotions, including all varieties of joy, fear, anger, and sorrow. Emotional experience is much like a wave that passes through us. It builds and grows in intensity until it reaches a peak; then it subsides and we return to our usual state of being. Often we are refreshed or renewed for having released this energy in ourselves, even if a bit tired from the intensity of the experience. I think of emotion as the technicolor of life. Without it, life is drab. At the other extreme, if emotions are excessive and out of control, life is hell. Emotion has an essential function of releasing our energies and tensions and alerting us to where we need to act for our well-being. If this natural function is blocked, we suffer psychologically and physically.

Confusion about how to handle emotion is common. Families and cultures create strong ideas about what we should be. Frequently these ideas conflict with our basic natures, especially with our emotional natures. We can mold and control our emotional response to a certain degree, but if done excessively, we create significant internal conflicts and pressures.

Dorothea's sense of her sexuality was a very important part of her emotional reawakening. Both her family and religious training taught her to feel conflict about the place of sex in her life, in spite of the fact that she was always an attractive, sensuous woman. The polio made her body into an embodiment of pain and embarrassment. In retrospect, given all she had to overcome, it was a tribute to her essential healthiness that she ever threw herself into the courtship arena.

In her therapy, she boldly struggled with all of the confusion and conflict she had about her body. She looked at the terrible things that had happened to her body, and how she had rejected it. Now, the psychological barriers against enjoying herself as a woman collapsed. When she claimed her right to full womanhood, she regained complete capacity for pleasure and sensuality as a physical being. She and Michael were delighted that she had "come home" to her body again. Her therapy had been a long series of stories. In the telling, she had filled in the missing chapter on her femininity.

Much of psychotherapy is about telling our stories. Layer by layer, we discover and declare ourselves. The wounded self is healed and empowered through this process. Therapy is not about changing ourselves so much as it is about claiming ourselves, allowing the full expression of all that we are. We may be constricted, and thus "less" than what we are. We may be inflated, and thus "more" than what we are. But to achieve wholeness, we must come to accept that we cannot be other than what we are.

Laurens Van der Post, the South African writer, wrote about the task of telling one's story as a crucial aspect in the life of the Bushmen of Africa. To the Bushmen, telling one's story is as important as living it. In the telling, life achieves meaning and integration within each person. A transformation can take place. As people tell their stories, they claim the life they have lived. As they grapple with life, it demands their acceptance.

We often resist the pure telling of our story. We want to tell the story as we think it should be and edit out the parts which make us uncomfortable. But this doesn't work. We must be honest and complete. We must acknowledge even the parts we don't like. In fact, where we have the most resistance is exactly where special attention is needed. Our resistance signals where we may discover the most important things about ourselves. There is no part of ourselves we can afford to discard. Every part is crucial for wholeness and has value to us.

When we review our life thoroughly, we return to the present with a renewed sense of meaning and possibility. We catch up with time by finishing what is past. The indisputable truth is that nothing in the past could have been different than it was. The past cannot change. But in telling our stories, our understanding of the past can change enormously. Seeing the past in a completely new way transforms how we view ourselves in the present. Failing to look at our past thoroughly and accept it totally, we may unconsciously repeat faulty patterns.

This immutability of the past gives many people trouble. There is a widespread tendency to hang on to the past. The entire color of an individual's personality sometimes reflects this preoccupation with unfinished business. Chronically nostalgic people always long for the old days, while guilt-ridden people are caught in obsessive regrets. Angry and bitter people, stuck in past injustices and disappointments, become experts in ferreting out unfairness, thus carrying their past hurts endlessly forward in time.

But the past does not exist. It is no more. The remains of the past exist only in our memories and in the psychological patterns or lessons that we formed then and carried forward. Our memories are a specialized form of history. They don't accurately tell us what happened in the past, only what we remember about how it appeared to us in those moments. Yet, here is a paradox. Our memory of the past is our psychological truth. We act on those memories and lessons as if they are *absolute truth*. This is why it is so important that we grapple with our past.

Dorothea had completed the telling of her story and had found new meaning in it. But the euphoria she experienced for a few weeks passed and she began slipping into a new depression. This was terribly disappointing and confusing to her. She knew that the changes she had experienced were real and substantial. She didn't doubt the success of the hard work she had completed. It did not feel to her that there was more from the past that required attention. So she was puzzled at this new miserable mood state.

In her effort to sort out these feelings, Dorothea achieved an important understanding of her ambivalence about her "dream house." She discovered that it had layers of hidden meaning. She realized that, unconsciously, the house had been a compromise, a substitute for what she had really yearned for—a second baby. She wanted another child even though she was fully aware that it was not physically practical to have one. Because she hadn't allowed herself to acknowledge this desire and accept it, she could not let it go and feel natural sadness and grief over the loss of possibility.

The house symbolized another reality. It was custom designed and built to accommodate Dorothea's handicap with level floors, gentle ramps, and a minimum of obstacles. In creating the house, she and Michael had identified the limitations they had to live with for the rest of their lives. This was the dark side of the dream house.

During the dreadful Ashland vacation, they were both confronted by the unchangeable realities of the polio handicap. They became irritated and alienated, fought bitterly, hated each other and themselves, and finally quit the vacation and returned home. What a contrast to the Sunriver vacation which had been filled with such a sense of possibility and joy.

Dorothea experienced despondency. During a conversation with a close friend at the beach, she wondered if life was worth living, whether she should go on.

During the psychotherapy of depression there are times when the use of anti-depressant medications may be indicated and useful in managing the symptoms. Patients who are successfully proceeding through psychotherapy sometimes encounter periods of profound despair. If the depressive symptoms begin to overwhelm them, they can cascade down into a nearly paralyzed condition. In this state, the psychotherapy becomes blocked and they may need chemical intervention to assist them through the crisis. It is important to anticipate the danger of such a free-fall into a major depression. Control of the symptoms is easier to affect before they become too severe. It serves no useful purpose to delay chemical treatment if it is needed.

On the other hand, serious and painful depressed feelings are not always an indication that anti-depressant medication is necessary. There are numerous factors to consider. If the depressive episode occurs in the context of a dynamic therapeutic process, it very well might be an expected development. In these situations, the therapist must carefully evaluate whether the patient has the personal and social resources at hand to move through the crisis unaided by medication. Emotional turmoil is often an important aspect of the psychological reordering which is taking place. The term "depression" implies that the person is in a condition which must be stopped, alleviated and reversed. This is not always true. Life sometimes leads us to encounter "a dark night of the soul." We need caring support during these passages, but we do not need to be rescued from them.

I have seen situations where the use of medication was an impediment to the natural emotional processing of a life crisis. For example, normal bereavement may produce periods of depressed mood which are integral to the grieving task. There is a danger that normal psychological reactions to life events can become pathologized, viewed as symptoms of a disease process which must be cured. Some biomedically oriented professionals tend to view personal distress and impairment as biochemical problems to be solved. And some psychologically oriented professionals err in the other direction, seldom or never considering the value of psychotropic medications for their clients.

But this is not an either/or issue. Many personal factors must be considered in evaluating when to suggest medication. An individual's life circumstance might be so stressful that he cannot manage his depressed feelings and he needs relief now. If suicidal preoccupations exist in the absence of a secure, social support network, the risk factor might be too high to go through the crisis without chemical support. Some people are disinterested in the wider meaning of their condition; they simply want to get rid of it. Other people are adverse to the use of psychotropic drugs, even when they need them.

Dorothea, like many people, felt embarrassed when she told me about her suicidal thoughts. She felt like she was revealing a shameful aspect of herself. I listened carefully and inquired about the issues which must be considered to evaluate the possible danger that can accompany such despair. As she talked, the frightening specter of the preoccupation began to lessen, and the underlying meaning of her thoughts began to become clearer.

Together we concluded that, as painful as the feelings were, she was not in danger of killing herself as the solution to her problem. "I wish I were dead" is an exquisite statement of feeling, but it is not always an intent to die or an indication that one might lose control and act on the feelings. Nevertheless, because of the possibility, such thinking and feeling has to be taken seriously and evaluated.

As we reviewed what she had been thinking about during the time I was away on vacation, the broader meaning of her anguish began to emerge. Dorothea was experiencing a kind of depression which occasionally takes place towards the end of an emotionally charged course of therapy. In the telling of her story, therapy had taken Dorothea on a detailed journey through her life. As the charged memories surfaced, she allowed unfinished emotional stress to be brought into the present and expressed. As difficult as this was, she usually was rewarded with a tangible sense of lightness and relief soon after each story episode was over.

After a year, she had completed the journey through her life. She was up-to-date. Now she was experiencing what I call a "retrospective grieving." It is the last step in the long process of taking in the full measure of the suffering that her life had required of her. Now that she had seen it all, she grieved for how painful it had been. This grieving is the last step in the movement to full acceptance.

In the depth of her despondency, Dorothea had a dream in which an older woman told her to execute four little girls who were standing in coffin-like cartons. She was to kill them with a "transparent gun" filled with "gray bullets." The dream repeated itself on a subsequent night and, this time, Dorothea recognized the girlhood version of her beautiful woman. This truly nightmarish drama about the horrors of her past reflects the despairing state of her grief.

Let's read the dream. She is to finish off the past, execute the child aspects, put them into coffins and let it be done. The transparent gun is a deadly instrument, yet a weapon capable of transmitting light. Dorothea struggles with the dream and she sees how she has been shooting herself, punishing herself for the reality of her life. The gray wall returns, but now in the form of gray bullets. She cannot obliterate the past. It was what it was. It is finished. And Dorothea is who she is, in the present, at the threshold of the future.

During this time, Dorothea also feared the dependency feelings she felt towards me in the therapy relationship. Although her treatment had not been lengthy, it had been emotionally intense and stressful and she had formed a sense of dependency on our relationship. This dependency had been important in creating the secure emotional environment in which she could let go of her defenses and encounter everything which had to be resolved. Now she feared that without the relationship, she might revert to a constricted, frightened state.

These feelings of dependency are normal and we talked about them frequently during the last months of therapy. Intellectually, Dorothea knew she was completely able to handle her life and would do so. But emotionally, she was less confident.

One day, alone, she returned to the ocean vista where she had earlier confessed her despondency to her friend. While looking at the tidal movements she reflected on herself and realized a final truth. In her life she had been helped by many people through difficult periods. She was loved by many people. But in her inner struggle with Dorothea, she was alone. She asked: "If I let the tide take my last illusion, what might that be?" If she accepted the impact of the polio in her life, the polio wouldn't matter—acceptance would make the loss not count. She confronted this illusion and realized there was no magic. She must accept her reality as it is.

Human beings hunger for the magical solution—like the apostle Paul's transformation on the road to Damascus, to have everything changed in a flash. But miraculous breakthroughs merely begin the real work of change. The rest of the journey unfolds in time, through daily life challenges, where we carry on the search for an authentic experience of ourselves and open, loving relationships with others.

19

DOROTHEA

LEAVE TAKING

Near the end of October, I told David that small poems were happening in me almost daily. I had kept a journal for almost a year now. In the beginning, I wrote to steady my fear of madness. I had hoped that if I put the words on paper, the frightening thoughts would lose their power. This strategy had worked quite well. I watched words become phrases, phrases become coherent sentences, and then fluent paragraphs. But I had never written poetry and these poems surprised me. I recited a few to David and felt awkward reading them aloud.

"It's like magic," I laughed, standing to put on my new blue cape. I struggled to balance my purse, poems, and cape all at once. David helped me fasten the cape so it wouldn't slip off. "It's okay," I protested, dropping my purse on the sofa. "I'm not in kindergarten. I can dress myself, for God's sake!"

"Oh yeah?" he countered. "What's the matter, Dorothea? Afraid if I help you with this you'll travel down to dependency hell?" He laughed.

"Of course not," I said. "It just feels stupid standing here letting you help. I guess I'm used to doing everything I can by myself. Kinda' makes up, maybe, for things I can't do."

"You don't have to make up for anything, you know. You're terrific the way you are." David smiled in admiration and I left his office glowing.

The light turned golden yellow on the drive home. Colored leaves whipped themselves into frantic circles along the roadway. More and more, everything was finishing. Now therapy sessions were followed by good moods or bits of insight instead of anguish or fear.

I laughed at myself. How could I depend on others—on Michael, family, friends—to help me accommodate new physical losses if I blushed when David helped fasten my cape. Such a simple act of kindness, so easy for him and so comfortable for me. Though I knew how much I had needed him—had gone on needing him well beyond when I had deemed my time was up—I wasn't comfortable with dependence. I had always been fiercely independent. Now, depending had to become part of my style.

The image of dependence was unpleasant to me. Helping others didn't seem so hard. It was the sense of burden surrounding it, the bitching many adults did, even unconsciously. I had worked to be independent, partly to avoid feeling like someone's burden. I had been very successful at it. Able-bodied people spoke about "those people" when referring to wheelchair users. "Those people" were from another planet. I didn't want to go there. Dependence meant sheltered workshops and crippled people. Exile.

I recalled the frequent hospital stays and rehabilitation periods that had laced my adolescent years. I had met other teenagers in wheelchairs. We had spent months together following recovery from surgery. We had shared pleasure and fun, a real social life beyond our physical limits. But I never carried those friendships forward. Why? Looking back at it now, I grew uneasy with tension in the pit of my stomach, the kind I'd had when my mother pushed me to "try, try harder."

Since I had gotten polio, my parents cheered each physical advance, every inch forward, but the most important word in our new vocabulary was *independence*. It rang out everywhere with exhaustive urgency. My mother especially was like a drill sergeant:

"Mom, I want a drink of water?"

"Do you have your braces on?"

"Yeah."

"Then get up and get it yourself!"

She insisted that I walk. In our four-room apartment in New York, it took five minutes to haul myself up and walk to the kitchen for water. But she made me do it. I hated her for it. I didn't understand how she could be so mean.

Other adults didn't understand her meanness either. My grandmother often wailed, "How could you be so hard on her, the poor thing!" But when I eavesdropped on her conversations, she always answered grandma the same way. Her words formed a protective shield against criticism from outsiders, even family.

"Listen, these are doctor's orders! We were told, when you take her home from the hospital, treat her as if you'd die in an auto accident tomorrow. Remember, no one will take care of her the way you would. You have to make her independent, as soon as possible. That's the best thing you can do."

I heard that story frequently after I came home from the hospital. It frightened me to hear my mother's anxious tones. In bed at night I worried. I was not yet 11 years old. What if my parents died the next day? I would lose them. Who would take care of me? I had to do my exercises, try harder. If I failed, I would become dependent and that was as good as dead. I better never depend on someone else. It was nasty, weak, shameful. I squeezed my eyes tight, wishing mother were talking about someone else. Sometimes I wished my mother were someone else, someone who would feel sorry enough for me to bring a glass of water to my room.

Recalling my old fear of dependence, I shuddered. Stories of survival had fascinated me as a child. On my 10th birthday, while I was still in the hospital, someone had given me an illustrated children's biography of President Franklin Delano Roosevelt which included, of course, great emphasis on his courageous battle against the ravages of polio. The book inspired me, but the moments of comfort and kindness had soothed my fear. Scenes of compassion were powerfully attractive, especially when they transgressed unspoken boundaries of behavior.

As a literature teacher, I had often discussed Tolstoy's "The Death of Ivan Illych." The story traces the awakening of a colorless civil servant who perceives his life as valuable only at the onset of a mysterious illness. While Ivan's family and friends are consumed by temporal whims and pleasures, Ivan's suffering leads him to examine his life and reclaim his spiritual self. When I taught this story, I was moved by Ivan's peasant valet, Gerasim, who cared for Ivan when others abandoned him. He sat all night, rubbing Ivan's legs and holding them over his own strong shoulders. I saw this as a Rembrandt painting—the dark, curly-haired Gerasim sitting on a low stool, half asleep, bearing the weight of Ivan's legs on his young shoulders. He simply gave comfort. Ivan simply received it. A perfect balance.

Comfort was missing from my experience. I saw that my fear of dependence had marked major events of my life when I had neither asked for nor received help. From my parents, and the adult world as I knew it, came the largely unspoken dictum that being strong and independent was good. Needing comfort, wanting to be held and loved, needing to lean on anyone, was weak. Winners stood alone. They were hard, fiery, feisty. I was a winner. I could see now that I needed to learn to depend, and that this would take time. I could practice on David before leaving him.

Throughout November, more poems poured out of me. I got up in the night and wrote in the kitchen. I nicknamed myself the "Mad Poet of Portola Valley." Driving to work, I avoided the freeway and took Arastradero Road, a winding country road where I saw hills, wild horses and hikers, not cars and concrete. New poems started here where the sky fanned out like colored feathers and the light glowed. Often I pulled off the road, parked on the grassy shoulder, and wrote on envelopes, old shopping lists, whatever was handy. I had fun and enjoyed myself.

The poems were short and lyrical. I wrote about my legs, about marital joy and strife, about my daughter, even about my own name. There was joy, pain, sadness and fragile beauty. Sometimes, bizarre humor. As I let go of the past, the feelings finished in a poem. I read my poetry to David during our hours together. He appreciated them and I enjoyed sharing this new part of myself with him.

Strangely, this writing and reading aloud was teaching me about depending on and trusting myself—speaking personal truth, taking risks that required exposure. I heard my new voice. David heard it. I knew every author needed an audience. It didn't have to be large, but for a story to be heard, a writer had to depend on others to complete the connection.

One day I wrote a poem about David. It was clearly a gift, as magical as my dream about the jewels almost a year earlier. It summed up my therapy experience and pointed to its conclusion. I named the poem "Leave Taking." It was only 14 lines, written quickly. Creating it, I felt like an instrument bringing forth something which I did not yet grasp. The imagery was graphic, the words laden with feeling. I put it away quietly. I could not read it to David. I wasn't sure I was ready to leave yet.

I wished I could just toss out all my fears, stamp my foot, demand that they leave. Now that I understood my fear of dependence, I simply wanted to accept it in my life. I wanted to trust my own strength to sustain me when I left the sanctuary of David's office. Once I left, I didn't want to return, at least not to relearn the same lessons. One day, feeling anxious and stressed, I sat in David's office feeling overwhelmed by self doubt. He looked at me long and hard then said, "Dorothea, I'd like to try hypnosis with you today."

"Why?" I shot back defensively. We hadn't done any of this kind of work for a long time.

"Because something's troubling you and we can't seem to get at what it is. Do you recognize this as one of your patterns?"

"Yes," I answered, this time more openly. "You know I'll work out of it. Something's there, I guess. It won't kill me."

"Of course it won't," he agreed. "But getting past those barriers you've set up would help you. Hypnosis is a simple way to do that. If you'd rather not, that's okay too."

My knee-jerk resistance faded as I saw the opportunity. When I closed my eyes and followed his instructions, it was easy to relax and pay attention to what was there. Almost immediately, I encountered fear.

"Stay with it," David said, softly. "Look at it. See that it can't hurt you. Just let it be. Let it come and go. Just move through it. You don't have to do anything. Just let it be."

After some time, the fear subsided, but I continued to move beyond it. In an occasional suggestion, David encouraged me to stay with it, to continue to relax. I spiraled downward in a gentle free-fall, floating through swirls of colors, shades of pink, crimson, rich blue, and deep purple. Light passed through the colors as they swept around me and I floated through them easily. I was totally aware of sensation, but quiet and awash in relaxation.

Accompanying the fall was a gentle whirring sound and some ancient music, totally unfamiliar but mellifluous, running up and down inside me like a light caress—asking for nothing, free of urgency, just letting me know that I was hearing new music.

I came to rest on the smooth velvety bottom of the sea. In this quiet place I felt tingling sensations all over. I was wrapped, held, safe—the water held me in great enveloping arms, showing me everything held inside me, contained. There were no questions, no human voices. But sensations of touch and sound came into me and flowed out, leaving me knowing who was there in a way I've never known before.

There I met fear and sadness in a new way, simply asking to pass through. When I saw fear, my body struggled against it, but it relaxed when I refused to fight. I saw that any controlling from me was simply interference. In this incredible quiet place inside myself, I saw that wholeness did not permit exclusion of any emotion or experience. If I went far enough, I could go beyond fear to pleasurable places. I could actually take myself there.

I was awed to see that special place in myself. I wept. "I have to tell you," I said, taking David's hand in both of mine, "that this is so good, so good. What I've just seen inside is so beautiful. And it's me." I believed it. I wiped my eyes and blew my nose and looked at him.

"Teach me how to go there again," I asked. "I want to know this like an imprint, something I'll never forget. Then, no matter what happens in my life, ever, even if I can't move a muscle, I'll still be able to give my real self to myself. If I can do that, I'll always be able to save myself. And I'll always be safe."

And so he did. On my own, I practiced. Sometimes I got distracted or ran from things I didn't want to see. Mostly I got so relaxed and full of pleasure that I just felt good about the life I had, even if the circumstances weren't ideal. Often when I visualized at night, I simply fell asleep.

Nighttime writing forays continued in earnest. In the week following my journey beyond fear, I wrote:

The great crippler
twists, gnarls,
tears, chokes,
festers, freezes
all aliveness—

the Great Crippler:
fear.

In daylight, I felt rushes of excitement. Sometimes I felt as if I were standing on a platform hearing the whistling of a fast-approaching train, feeling the wind of the great engine cutting the air, blowing my own hair back from my face. Other times I was the train rushing forward—bold and big with energy and joy.

Simple events moved me to write. In October, Michael had planted a bed of Iceland Poppies to cheer me. He often said I love you by planting something beautiful. Now, in December, the poppies bloomed all together like a surprise defying winter. One warm sunny morning, I sat at the kitchen table admiring the profusion of blooms.

Iceland Poppies

Poems keep happening in me
Plants coming to flower

I watch you reseeding for me
before the long slow winter
your planting hands working
the rich ready soil
spreading the gifts
calling forth the promise

178

My body thanks you
for the champagne bubbles
all golden bright crayon yellow
blushing pink scarlet crimson
their swaying stems, papery petals
almost translucent.

"It's crazy!" I told David one morning. "Here it is December, almost Christmas, and the poppies are blooming!" I was drunk with pleasure. There were so many flowers that I showed up for therapy with an arm-load of poppies hoping that he, too, would delight in the elegant simplicity. He did.

Along with the abundance of daily delights, my dreams had become rich sources of pleasure. One night I dreamed I visited David in another office, a new place on an ocean-front, very light, airy, open. In the dream I was troubled and asked him to help me by holding my head in his hands. My head felt so heavy that I couldn't hold it upright. He smiled and said, "Sure, I can do that." With his hands on my head, I felt warm energy in my skull and I began to cry softly. In the midst of tears I said, "I feel a fear coming."

"Good. Why don't you look at it?" he said.

I did. I didn't run. Then I said, "I can stand up to my fear and beat it back as if I were crossing a tall grass prairie." We both laughed at the image of my doing that. I went on. "I know I can't go back and get what I lost. But I think I'm afraid I'll die if I don't get what I need now. And I don't know how to ask for it." We sat together quietly. I stopped crying and started grinning a little. I took David's hand and said, "Let's go outside."

He came along happily, like a dear friend. Then a magnificent thing happened. There in the sun on the beach, I began to walk. No crutches! Just a brace with a bending knee joint. Then I ran back and forth between the edge of the surf and the dry sand like those unleashed dogs you see playing on the beach. I yelled, "I'm mad, I'm completely mad, you know? What am I going to do?"

David laughed heartily and clapped his hands. "You're going to keep beating down the fear! You're going to keep dancing! What a wonderful dancer you are!" As he spoke, I noticed that I'd gone from running to dancing. "And you're going to get what you need, but I don't know how in hell that's going to happen either. You can't know everything, Dorothea!"

As he spoke, David took off his shoes and danced bare-legged in gray bermuda shorts and a fisherman's heavy knit sweater.

"And its okay to go on needing you to help me learn and grow?" I shouted out. "You'll come if I call you? I shouldn't feel weak or ashamed if I need to depend on anyone for the whole rest of my life? I have begun with you. I'm safe now with me—and with you. That's twice safe!"

"Yes!" David shouted across the wind blowing between us. "That's right. Now you've got it! Just keep trusting yourself, holding onto yourself. I can be one of your people. I already am, you know. And there are many others. You may not see them now, but you half know."

In that flashing moment of freedom and well-being I felt complete and perfect love for myself and for each person in my life. I saw the years to come, full of joys and sorrows, confusion and clarity, pain and pleasure. But incredibly rich, spun out with a whole new dimension. We danced on until the scene faded out. I awoke feeling as if I had just been to a great feast.

In mid-December, shopping for Christmas gifts, I saw a simple watercolor print of Iceland poppies. Next to the print was a tall roll of gold Mylar wrapping paper. I bought the print and in careful script wrote "Leave Taking" on the back side of the stiff cream paper. When I wrapped the gift in shiny gold mylar, I knew I was ready to give it away.

Weeks preceded the giving. I was surprised to feel loss and sadness at the thought of leaving. I read and reread the poem, thought about the months of struggle, fear, and pain, about the vigil David had been willing to keep with me. He'd had faith when I wavered. He had guided me to insights of my own—sometimes with deliberation, sometimes with a simple spontaneous response. I was touched deeply by the experience we had shared and there was a certain sadness in having to say goodbye. I was healed. I didn't need him anymore.

The day before the Winter Solstice was clear and cold. I arrived at the office early, bearing my gift, feeling partly self-conscious thinking, "I wish I weren't doing this," and partly like one of the three Wise Men delivering gold. I recounted a wonderful dream about revisiting my childhood home, which was aflame in the dream. My job was to revisit each and every room of that four-room apartment, memorize what was there, and then leave, taking nothing and saving no one but myself. Later in the dream, I found myself drinking beer with some women friends at a local hangout. "Did you read about the spectacular fire in that historic New York apartment?" one friend asked me. "It's amazing that everyone got out alive, isn't it?" I smiled and nodded yes, but said nothing.

"Well, that's a real finishing dream, isn't it?" David said.

"I don't know about that. But I think this is a real finishing gift," I said, handing forth the square mylar package. He looked pleased and surprised as he took the gift and opened it in happy anticipation. The print was unframed, mounted on simple matting. He looked at the field of poppies in their crimsons, pinks, and yellows, and broke out in a broad grin. Then he turned the print over in his lap and saw the poem.

I couldn't bear to watch him read it. What will I do if he doesn't like it? What if he doesn't get it? Misunderstands it? How will I get past this gracefully? But before I could do damage to myself, David said, "This is beautiful, Dorothea. Really beautiful. How did you write it?"

I flushed with pleasure and relief. "It wrote itself really. I mean, it came from the new place in myself. I wrote it down, and worked to shape it a little. But I didn't do too much with it. It just came out that way, through my hand and my heart." I paused and took a breath. "Would you like me to read it to you?"

"Very much so," he said softly, tilting his head just slightly and moving his chair a little closer to where I sat on the sofa.

Leave Taking

If I should meet you in some future year
Beyond this one so marked, so steeply bound
By jagged cliffs, by canyons high and deep,
By darkest nights, by fearful broken sleep,
If I should raise my eyes and catch your own
Laughing unawares or lost in thought,
I think that I would gasp, and pause, and stop
To glimpse a never quite forgotten time
When tumbling over in a dark abyss
You caught and held me lest I broke in two,
Then led me through a maze with gentle song
And let me cry my tears so deep, so long.
We live together in that private space,
My other loves live in another place.

Reading the poem aloud to David, I felt the intensity of all the work behind me and the simple acknowledgment of all I could never say. Awed by the very special love that had grown out of my journey to wellness, I fell quiet when I finished reading. David's reflective expression told me that he, too, had heard my poem as if it were a new life in the room. He picked up the watercolor, turned it over, and asked, "How did you do this? It's so special. Amazing."

"It's what I felt and saw and knew....I love it when things just come out of me without theory or understanding." I knew this new voice was the awakened part of me, the voice that I had neglected and ignored for so long. I needed it for more than poetry. But I trusted myself for what I needed now. And I had learned to trust others as well.

"It's going to be a great Christmas," I said as I rose to leave. "Now all I have to do is learn to walk on water!" I laughed.

"No, you've already done that," David answered. We shared a warm heart-felt hug and then stood apart. "You have done your work well. You have done it beautifully. I'm so glad you came to me to do it," he said.

My eyes swept his office, gathering up anything I might need to go on with my journey. We had finished our work; it was clear in the writing and giving of the poem. That was the gift to both of us. In taking my leave, I balanced carefully on my crutches. I turned the doorknob and glanced down to survey my next step. Then I moved forth alone to gather the gifts that lay ahead.

20

DAVID

INTEGRATION, CREATIVITY AND CLOSURE

I find it fascinating to observe the ending of a therapy process. It seems as though it should be a simple and straightforward event. Only occasionally is it so. In brief therapies, with very specific limited goals, knowing when the task is done is fairly easy. But in therapies which involve an in-depth examination of the past and the resolution of difficult emotions, the question, "When are we done?" can be complicated to answer.

In clinical jargon, ending therapy is called termination. I always thought this was a strange and grim way to describe what should be a joyous event. Imagine it applied to other transitions such as College Termination or Career Termination (for job changes or retirement).

In the technical literature, much is written about this aspect of psychotherapy. There are important issues involved. The changes accomplished in the treatment must successfully integrate into the ordinary life of the patient, and not be dependent on the existence of the therapeutic relationship. Timing is very important here, as errors can be made both by ending too early or by allowing the treatment to continue too long. Termination also means ending the relationship between the patient and the therapist. Even though this has been a business/professional encounter, it is nonetheless a rich human relationship. The loss of any important relationship has many psychological meanings and needs to be handled sensitively.

With some patients, termination is a lengthy, difficult process replete with anxiety, fear, and sadness. The therapy experience may have been the first fully trusting relationship in their life. There can be a strong bond of affection for and dependence on the therapist. The ending of such a close relationship involves a gentle series of steps during which the emotional investment is gradually withdrawn and shifted into real-life relationships and activities.

Not all therapy experiences are emotionally difficult. Termination can be uncomplicated. Sometimes, the sense of completion just unfolds, and termination is a simple and joyful experience. There are some people who engage in therapy with a business-like efficiency, and their termination process has a matter-of-fact quality.

Dorothea's "retrospective grieving" resolved itself as she faced those aspects of her life which would never change, no matter how solidly she completed the past and learned to be fully responsive to her life now. The depressed feelings ended and her energy and optimism gradually returned. Periodically, she talked about being afraid she was dependent on me and the therapy. Because of the intense nature of her experience, the therapeutic relationship had acquired a special and secure quality for Dorothea.

In talking through these anxieties, she was psychologically orienting herself to the future and it gradually became clear that she was nearing the end of therapy. Increasingly, her preoccupations became focused on practical, real-life issues. These included discussions about the possible future decrease in her physical capability due to the post-polio syndrome. These possibilities were unpleasant for Dorothea to contemplate, but they no longer triggered significant emotional distress. As she sorted through these projections into the future, she also contemplated life without therapy and came to feel comfortable about it.

The completion of an intense therapy process also affects me, but differently than is true for my client. I became intensely connected to Dorothea as she struggled through her memories and emotional traumas. But the ordeal was hers, not mine. I was touched by it emotionally, felt the important role I carried out as she worked through her life issues, but I remained outside of her life. Here is a paradox in the therapeutic relationship. It is special and personal, yet for the therapist, the relationship is founded on a professional and objective basis. Intense relationship is the context of my professional life, and the most fundamental tool in my repertoire of therapeutic skills.

I often felt warm affection and empathy for Dorothea. At other times I felt irritated or annoyed. These feelings were not technique; they were genuine. But their meaning was specific to the context of a consciously goal-directed relationship.

On the other hand, there is a contradiction to all of this objective perspective. Maintaining an objective frame provides an important foundation for the therapeutic relationship. Nevertheless, it does not erase the fact that the people involved are simply human, and the relationship they create is a genuine human relationship. When we stand guard with a fellow human passing through critical life experiences, we are changed by the encounter, regardless of the context. When our clients or patients break through to new possibilities, we feel empowered too.

During the time of Dorothea's therapy I was treating numerous other clients. I maintained a unique and personal relationship with each of them. Each relationship had its own character. Some were warm and personal, others were formal and business-like, depending on the client's personality and the kinds of problems involved.

By nature, I am an affectionate person. If I spend much time working with nearly anyone, I soon develop warm feelings for them. I like this about my work. Each day I look forward to seeing my clients, discovering what has unfolded for them since the last session, and seeing what will emerge in this one. When I am with a client, it is as if he or she is my only client. My duty is to be psychologically and emotionally available, fully present in the moment as much as is humanly possible. In the truest sense, the fundamental goal of my work is for my client to no longer need my services.

How do I know when the work is complete? Therapists have different approaches to this question. My own comes from a basic belief that therapy should be as brief as is needed. Psychotherapy is a specialized relationship, designed to achieve specific goals. Once those goals are reached, the relationship needs to come to a conclusion and recede into the past. Other therapists have different approaches to this issue. The well-publicized cases of famous people who seem to remain in psychotherapy for 20 years or more are not representative of contemporary therapy approaches.

To be called a mental disorder, a person's symptoms must cause "subjective distress and/or functional impairment." Therapy has succeeded when the client is no longer in distress or impaired by his mental symptoms. The judgment of when this point is reached must take into account the habit-driven nature of psychological functioning. We evolve our psychological and behavioral patterns over a long period of time, always striving to ensure emotional security and survival as best we know how. Our brain releases old habits reluctantly. It is a conservative system. If therapy ends prematurely, there is a strong possibility that the new coping behaviors will be overcome by the sheer force of the old habits.

Throughout the therapy work, Dorothea expressed worry that she was taking too much time. Periodically, I was concerned she might end therapy prematurely because of these feelings. Actually, her sixteen months in treatment is not a long time by many standards.

Her creative flowering gave me a signal that Dorothea was nearing the end of her therapeutic work. I remember the day when she reported with great excitement that she had written some poems. "I had just pulled into a parking space. An autumn leaf dropped from a tree and landed on my windshield. Suddenly this poem began pouring into my mind and it was all I could do to find a pen and paper to write it down."

This was an exhilarating experience for her. It had occurred so spontaneously that she hesitated to claim the poem as her own. She looked at those early poems almost as if they were visitations from a distant planet. She frequently described the writing of her poems as "happenings." It's hard to imagine a more delightful experience than this for an English professor, a teacher immersed in literature for 25 years. Until now, she had done little writing of her own, and poetry held a unique significance for her because she had met her beloved Michael in a poetry class.

Throughout the therapy process, Dorothea's dreams and daytime reveries had frequently given her new themes to explore. Sometimes her dreams gave her reassurances, as if her unconscious mind were patting her on the back and saying, "Good work, Dorothea. You are on the right path."

Now her poems were fulfilling the same function. With each new poem, Dorothea's sense of security deepened. It was obvious that significant changes were taking place. A new voice was speaking, and it was doing so in a very elegant manner. Dorothea loved her new voice, and I was delighted to witness its birth.

Freud, Jung, and many other observers of psychological phenomena considered creativity to be a natural outcome of successful therapeutic experience. In my work I have seen that when people break down the barriers of fear in themselves, they release resources of energy formerly constricted and blocked. Spontaneity, creativity, and emotional liveliness are signs of psychological integration. When we are free of fear and distress, our essential self, our real self, expresses a joyous response to life.

This joyous response took the form of poetry for Dorothea. Creativity can blossom in any endeavor of significance to a person. Each of us is unique and we have our own special genius, whether it is art, science, business, relationships, gardening. Sometimes, the expression of creativity is a total surprise to us.

There was one nagging problem which continued to bother Dorothea. She still struggled with occasional bouts of anxiety and fear. When she encountered strong negative feelings, her knowledge was difficult to put into action because she became insecure. She needed a means of establishing security for herself at these critical moments. She had all the psychological skills and resources she needed, but could not access them when under stress.

Using hypnosis, I led her on a guided visualization to find an "inner sanctuary," a place she could return to in times of fear and stress. As was usual with Dorothea, she quickly moved past her initial nervousness and connected with the spirit of the meditation.

Not surprisingly, she found herself drifting downward to a previously visited place of contentment. In her visualization, she once again found herself at the bottom of the sea. This was where, in a dream, she discovered a treasure chest filled with precious jewels and a magic ladle with which to sprinkle the jewels on all of the important people in her life.

This time the jewels take a more specific form and she encounters the emotions of fear and sadness, face to face. She realizes that they are not dangerous. They are simply feelings. They ask only for acceptance. Dorothea discovers that the ladle is a metaphor for that acceptance. There is no need to control, no need to resist. I show her how she can use this visualization on her own. It becomes a method by which she can directly access her inner strength and security.

This hypnotic procedure is a directed experience which mimics something done naturally by many individuals. The procedure establishes a "resource state" in the mind which can be reached in critical moments to overcome personal self doubt and fear. Good salesmen know how to do this well and coaches know how to teach this to their players. It is not magic. It is simply a method to get in touch with strengths already developed.

Dorothea creates such descriptive metaphors and symbols in her dream and intuitive processes. It was in keeping with this creative spirit that Dorothea came to a later session with the wonderful poem *Leave Taking*. The beauty of her sonnet stunned me. How could the complex experience we had shared during the past 16 months be so exquisitely summed up in 14 lines? But it had, and when I thought about the message of the poem, I saw that she had moved forward to the future.

In the poem, Dorothea had projected herself into the future and, from there, looked back to the time of her therapy experience. This was a powerful signal that the transformation from this process was deeply embedded in her unconscious mind. There was little else to do now. Her work was finished.

It reminded me of the experience of completing my own therapy work many years earlier. Following the initial surfacing of unexpressed grief and guilt about my brother John's death, I subsequently had a series of memories which contained other aspects of that loss. Each of these helped me to understand more of what John's death had meant to me and led to further emotional unloading of the memories.

After some years, I had the chance experience of meeting a young mother who was still deep in the terrible process of grieving the death of her own child. I heard her tell her story to a group. Later that day, I felt powerful feelings rising in myself, and when they spilled out, I found myself grieving for my mother and my father. Having felt the full measure of my own pain, I now understood the depth of their pain. This led me to understand everything which had stood between us for so many years. When this final understanding took place, I was filled with relief and wept tears of profound sadness.

A strange thing happened during that final weeping. I came to the end of the process. My mind became blank. There was no more content to the grief. I continued to weep in a state of psychological silence. No longer weeping for Johnny, myself, or my parents, I was simply in contact with an empty place inside that once had been where I kept the love for my brother. No longer a wound, it was now just part of my inner psychic landscape, a vital part of my wholeness, a part of my self.

And so, I heard in Dorothea's poem, a premonition of a future time. A time when, no longer "tumbling over in a dark abyss," she could "stop to glimpse a never quite forgotten time." That never quite forgotten time was now finished.

DOROTHEA

AFTERWORD

"I wake to sleep, and take my waking slow.
I learn by going where I have to go."
—T. Roethke

What happened next? Life went on. While I walk more slowly than I did when I left David's office six years ago, I still walk. My husband, my daughter, and my career all thrive. Therapy did not change the negative realities—pain, fatigue, loss of strength, and decreased mobility are all with me. Therapy doesn't cure crippling, although it helps to heal the wounds so mind and body and emotions can coexist. I now have access to all of my feelings. I came home to my body exactly as it is. I learned to understand and cherish myself better. For me, the tangible limitation has been polio—for others, it may be another crippler of mind or body, another disease or emotional trauma.

As with history, failure to remember the lessons of therapy dooms us to repeat the same mistakes. So the lessons must be practiced long after they first have been learned. Developing full acceptance of my limitations has not been easy. Especially since I started out knowing I had already accepted the facts of my disability. Much in our culture trains us to seek perfect well-functioning bodies, encourages us to crave control, drives us to make things happen in a way we think they should. I've found that imagination and detachment go a long way in diluting the frustrations of confronting limits.

While I still fear falling, I have learned to handle this danger differently. Because I respect my body's fragility, I no longer take unnecessary risks to prove that I can do anything. So I no longer spend huge amounts of energy on fear. I can spend that energy being more honest and open with Michael and myself. I can accept his help when he offers it or request his help when I need it. My ability to depend on him has drawn us closer. With a balanced perspective, I am learning the wisdom of acceptance. This simple lesson is difficult to learn.

My writing adventure, in this book and in poetry, says a great deal about the changes in my life. To write well I have to wrestle and stay with truth, and be willing to go to every imaginable place. When I write, I must first venture out into the entire spectrum of human experience. Later, I must reflect, assess, and shape. This adventure requires a kind of bravery I can now claim within my capacity.

Last week, I had a chance to appreciate the rewards of my new perspective in an intimate way. Rummaging around in my jewelry box, my daughter Kathryn picked out the exquisite brooch that I now call my "beautiful woman" brooch.

Lifting the graceful oval from the box she remarked, "You know, Mom, I think this is the most beautiful piece of jewelry you own. I really love it."

I smiled at her and said to myself, "I am that woman."

DAVID

AFTERWORD

We are living in an era where the use of psychoactive medications is being widely promoted as a solution to the age-old problem of depression. Every month magazine articles, feature stories, and news releases appear describing the "chemical revolution," with predictions for the future when even better substances will be created to treat mood disorders with more reliable results and fewer side-effects. It is clearly true that anti-depressant medications have improved and will continue to improve.

This is good thing. We need medications which work well to assist individuals who become mired in serious depression and cannot find their way through the despair.

But it is also true, in my opinion, that for most people depression is a sign that there is some critical area of life that needs serious attention. It might be, as in Dorothea's case, that unexamined traumas from the past require discovery and release. Or it might be that the manner in which daily life is being lived is significantly out of balance, that psychological or emotional needs are not being met, and that too many stresses are overwhelming the body's ability to cope. In all of these cases, medications may provide relief but they will not address the issue of personal functioning that needs attention.

We are a society that often looks for the easiest solution, the short-term profit, the method that doesn't require us to confront uncomfortable realities. I fear that the future of more and better psychoactive chemicals could lead to a dependence on these kinds of interventions, at a cost that can only be measured in terms of personal human maturation and development. It is indisputable that certain substances can make us feel good. This is one of the joys of living, the delights of

191

drinking an enjoyable beverage, sharing a gourmet meal with friends, or eating a delicious dessert. But is this the same thing as taking a chemical each day in order not to feel bad?

This book describes a drug-free psychotherapy for depression. While much of the story revolves around polio and the profound effect this disease had in Dorothea's life, it is important to clarify that the fundamental basis of her depression was not related to polio per se. It was the effect of unprocessed emotions caused by traumatic events. Polio is not common, but excessively stressful or traumatic life circumstances are. Therefore, the depression depicted here is very much like the depression suffered by many individuals.

Dorothea's therapy is an interesting and clear example of a successful psychotherapy. If the broad range of therapy strategies I used with Dorothea had not worked, I would have tried others including, possibly, the use of drugs. But the process of a talking therapy, when it works, produces results not achievable by drug therapy alone. Psychotherapy reorders the individual's orientation to life experience—past and present—in such a manner as to create a safeguard against future depressive states.

Depression is a miserable condition that distresses millions of people at some time during their lives. It is eminently treatable, but requires active and serious engagement. A tragic fact is that many people live with this terrible emotional blight, assuming perhaps that life is simply grim and they must bear it. I hope this book contributes to a greater understanding that if life does indeed seem grim, then, perhaps, it is due to depression.

Depression should be treated.

SUGGESTED READINGS

Depression

Breggin, Peter R., M.D. *Talking Back to Prozac: What Doctors Aren't Telling You About Today's Most Controversial Drug*. New York: St. Martin's Press, 1994.

Burns, David D. *The Feeling Good Handbook: Using the New Mood Therapy in Everyday Life*. New York: W. Morrow, 1989.

Copeland, Mary Ellen. *The Depression Workbook*. Oakland, California: New Harbinger Publications, 1992.

Kramer, Peter D. *Listening to Prozac*. New York: Viking, 1993.

Slagle, P. *The Way Up From Down*. New York: St. Martin's Press, 1988.

Styron, William. *Darkness Visible: A Memoir of Madness*. New York: Random House, 1990.

Psychology

Frankl, Victor E. *Man's Search For Meaning*. Boston: Beacon Press, 1959.

Jung, C.G. *Memories, Dreams, Reflections*. Boston: Beacon Press, 1959.

Jung, C.G. *Man and His Symbols*. New York: Doubleday & Co., 1964.

Jung, C.G. *The Structure and Dynamics of the Psyche*. Princeton University Press, 1960.

Lerner, H. *The Dance of Anger*. New York: Harper & Row, 1986.

Peck, Scott. *The Road Less Traveled*. New York: Walker, 1985.

Singer, June. *Boundaries of the Soul: The Practice of Jung's Psychology*. New York: Doubleday & Co., 1973.

Living With Disabilities

Beisser, Arnold. *Flying Without Wings*. Boston: G.K. Hall, 1992.

Black, Kathryn. *In the Shadow of Polio: A Personal and Social History*. Reading, MA: Addison-Wesley, 1996.

Gallagher, Hugh G. *FDR's Splendid Deception*. Arlington, VA: Vandamere, 1994.

Gould, Tony. *A Summer Plague: Polio & Its Survivors*. New Haven, CT: Yale University Press, 1995.

Kaysen, Susanna. *Girl Interrupted*. New York: Turtle Bay Books, 1993.

Mairs, Nancy. *Remembering the Bone House*. New York: Harper and Row, 1989

Mairs, Nancy. *Carnal Acts*. New York: Harper & Row, 1990.

Milam, Lorenzo W. *CripZen: A Manual for Survival*. San Diego: MHO & MHO Works, 1993.

Sass, E.J., Georg Gottfried and Anthony Sorem. *Polio's Legacy: An Oral History*. Lanham, MD: University Press of America, 1996.

Stegner, Wallace. *Crossing to Safety*. New York: Harper & Row, 1990.

Tolstoy, Leo. "The Death of Ivan Illych," in *Fiction 100: An Anthology of Short Stories*, 3rd ed. James Pickering, ed. New York: Macmillan Publishing Co., 1982.

Personal Growth and Healing

Dienstfrey, Harris, ed. *Advances: The Journal of Mind-Body Health*. Kalamazoo, MI: The Fetzer Institute.

Moyers, Bill D. *Healing and the Mind*. New York: Doubleday, 1993.

Young-Sowers, Meredith L. *Spiritual Crisis: What's Really Behind Loss, Disease, and Life's Minor Hurts*. Walpole, NH: Stillpoint Pub., 1933.

Post-Polio Syndrome

Dalakas, Marinos. *The Post-Polio Syndrome: Advances in the Pathogenesis and Treatment*. New York: New York Academy of Science, 1995.

Eulberg, Halstead and Perry. "Post-Polio Syndrome: How You Can Help." Directive to Physicians on physical and psychological implications and treatment suggestions. *Patient Care* magazine, June 1988.

Frick, Nancy and Richard Bruno. "Post-Polio Sequelae: Physiological and Psychological Overview." Features history, sequelae, treatment, and psychology of acceptance. *Rehabilitation Literature*, vol. 47, May/June 1986.

Headley, Joan, executive director. Gazette International Networking Institute (GINI). Coordinator of International Polio Network and International Ventilator Users Network, 4207 Lindell Blvd., Suite 110, St. Louis, MO 63108-2915, email: gini_intl@msn.com.

Park, Alice. "Reliving Polio." *Time Magazine*, March 28 1994, pg. 5455.

International Polio Network Support Groups. A support group leaders' workshop booklet offers philosophy, guidelines, and resources for PPS support groups. Send $5 to IPN, 5100 Oakland Ave. #206, St. Louis, Mo.

Polio Society Newsletter. Published by the Polio Society, 4200 Wisconsin Ave., NW. Suite 10623, Washington, DC 20016; (301) 897-8180.

Post-Polio Sequelae Bibliography. B. Hatfield, 2 Coral Way, Half Moon Bay, CA 94019. Note: comments by B. Hatfield following titles of articles are unsolicited, nonbinding, and merely serve as a descriptive aid. Hatfield's bibliography provides a 30-page annotated list of sources on dysphagia, fatigue, neurology, occupational therapy and rehabilitation, physical medicine, physical therapy, psychology, respiratory post-polio syndrome, and areas of general information.

Internet Resources

Depression

Finding Help: How to Choose a Psychologist
http://www.apa.org/pubinfo/howto.html
The American Psychological Association discusses when you should consider psychotherapy, what you should look for in a therapist, what questions to ask, and related issues.

Clinical Depression Screening Test
http://sandbox.xerox.com/pair/cw/testing.html

Depression and Mental Health Links
http://drycas.club.cc.cmu.edu/~maine/depress.html

Depression and Mental Health Sources on the Internet
http://stripe.Colorado.EDU/~judy/depression/

Depression FAQ
http://avocado.pc.helsinki.fi/~janne/asdfaq/index.html
This self-proclaimed "depression primer" includes causes, treatment and resources.

Depression: Uni/Bipolar Disorders Page
http://www.duke.edu/~ntd/depression.html
Many links and lots of information on major depression.

Dr. Ivan's Depression Central
http://www.psycom.net/depression.central.html
Clearinghouse for information on depression and other mood disorders, broken down helpfully by topic. Includes an area with a large introduction to depression, especially how it is defined, how it is treated, FAQs and more. Links to material on depression in Spanish also provided, as well as a special section devoted to Women and Depression.

Internet Depression Resources List
http://www.execpc.com/%7Ecorbeau/

Online Depression Screening Test
http://www.med.nyu.edu/Psych/screens/depres.html

Psychiatry On-Line
http://www.cityscape.co.uk/users/ad88/psych.htm
The *International Journal of Psychiatry.* Presents the latest articles, papers, and news; as well as forensic psychiatry on-line, child and adolescent psychiatry on-line, transcultural mental health on-line, and more. Information on other world-wide web psychiatry resources is provided.

Warning Signs of Trauma-Related Stress
http://www.apa.org/ptsd/html

Psychology Self-Help Resources on the Internet
http://www.gasou.edu/psychweb/resource/selfhelp.htm
Links to non-commercial sites providing information and help about specific disorders related to psychology.

Polio/Post-Polio Syndrome

Dave Graham's PPS in Under Two Minutes
http://www.polionet.org/Pl1-94JA.htm

Tom Walter's What Is PPS?
http://www.zynet.co.uk/ott/polio/lincolnshire/#whatpps

Polio Reference Page
http://www.eskimo.com/~dempt/polio.html

Polio and Post-Polio Information Page
http://members.aol.com.harvestctr/pps/polio.html
An informative site authored by Drs. Bruno and Frick.

Post-Polio Syndrome Links
http://www.geocities.com/HotSprings/1161

The Polio Pals Place
http://www.radiks.net/jschoen/index.html or
http://www.webslnger.com/jschoen
Sponsored by the Polio Survivors Resource Center, offers help and direction.

Polio Internet Mailing Lists
polio@maelstrom.stjohns.edu
The purpose of this list is to supply information and provide support and friendship in an informal and friendly environment.

polio-life@eskimo.com
A forum for sharing experiences or insights on a broad range of topics, not limited to medical issues.

DOROTHEA

EPILOGUE

T en years ago, when I was in psychotherapy, I gave David a gift: a small stained-glass kaleidoscope that had sat on my desk at work for years. During that difficult autumn of therapy conversations, I had often twirled the multi-colored glass toy, scanning the sweep of the hills beyond campus, breaking them into new patterns.

That gift was a symbol. It was time, I thought, to see the patterns without the mirrors, to see life without distortion. I was grateful to have found someone who allowed and encouraged me to speak freely of the trauma of polio; to speak freely of the losses, the pain and the depression. I gave the kaleidoscope to David with a note that said, "Thank you for helping me to see things differently."

Today, this practice of looking at things differently and seeing things clearly is reaping tangible harvests in my life. It enables me to keep moving forward, living each moment, and letting go of the past to make room for the future. While metaphors for change, such as the kaleidoscope, are useful and inspiring, actual change and acceptance of loss takes place in real time, on a daily basis, and in small, specific actions.

This can be illustrated by two different trips that I took to Europe with Michael.

In 1989 we spent three weeks in Great Britain. We decided on this trip spontaneously and looked forward to it with great anticipation. I had not yet travelled with a wheelchair, but within a day of our arrival in London, we both knew I needed one. Luckily we found a neighborhood supply house near Mayfair and rented one for the duration of our trip. We left the store with a rickety old variety that made me vibrate all over.

The streets were impossibly narrow and there was construction going on everywhere. The chair had a tendency to suddenly turn right, frustrating and exhausting both of us. Every outing felt like taking on a new battle against unruly crowds, impatient vehicular traffic, endless obstacles, and the occasional, unexpected right turn into traffic. Getting into buildings usually involved following a mysterious path to a service door that was often unattended. Once inside, there were still more barriers. I remember exploring the National Portrait Gallery by wheelchair and, in the middle of a floor between rooms, a small set of stairs much like a sunken living room left us stranded.

Things did not improve much when we picked up our rental car and left London. In our earlier travels, we had enjoyed staying in bed and breakfasts, stopping when we wanted and searching for cozy little out-of-the-way places. But I could no longer climb more than a few shallow stairs, which precluded traveling this way. We began to settle for the Trust Houses with their standard accessible rooms and their predictable hotel meals. Everywhere we went there were crowds and obstacles. I often pushed myself harder and further than was good for me. Frequently I wept or withdrew in sheer frustration and exhaustion.

We made the best of it and certainly appreciated all we could do because we were both creative, imaginative, problem-solving people. However, that journey made clear the fact that we were going to have to travel differently if we were going to continue traveling together.

Michael and I began a realistic dialogue about future travel. As a result of this shift in perspective, I was willing to venture to Europe again, this time to the Continent to celebrate our 25th wedding anniversary. We planned a trip that took my limitations into account, and still allowed us to enjoy exploring.

We had an opportunity to spend a week in a residence hotel converted from a 16th century monastery in Aix-en-Provence. We both saw it as a chance for a new adventure. This time, we faxed the hotel to inquire about access for me. Were the doorways wide enough to permit a wheelchair, even in the bathroom? Were there any stairs? Through making the right inquiries, we found that while not totally ideal, the hotel was accessible. We signed on for a week in late April and shopped for off-season air fare. We also purchased a hotel chain package for a week in Italy. All our lodging was confirmed in advance, something we had never done.

This time, planning with the reality of limitations paid off in pleasure. The week in Provence was about as idyllic as we could get for traveling with a wheelchair and sharing the late April showers with other off-season travelers. Each day we made plans that matched our energy levels. On rainy days, we took car trips through the surrounding countryside to get the feel of where we were. When the weather was clear, we enjoyed exploring local markets and boulangers and often brought simple meals back to the monastery.

One day, we ventured out to St. Remy to visit the asylum where Vincent Van Gogh had completed more than 150 paintings, including "Starry Night." That day-trip was particularly memorable because my own wheelchair was able to handle many of the paths and small gates. Still there were limitations. When Michael wanted to see an adjacent Roman quarry that was clearly inaccessible for me, I asked him to leave me on a knoll overlooking a picture-perfect pastoral setting. I had about an hour there with the beauty of the wildflowers, the sound of the wind, and the amazing changing light. I experienced what had inspired the painters of Provence. It would not have been possible had I not accepted the confinement, and paradoxically the freedom of the wheelchair.

During our week in Italy, we traveled long days by car. From the beginning it was more ambitious and it turned out to be less satisfying. The small towns on the Italian Riviera and the four balmy nights in Florence were spectacular—but they were also exhausting. The interior of the hotel in Florence was entirely accessible, but there were a dozen daunting marble steps from the street. We took taxis to the center of the city, but between churches and museums the wheelchair often had to be pushed over ancient cobblestones. Michael got plenty of exercise and my bones felt shaken up and rearranged. While we both cherished the riches of Florence, we concluded that we were better suited to travel in the country than the city.

This discovery has not been easy. I am somewhat of a city girl at heart while Michael is a country boy. But my realities of travel have required changes in both of us. Had either of us been unwilling to change, we would have had to give up travel as a shared adventure. Now, while our trips are curtailed by my increasing physical limitations, we can still enjoy them so long as we maintain balance between our overly ambitious imaginations and the reality of our abilities. There are times when we feel bad about the losses, the mounting pile of things we cannot do and places we cannot go, but that is just a fact of our lives. Our energy goes to what is possible. I can choose to look at what I have lost, or twirl the kaleidoscope to see what I can have. The choice is mine, but I must often remind myself to turn the wheel.

My daughter has also moved from joining me in a conspiracy of denial to gracefully and creatively accepting new ways of living with polio. In 1987, when I began to do my therapy work, Kathryn was in fifth grade and said things like,

"Mom, I hate it when you park in those blue spots with the wheelchair symbol!" Now she drives my car often and is happy to find a "blue spot." What is important to us is that we have our mother-daughter talks, our shopping trips, our coffee dates, and our shared movies and books. She tells me, "I can be your legs now" as she loads and unloads the wheelchair into my trunk, and together we go wherever our hearts and imaginations take us. Like Michael, she has grown to accept a different kind of travel.

While my world seems to shrink due to physical limitations, it has also expanded through personal changes. I have connected with the polio community as I never did before, and am excited about growing in the direction of advocacy.

In May 1997, I joined hundreds of other people living with similar limitations at the 7th International Post-Polio and Independent Living Conference in St. Louis, Missouri. The conference was organized by the Gazette International Networking Institute based in St. Louis. This is a powerful organization whose purpose is to support the independent living, self direction, dignity and personal achievement of people with disabilities. It is dedicated to the collection and dissemination of information, and to connecting people with people.

Assembled were 75 health care professionals from nine countries who had focused their careers on helping the almost-forgotten survivors of polio, survivors who were now facing new losses. Several-hundred people with polio had come to listen and learn and share their strengths with one another. For me it was a giant "coming out" to join others who, like me, had been systematically separated from one another after our hospital and rehabilitation experience. There was laughter, intelligence, courage, and compassion. For the first time as an adult, I was among a group of people from whom I did not feel "different" in some visible way. There was strength in this assemblage. And as Tony Gould, author of A Summer Plague: Polio and Its Survivors, observed, maybe those of us who were old enough to remember "before polio" and "after polio" are only essentially different in one way: "We know the precise moment after which everything was changed forever."

The conference moved me to feel socially connected in a different way, and has inspired me to use my energy in political action on behalf of the disabled community. At the concluding session, Cyndi Jones, publisher of Mainstream magazine, gave a vibrant talk that encouraged us to follow our bliss by responding to our own needs and championing universal change. She urged us to engage in creative action that will allow us to be empowered. Speaking from her wheelchair she said, "Polio never goes away. Dare to listen, to educate yourself, to continue on your journey. This is how I learned to move on."

Glancing back at the years, I see a whirl of colors and pictures. The trauma of polio was certainly one of the defining events of my life, but there were others as well—marriage, motherhood and a career. Once again, I can choose to look at what I have lost, or what I have had. I think my depression narrated in Healing the Blues ultimately helped me learn to accept the pain in my life and transform it, when I could, into something new. This is not to say that I would wish depression on anyone! But people who come through depression, with or without the use of drugs or formal counseling, are forced to confront their demons. In so doing, they awaken, grow, change and ultimately see things differently.

When I completed therapy, I truly hoped that I would not have to deal with depression ever again. But dealing with new losses, I still must remind myself not to shut down and deny the life that I have. We are who we are. At least I know the way out of depression, and I know the work is never done. Pain and loss, whether from polio or some other traumatic event, are tangible and call out for acceptance that is whole and healthy, sad not stoic. Sometimes a simple event can still call up great sadness that must be looked at, however privately, but not set aside or buried.

One bleak January afternoon this past winter, an old acquaintance stopped at my house for an unexpected visit. I had been sitting at my computer for hours and felt particularly "creaky" as I maneuvered crutches and brace across the room to greet him. He, in contrast, was robust and vigorous, grinning and panting at having biked over steep hills to arrive at my door. In our short "catch-up" conversation, he told me he was in training for a marathon. As he talked, I felt a vague discomfort growing in me. When I rose to see him to the door, I felt like a fossil, ancient and embedded in a piece of stone.

That evening I alternated between irritability and sadness. I called a friend and told her about the visit. "I have absolutely no idea what it would feel like to run in such an event, especially now that I'm having trouble even walking across the room!" I said. "How could he come by here and talk like that to me? Why, he has no idea how difficult it has become for me, how I have slowed down since I last saw him, how many more losses I've had to accept!"

My friend interrupted my ranting. "Don't ever even think you don't know what an athlete's training is like," she said. "You have been training every day for almost 50 years, every day since you had polio. You are an Olympic medal winner. Nothing less. Not ever!"

In the past, the singularly cheerful Dorothea would have ignored her own anger and buried it, joked about it or even made fun of herself. Now I could accept the distance between our abilities, the discouragement I felt from my decreased mobility, and my overly sensitive response to his casual remarks. As I regained my perspective by looking at the situation in a different way, his seeming heroic athletic accomplishments appeared in a new light. All people are different in abilities, I reminded myself. And people who have survived polio and its aftermath are athletes of Olympic medal status. I have run the race each day of my life and continue to do so.

The lessons I have learned from polio parallel those needed to heal depression. In moving through both physical and mental obstacle courses, I have learned that the race is not so much to the swift as to the enduring. While the work is ongoing, healing depression requires acknowledgment of pain, shifts in perspective, action, and acceptance of the lives we are given.